Lenin

"A welcome gift: guidance from a generous, experienced, and wise comrade when we need it most … Le Blanc brings out the practical activism, principled politics, and revolutionary patience crucial to organizing the oppressed on a rapidly over-heating planet."

—Jodi Dean, author of *Comrade: An Essay on Political Belonging*

"Fantastic, very interesting and important for our times."

—Tamás Krausz, author of *Reconstructing Lenin: An Intellectual Biography*

"Crackling with intellectual life … Paul confronts opposing views, brings in evocative quotations from dead witnesses and living scholars, and wrestles with the most difficult interpretive questions. Don't read this book to learn 'the truth about Lenin', read it to enter into Lenin's world and to face the choices that he too faced."

—Lars T. Lih, author of *Lenin Rediscovered*

"An incisive, engaging overview of Lenin and his revolutionary ideas."

—Eric Blanc, author of *Revolutionary Social Democracy: Working-Class Politics Across the Russian Empire, 1882–1917*

"Well-researched and dutifully contextualized, Le Blanc paints a striking portrait of Lenin as an unwavering champion of democracy."

—Cliff Connolly, *Cosmonaut*

"From feminists to environmental activists, from trade unionists to those active in the movement for Black Lives, or justice for Trans, there's something here for all who believe that forging revolution and transformation of society will be necessary to … win liberation for all humanity."

—Linda Loew, longtime socialist, feminist and union activist

"Brilliant … a tireless catalogue on the past and future of Lenin, Leninism, and revolution, offering indispensable insights into what is to be done amid the cascading catastrophes of today and tomorrow."

—Ankica Čakardić, author of *Like a Clap of Thunder: Three Essays on Rosa Luxemburg*

"A wonderful sketch of Lenin's life and times, illustrating both Lenin's complex personality and his remarkable insights … With an excellent timeline, biographic sketches of the main characters, and a thorough bibliography … this book is perhaps the best introduction to Lenin available in English."

—Michael D. Yates, Director of Monthly Review Press and author of *Can the Working Class Change the World?*

"Historian and activist Paul Le Blanc considers what the author of *What Is to Be Done?* has to say to today's radicals. What emerges are valuable contributions to the struggle against the ongoing catastrophes of war, poverty and climate chaos."

—Alex de Jong, co-director of International Institute for Research and Education, Amsterdam

"In lucid, jargon-free prose, Paul Le Blanc forces us to question what we thought we knew about the great revolutionary … The result is a Lenin ripe for rediscovery, whose ideas are less distant than we might think."

—Alan Wald, H. Chandler Davis Collegiate Professor Emeritus, University of Michigan

"This fresh and nuanced examination … is essential reading for anyone seeking to understand Lenin's historical role and his relevance to today's movements for transformative change."

—Ian Angus, author of *The War Against the Commons: Dispossession and Resistance in the Making of Capitalism*

"A well-written, readable, and useful introduction to Lenin and Leninism, presented in a way young political activists will be able to relate to."

—John Molyneux, author of *Marxism and the Party*

"Produced, with great skill – a compressed and very readable account of Lenin's life and ideas which is honest, attractive, and non-hagiographical."

—Mike Taber, editor, *Under the Socialist Banner: Resolutions of the Second International, 1889–1912*

"With great power of synthesis, the book addresses and clarifies fundamental issues of the Leninist struggle and is indispensable reading for the international left.'

—Flo Menezes, Brazilian composer, musical scholar, and revolutionary militant

Lenin

Responding to Catastrophe, Forging Revolution

Paul Le Blanc

First published 2023 by Pluto Press
New Wing, Somerset House, Strand, London WC2R 1LA
and Pluto Press, Inc.
1930 Village Center Circle, 3-834, Las Vegas, NV 89134

www.plutobooks.com

British Library Cataloguing in Publication Data
A catalogue record for this book is available from the British Library

ISBN 978 0 7453 4834 6 Paperback
ISBN 978 0 7453 4835 3 PDF
ISBN 978 0 7453 4836 0 EPUB

This book is printed on paper suitable for recycling and made from fully managed and sustained forest sources. Logging, pulping and manufacturing processes are expected to conform to the environmental standards of the country of origin.

Typeset by Stanford DTP Services, Northampton, England

Simultaneously printed in the United Kingdom and United States of America

Contents

Acknowledgments and Dedication

All books are a collective effort, and to acknowledge everyone who is part of this book's collective would require pages of names. I restrict myself to naming only a few.

First, there is my life partner of many years Nancy Ferrari, whose loving friendship helped make it possible for me to live long enough to write this.

Second, there is Rida Vaquas—a valued collaborator within the wondrous collective that is engaged in producing the Verso complete works of Rosa Luxemburg. She reached out to me to initiate this project and has been immensely supportive.

Third, there is David Castle of Pluto Press, whose heartening response was essential to this book coming into being, and who provided much useful advice. Also much appreciated are efforts of all the laborers of hand and brain at Pluto Press who made this book possible, including head of production Robert Webb, copy-editor Elaine Ross, typesetter David Stanford, and cover designer Melanie Patrick.

Special thanks to those who agreed to look over earlier versions of the manuscript and provided feedback: Nick Coven, Alex de Jong, Nancy Ferrari, Noah Gonzales, David Hayter, Ginny Hildebrand, Thomas Hummel, Lars Lih, Christopher (Kit) Lyons, the late John Molyneux, Bryan Palmer, Eric Poulos, John Riddell, Bill Roberts, Nancy Rosenstock, Lynne Sunderman, Mike Taber, and Rida Vaquas. Helpful input of anonymous readers lined up by Pluto also contributed to what is presented here. (It should not be assumed that any of these readers necessarily agree with everything in this book.)

Use of the Marxist Internet Archive, an incredibly rich resource, contributed to the composition of the present work.

Thanks to the many comrades over the years whose life efforts shaped so much of what I know, and to the waves of students who pressed me to be clear and honest in what I was trying to share.

Finally, there are those who really hope to understand the past, and perhaps to do something to help create a future of the free and the equal. This book is dedicated to you.

Prologue: What's the Point?

> Lenin was very tough, and he was for the workers.
>
> —Gus Le Blanc (trade union organizer) in 1960, responding to questions from his 13-year-old son

In my twilight years, I envision future catastrophes. Those who outlive me will experience these in ways I will not. Studying an outstanding revolutionary who sought to make his way through past catastrophes might be helpful to people I leave behind. If the future turns out to be far rosier than I fear, I still believe understanding past struggles may benefit those engaging in future struggles, and those simply seeking to make sense of the past. For such activists and scholars, I offer this small book. Some heads may shake or assume a quizzical cock, with the thought: "What *was* he thinking?" This prologue offers a partial answer.

LIFE

Like so many in our times, I have been subjected to multiple shocks.

There were shocks in my early teens as racism was being challenged in militant struggles for the "liberty and justice for *all*" I had been intoning with my public-school classmates every morning as we pledged allegiance to the flag of the United States of America. Then I saw that same flag being used to justify a dirty war in Vietnam. This was not the country I'd thought it was when I was a little kid. With others of my generation, I committed to changing that.

A different shock came when, as a 19-year-old activist in a vibrant "New Left" of the 1960s, I spent a summer working in the national office of Students for a Democratic Society (SDS). With its catchwords of "let the people decide" and "participatory democracy," and its opposition to the Vietnam War, racism and poverty, SDS was growing phenomenally. But my intimate involvement at the organization's center provided devastating insights into terrible inadequacies: amateurishness, disorganization, and multiple confusions. This guaranteed that its seemingly stunning successes would soon lead to chaos, collapse, and fragmentation.[1]

Yet another shock came shortly after my stint in the SDS national office, during an illness when, bed-ridden and with time on my hands, I read Lenin's classic *What Is to Be Done?* —posing a question that seemed as urgent to me in 1966 as it was to him in 1902. Many "New Left" authorities had assured me Lenin was passé. Yet his text spoke to me with a compelling relevance I had not expected.

Other shocks resulted in my becoming active, by the early 1970s, in an organization which proudly emphasized its adherence to the Leninist tradition and helped bring an end to the U.S. war in Vietnam.[2] In the wake of its success, however, came uncertainty and disorientation regarding what to do next. In the name of "Leninism," some of the ascendent leaders transformed the group into an authoritarian sect. It would soon embark on an expulsion campaign to rid itself of those who disagreed.

A veteran Trotskyist resisting that development, George Breitman, was one of my mentors. He asked me to develop a study of what Lenin had actually said and done in helping to forge an organization capable of leading the Russian Revolution of 1917. In writing *Lenin and the Revolutionary Party* in the 1980s—as I combed through Lenin's texts, studying how they related to the actual historical contexts—I experienced yet another shock. My understanding of Lenin, and that of many comrades (though not a seasoned few, such as Breitman) had been stilted.[3] It was disconnected from the actual struggles of large numbers of past activists in very particular situations. In my continuing study of Lenin and his times, I have been struck by a complexity and richness in his thinking, and that of his comrades, that had eluded me in earlier decades.

Yet the shocks never stop coming.

Lenin lived over a century ago. How could he possibly be relevant to our own times? In the twenty-first century the people on planet Earth live in wondrous times indeed. At our fingertips are amazing technologies connecting us with each other as never before, with immense quantities of knowledge, and with capacities to do and create things far beyond what previous generations had imagined.

We live in terrible times as well. The structure and dynamics of the global economy generate deepening inequalities, instabilities, and destructiveness that throw into question the future of human civilization—and even humanity's ability to survive. An eroding quality of life for more and more of the world's laboring majorities is matched by growing authoritarianism, irrationality, and violence. A voracious market economy designed to enrich already immensely wealthy elites is intimately connected with environmental destruction engulfing our world.

On this last point, it seems there is good news and bad news.

The Good News: A scientific consensus projects that climate change—currently being driven by the immensely powerful fossil fuel industries—might still be halted, preventing our being overwhelmed by cascading catastrophes, provided that dramatic, decisive action is soon taken on a global scale.

The Bad News: The necessary changes will be too costly, in the short run, for the businesses and governments that make the decisions. So far, the necessary changes are not being implemented.

More Bad News: The scientific realities will not fade away despite strident denials, eloquent rhetoric, empty promises, or "pragmatic" compromises. Nature doesn't compromise. Nor are the relatively limited protests (some of which I have been part of) likely to prove adequate to save the situation. We must prepare for catastrophe.

Even aside from climate change, a majority of laborers and consumers, whose lives enrich the elites, face increasing and sometimes horrific difficulties. Perhaps things are not quite that bad—or perhaps (as I suspect is the case) they are even worse. Either way, many already seem to feel the old ways of doing things no longer work, and this feeling will probably intensify and increase. With growing urgency, the question is being posed: *what is to be done*?

Sometimes our protests against social and environmental injustice and destruction assume mass proportions, yet I am reminded of the impatience, half a century back, of the sophisticated and highly political literary critic Philp Rahv when he wrote (shortly before his death) about the mass movement of young activists arising in the late 1960s:

> Historically we are living on volcanic ground. … And one's disappointment with the experience of the New Left comes down precisely to this: that it has failed to crystallize from within itself a guiding organization—one need not be afraid of naming it a centralized and disciplined party, for so far no one has ever invented a substitute for such a party—capable of engaging in daily and even pedestrian practical activity while keeping itself sufficiently alert on the ideological plane so as not to miss its historical opportunity when and if it arises.[4]

Rahv was drawing on his own residual Leninism of the 1930s—yet even now his comment seems to resonate.

PERSONALITY AND HISTORY

Many historians go out of their way in exposing Lenin's supposedly abhorrent character. The conservative scholar Stefan Possony condemned him as:

> Self-righteous, rude, demanding, ruthless, despotic, formalistic, bureaucratic, disciplined, cunning, intolerant, stubborn, one-sided, suspicious, distant, asocial, cold-blooded, ambitious, purposive, vindictive, spiteful, a grudge holder, a coward who was able to face danger only when he deemed it unavoidable—Lenin was a complete law unto himself, and he was entirely serene about it.[5]

But the way Possony saw things was conditioned by the conservative conviction that some people, some classes, and some races are superior to others, as he argued in a book co-authored with Nathaniel Weyl, *The Geography of Intellect*. Possony despised revolutions driven by ideas of "equal rights" and "rule by the people." From this standpoint, Lenin—committed to overturning the present social order to create a radically democratic society of the free and the equal—was a monster. Denouncing this radical democrat as an "architect of totalitarianism" has been a device employed to shoo people away from his ideas—but perhaps his personality and ideas are not so repellent after all.

The free-spirited Rosa Luxemburg, a humanistic and democratic revolutionary who would have wasted no time with the terrible person described by Possony, had a rather different impression of Lenin: "I enjoy talking with him, he's clever and well educated, and has such an ugly mug, the kind I like to look at." An opponent within the Russian revolutionary movement, the Menshevik leader Raphael Abramovitch, who was Lenin's guest when he and Lenin were both living in Swiss exile in 1916, reported: "it is difficult to conceive of a simpler, kinder and more unpretentious person than Lenin at home."[6]

Angelica Balabanoff, who had worked closely with Lenin, was able to specify—many years after she had broken from him—precisely the qualities a conservative such as Possony would have found so monstrous: "From his youth on, Lenin was convinced that most of human suffering and of moral, legal, and social deficiencies were caused by class distinctions." She explained: "he was also convinced that class struggle alone … could put an end to exploiters and exploited and create a society of the free and equal. He gave himself entirely to this end and he used every means in his power to achieve it."[7]

From a location on the right end of the political spectrum, Winston Churchill sought a balanced measure of his mortal enemy. He hated what Lenin represented no less than Possony, and even hailed Mussolini's fascist dictatorship in Italy for its "triumphant struggle against the bestial appetites and passions of Leninism." Yet he wrote of Lenin: "His mind was a remarkable instrument. When its light shone it revealed the whole world, its history, its sorrows, its stupidities, its shams, and above all its wrongs. … It was capable of universal comprehension in a degree rarely reached among men." It is worth adding an insight from sometime-sympathizer Max Eastman, who suggested that one of Lenin's contributions in "the theory and practice of Marxism" was a rejection of "people who talk revolution, and like to think about it, but do not 'mean business' … the people who talked revolution but did not intend to produce it."[8]

The shrewd observations of the knowledgeable anti-Communist journalist Isaac Don Levine capture an additional quality. "His mentality … may have been extraordinarily agile and pliant as to methods, his erudition may have been vast and his capacity to back up his contentions brilliant, his character may have been such as to readily acknowledge tactical mistakes and defeats," Levine commented shortly after Lenin's death in 1924, "but these he never would have ascribed to the possible invalidity of his great idea … the Marxian theory of class struggle as the form of the transition of the capitalist society to a socialist one." Levine himself judged the "great idea" to be invalid, but there were many in Russia and beyond who felt otherwise.[9]

Animated by such convictions, Lenin helped build a powerful revolutionary movement in his native Russia, culminating in the Russian Revolution of 1917, which he and his comrades believed was the beginning of a global wave of socialist revolutions. He was a key architect of modern Communism, designed to bring about such an outcome.

Yet many who shared his ideals were critical. Among revolutionaries in Russia there were standpoints in contradiction to those of Lenin's organization—for example, varieties of anarchists who joined with Lenin's forces to make the 1917 Revolution, but then came into conflict with the Communists afterward. An imprisoned anarchist in the United States, the soon-to-be-martyred fishmonger Bartolomeo Vanzetti wrote in early 1924: "Lenin has passed away. I am convinced that unintentionally he has ruined the Russian Revolution. He has imprisoned and killed many of my comrades." Vanzetti felt compelled to add: "And yet he has suffered much, toiled heroically for what he believed to be good and the truth, and I felt my eyes filled with tears in reading of his passing and his funeral." But in the end, and for reasons worth reflecting over, Lenin remained for him "my great adversary."[10]

However, around the world, many revolutionaries adulated Lenin. Among the many in the funeral processions was a young Vietnamese revolutionary in Soviet Russia, going by the name Nguyễn Ái Quốc (born Nguyễn Sinh Cung, later known as Ho Chi Minh). "In his life he was our father, teacher, comrade, and advisor," wrote the youthful Communist. "Now he is our guiding star that leads to social revolution."[11] Harlem Renaissance poet Langston Hughes expressed a similar sentiment years later:

Lenin walks around the world.
Black, brown, and white receive him.
Language is no barrier.
The strangest tongues believe him.[12]

These testimonies come from the twentieth century—an age of hopeful revolution, horrific civil war, often triumphant counter-revolution, and ongoing class struggles. But does Lenin's project offer anything useful for us in our own time?

This book, in its subtext suggesting an affirmative answer to that question, dispenses with six historiographical myths: (1) Lenin favored dictatorship over democracy; (2) his so-called "Marxism" was a cover for his own totalitarian views; (3) he favored a super-centralized political party of "a new type"—with power concentrated at the top, himself as party dictator; (4) he favored rigid political controls over culture, art and literature; (5) he believed that through such authoritarian methods a socialist "utopia" could be imposed on backward Russia; and (6) flowing naturally from all this, he became one of history's foremost mass murderers.* This book rejects all such *false negatives*—at the same time seeking to identify actual negatives which, inevitably, can be found in Lenin and the tradition to which he was central.

Faced with the complex swirl of Lenin's life and times and ideas, one can focus on matters, and select ideas, adding up to a "Leninism" from which decent people must turn away. This book's approach is different. In her critique of the Russian Revolution, Rosa Luxemburg emphasized her determination to "distinguish the essential from the non-essential," with her critique of the non-essential designed to help advance the triumph of what was essential in Lenin's revolutionary Bolshevism. In this brief study, the focus will be on what seems to me to be those essential qualities.

---

* There is also a repeated accusation that Lenin was an agent of Imperial Germany, with documentation of money and logistical aid accepted. Lenin certainly *was* a German agent, in the same way that (as I've shown elsewhere) George Washington was a traitorous agent of the French monarchy.

LENINISM

A left-wing critic of Lenin, John Medhurst once tagged me as a "soft Leninist,"[13] in contrast to one or another variety of "hard Leninism." There are certainly imperious militants who have, over the years, been "hard and unyielding" in defense of a revolutionary purity (see Nadezhda Krupskaya's comment in Chapter 4). There are also rigidities associated with Joseph Stalin and other authoritarians (see Chapter 10). But these distort Lenin's orientation. One can certainly find, in what Lenin said and did under one or another circumstance, things that were rigid or dogmatic or authoritarian or wrong or overstated. (Lenin himself later reflected that—as was common among émigrés—some of his thought in exile had been too "leftist," and he commented to Karl Radek when the comrade was looking through his old writings: "It's interesting to read now how stupid we were then!")[14] But the essential thrust of Lenin's thought and practice went in the opposite direction from such limitations. *That humanistic and democratic "opposite direction" has the greatest relevance for those who would change the world for the better.*

"No one understood Leninism better than Stalin," according to Stalin's close associate Vyacheslav M. Molotov, and many Communists and anti-Communists have seen things just that way. In the 1924 work *Foundations of Leninism*, Stalin asserted that Lenin had added to the tactical propositions of Marx and Engels "a system of rules and guiding principles." This has been touted as "Leninism" for almost a century, exerting a powerful influence on adherents, critics, and opponents. But that system has been fatal, certainly lethal, in the course of human events. And even though it has, for more than one reason, passed as an understanding of Leninism among millions of people, it fails to capture the actual dynamics of Lenin's thought.[15]

Another comrade, who had known Lenin longer and more intimately than Stalin, offered a different understanding. "Lenin did not write and could not have written a textbook of Leninism," noted Lev Kamenev, adding that "every attempt to … create any kind of a 'Handbook' of Leninism, a collection of formulas applicable to all questions at any time—will certainly fail." Lenin's writings were "permeated through and through with the anxieties and lessons of a particular historical situation," and since no particular historical situation is repeated, his approach involved an open, critical-minded, "active, vital character." More than once, Lenin emphasized that the Marxism he was utilizing should not be seen as a set of immutable doctrines, but rather as "a guide to action." Kamenev was suggesting a similar approach to the ideas of Lenin himself.[16]

The "Leninism" of Lenin is inseparable from the revolutionary party he played such a central role in bringing into being, known in the years leading up to the Russian Revolution of 1917 as the Bolsheviks. One of the keenest historians of this organization, Ronald Suny, has summarized some of what he has found: "Bolsheviks ... were an argumentative lot. They were Protestants without an infallible pope. Many were well-read in the classics of Marxism and kept abreast of the controversies at party congresses and conferences and in the party press." He notes they were inclined to dismiss pretentious intellectuals coming from outside of the working class, although many of them were, in fact, working-class intellectuals and all of them "were dedicated to the intellectual endeavor—using a body of political theory and historical interpretation to analyze the politics of the moment and predict possible outcomes."[17]

From this the Bolsheviks crafted an orientation to transform society. Far from being good little soldiers prepared to follow the Leader, the Bolsheviks were a dynamic revolutionary collective forging strategy and tactics through discussion and debate. The result was subjected to the test of experience, then collectively evaluated, refined, revised, adjusted to shifting realities.

The Marxism of Lenin contained a dynamic convergence of different elements. Boris Souvarine aptly quotes him during a moment when he reproached some comrades for "repeating a formula divorced from the series of circumstances which had produced it and assured its success, and applying it to conditions essentially different." Sometimes Lenin would "speak French" when Russian realities seemed to approximate those that had brought the French Revolution, and when realities shifted in the opposite direction, he would "speak German," advancing the patient organizational approach reflected in the German Social Democracy's Erfurt

Program. But "he never ceased 'speaking Russian,'" Souvarine tells us,* "sounding all possibilities, weighing opportunities, calculating the chances of keeping the Party on the right track, avoiding alike belated or premature insurrection inspired by romantic motives, and constitutional and parliamentary illusions." Souvarine concludes: "He was a disciple of Marx, but undogmatic, eager in the pursuit of science and knowledge, always alive to the teachings of experience, capable of recognizing, surmounting and making good his errors, and consequently of rising above himself."[18]

After Russia's 1917 Revolution, as he labored to build a Communist International that could help spread effective revolutionary struggles to other lands, Lenin sought to convey this approach to revolutionaries around the world. Warning against a "slavish imitation of the past," both in analyses and political tactics, Lenin stressed that genuinely revolutionary analysis and tactics require flexibility. "While the development of world history as a whole follows general laws," he acknowledged, one should assume that unfolding specifics and "peculiarities" require dialectical (dynamic, fluid, interactive) rather than doctrinaire approaches.[19] Lenin's orientation transcends the peculiarities of tsarist Russia.

While the global market economy and its vast labor force have evolved dramatically since the time of Lenin, some of the essential dynamics are still very much in evidence, even as they take new form. Then too, an accumulation of crises stirs deepening concerns: economic downturns, soaring inequality, unstable living standards, escalating violence, spreading right-wing authoritarianism, capped by pandemics and the multiple impacts of climate change. Because things are as they are, they cannot stay as they are.

Leninism is one of those words that, according to Louis Fischer, are like "empty bottles into which one person pours poison and another wine."[20] This book offers neither poison nor wine, but simply a consideration of the revolutionary named Vladimir Ilyich Ulyanov, known to intimates as Volodya or Ilyich, known to the

---

* Walter Rodney later emphasized this point as particularly relevant to the African liberation movement—that Lenin "had to take those formulations out of the specific cultural and historical context of Western Europe and look at Eastern Europe, at Russia, which was evolving differently, and apply them to his own society."

world as Lenin. *Here the word "Leninism" is meant to convey what he thought and what he did.*

Some ideologues on both ends of the political spectrum, as well as various historians who are either adoring or hostile, have been inclined to attribute to Lenin greater originality (for good or ill) than he deserves. We will see Lenin's own thinking and contributions evolved through interaction with others, as part of a revolutionary collective process. Some of "Leninism's" presumably distinctive ideas can be found in insights shared with Karl Marx, George Plekhanov, Pavel Axelrod, Vera Zasulich, Karl Kautsky, Julius Martov, Alexander Bogdanov, Rosa Luxemburg, Leon Trotsky, Nikolai Bukharin, Gregory Zinoviev, Lev Kamenev, Nadezhda Krupskaya, and many more. This collective process is inseparable from the actualities of what goes by the name of Leninism.

This is related to what some see as an essential and distinctive quality. "Lenin's capacity to build a leadership collective," reflects activist-historian John Riddell, "seems to me to be historically his most important feature—what set him apart from other exceptionally able individual leaders like Trotsky and Bukharin."[21]

The actualities of Lenin's orientation were incompatible with the "hard Leninism" so often attributed to him by most foes and all-too-many would-be adherents.

COMMUNISM AND FREEDOM

Essential to the "Leninism" of Lenin is the fusion of communism and freedom. In fact, such a fusion was envisioned by revolutionaries throughout the Russian Empire. "There will be a time when every person, without exception, will have the right to be human, to develop all of their abilities," wrote the Polish revolutionary Julian Marchlewski (a close comrade of Rosa Luxemburg who joined Lenin's Bolsheviks), adding that "art will cease to be a luxury, it will be an aspect of our daily lives, spreading into all areas of private and social life." Similar notions found their way into a leaflet of the Latvian socialists: "The struggle for people's freedom requires from us now all of our energy, our blood, our lives. But we go into this battle boldly and joyfully because it will bring victory and liberation to all slaves and servants."[22]

Such notions found expression in writings of the revolutionary novelist Maxim Gorky. His 1907 novel *Mother*, dramatizing the revolutionary underground, was saturated with these ideas. "I know the time will come when people will wonder at their own beauty, when each will be like a star to all the others," says one of the characters. "The earth will be peopled with free men, great in their freedom. The hearts of all will be open, and every heart will be innocent of envy and malice." Near the novel's end, the downtrodden and illiterate mother of a radicalized worker gives voice to her own radicalized consciousness: "Everything for all—all for everyone! That is how I see it. In very truth we are all comrades, all kindred spirits, all children of one mother, who is truth!" Lenin's young sister Maria later recalled "how avidly we read" Gorky's novel, and his companion Nadezhda Krupskaya stressed that Lenin "particularly liked" this work.[23]

Such ideas had long been in circulation in Russia. For example, the 1892 classic *The Conquest of Bread* by anarchist Peter Kropotkin inspired many thousands with the vision of a society of the free and the equal—for whose practicality Kropotkin made a compelling case. "We find in all of modern history a tendency ... to establish the Communist principle," he emphasized, going on to draw readers' attention to its contemporary reality:

> The bridges ... have become public property and are free to all; so are the highways ... Museums, free libraries, free schools, free meals for children; parks and gardens open to all; streets paved and lighted, free to all; water supplied to every house without measure or stint—all such arrangements are founded on the principle: "Take what you need."

Kropotkin argued that "the predominant tendency in modern societies, the pursuit of equality," is the source for both anarchism and communism, "Communism without government—the Communism of the Free."[24]

By 1917, aspects of Lenin's thought had drawn remarkably and explicitly close to aspects of Kropotkin's perspective. As was the case with his contrast of "bourgeois democracy" with genuine democracy, he was critical of the meaning that *freedom* assumed in class societies: "Freedom in capitalist society always remains about the same as it was in the ancient Greek republics: freedom for the slave-owners." He praised the way Frederick Engels defined the matter: "the proletariat needs the state, not in the interests of freedom but in order to hold down its adversaries, and as soon as it becomes possible to speak of freedom the state as such ceases to exist." In his 1875 "Critique of the Gotha Program," Marx made distinction between lower (immediate) and higher (more advanced) stages of socialism or communism. In the higher stage, democracy would become a habit among the free association of producers, not involving a set of laws enforced by the police. In *The State and Revolution* Lenin tagged the lower stage "socialism" and the higher stage "communism." The conclusion he drew converged with Kropotkin's position:

> Only in communist society, when the resistance of the capitalists has disappeared, when there are no classes (i.e., when there is no distinction between the members of society as regards their relation to the social means of production), only then "the state ... ceases to exist," and "it becomes possible to speak of freedom."[25]

The aging anarchist agreed to meet with Lenin in 1919—despite very sharp disagreements—in part because he was impressed that Lenin "puts forward a prognosis that the State and its rule would in the end wither away." Prominent Bolshevik V.D. Bonch-Bruevich, who set up the meeting, added "Vladimir Ilyich always looked upon Kropotkin with the greatest respect." The two engaged in animated discussion, with Lenin sharply challenging Kropotkin's stress on the importance of cooperatives (although we will see his thinking would later shift on this matter). In the final year of Kropotkin's life, his own criticisms of Lenin's government deepened, though as his death approached, he expressed the hope that Soviet Russia would eventually evolve, as Lenin envisioned in *The State and Revolution*, into a "communist stateless society."[26]

THE POINT

Three decades before Andreas Malm urged consideration of a catastrophe-driven "ecological Leninism," before Ian Angus and David Camfield emphasized Lenin as a reference-point in the environmental struggle, before Kai Heron and Jodi Dean spoke of "climate Leninism and revolutionary transition," Octavia Butler, in her powerful works of speculative fiction *Parable of the Sower* and *Parable of the Talents*, envisioned a future in which people were engulfed by catastrophes: "the growing rich/poor gap … throwaway labor … our willingness to build and fill prisons … our reluctance to build and repair schools and libraries … our assault on the environment … spreading hunger … increased vulnerability to disease …"[27]

The central character in Butler's novels is committed to survival, transformation, freedom, and community, insisting that "belief initiates and guides action—or it does nothing." Identifying a shortcoming in another admirable character, Butler wrote that "somewhere inside himself, he believes that large, important things are done only by powerful people in high positions," and therefore "what we do is, by definition, small and unimportant."[28] But that is wrong.

That gets to the point of this book. Lenin's ideas—when he's right and sometimes even when he's mistaken—provide an incredibly rich resource for those who are not "powerful in high positions." They might help people like us comprehend ways in which our own world emerged out of both the glory and wreckage of the last century's revolutions. They might also provide insights into *what is to be done* amid cascading catastrophes of today and tomorrow.

1
Who Was Lenin?

Like the great majority of Russia's peoples, Lenin's ancestors were serfs under the yoke of wealthy landowning nobles. His grandparents had broken free from the poverty this entailed—enabling his father, Ilya Nikolaevich Ulyanov, to get an education, and then become an educator, rising first to the position of a school inspector and then a director of public schools. In 1882 he was inducted into the lower-level service nobility.

FAMILY AND CHILDHOOD

Ilya Ulyanov's wife Maria Alexandrovna Blank was a physician's daughter. Trained to be a teacher, she was never employed but cultivated in her children enthusiasm for foreign languages, a love of music, and especially a passion for literature. The works of Pushkin, Gogol, Turgenev, and Tolstoy were highly prized by all the Ulyanov children. Also shaping her children were her industrious, economical, and highly organized qualities that provided a firm foundation for their household in Simbirsk, a provincial town on the Volga River. It is here that Vladimir Ilyich Ulyanov was born on April 22, 1870 (April 10, according to the Old Style calendar then used in Russia), the third of six children in a relatively happy family.

Inspired by the modernization and reforming policies associated with Tsar Alexander II, who freed the serfs in 1861, Ilya felt he could best realize his own liberal hopes for Russia's progress through bringing quality education to the children of peasants and the urban poor—loyal at one and the same time to the tsar and to the laboring majority of the people. And he adored his family. "Thus Ilya Nikolaevich was to his children an edifying example of 'service to the people,'" notes historian Isaac Deutscher, but "he was also accessible to them, friendly, humorous, full of stories and eager for games."[1]

"Both parents seem to have worked together in raising their children," comments the biographer of Lenin's sisters, Katy Turton, "and had an equal share of influence over the type of upbringing they received." Educational expectations were high in this household, for the daughters as well as the sons. The oldest two children, Alexander (Sasha) and Anna, set an example to the others—highly intelligent and incredibly hardworking. The intense and conscientious Sasha, in many ways the family favorite, and a prize-winning student, was clearly destined to become a brilliant scientist as he labored at St. Petersburg State University. Then there was the third child, Vladimir (Volodya), who showed himself capable of being maddeningly mischievous and, compared with Sasha and Anna, a bit lazy. Complaining that at times her father could be too severe, Anna reminisced this approach was "fully correct only for Vladimir, whose vast self-confidence and constantly distinguished achievement in school called for a corrective."[2] Philip Pomper, biographer of older brother Sasha, comments that "in a family of rigorists," Vladimir "seemed to be more boisterous and less serious and dutiful than the other children." He adds:

> Volodya, physically the spitting image of his father, showed no inclination to follow Ilya Nikolaevich—or Sasha—into the natural sciences. At an early age Volodya loved language, literature, music, and drawing, and he showed gifts for all of them. Although Ilya disapproved of his second son's habits, and worried about his preferences, father and son were quite alike temperamentally. They were confident of each other's affections. Just beneath the surface of Ilya Nikolaevich's severity, there was a streak of mischievous humor, a quality completely alien to his older son and characteristic of Volodya.[3]

Tragedy soon struck: the loss of the beloved father, Ilya. Not long before his premature death, however, Ilya's spirit broke: the liberalizing hopes and enthusiasms of the 1860s and 1870s were wiped away by a decisive rightward swerve. After revolutionary populists of *Narodnaya Volya* (People's Will) assassinated the reform-minded

Alexander II in 1881, the strong-willed successor Alexander III imposed a set of counter-reform policies based on the slogan "Orthodoxy, Autocracy, Nationalism." Its ideology reinforced the pre-eminence of the Russian Orthodox Church, the authority of the absolute monarchy, and despotically super-patriotic notions of Great Russia. Children of the lower classes were judged to be getting more education than was good for the traditional social order, and new policies promoted servility and unquestioning obedience at the expense of genuine education. Narrowly avoiding the loss of his job, Ilya Ulyanov witnessed the utter negation of his life's work. At 54, he died of a stroke, the same affliction which eventually brought down his son Vladimir at the same age.

Among the children, Katy Turton notes, there was a natural division into boy-girl pairs as playmates and confidants. The youngest—the "small fry" Dmitri and Maria—were viewed with "affectionate contempt" by the others. The oldest—Alexander and Anna— "had similar characters; both were quiet, reserved, and even melancholy." Neither had much patience for the mischievous Vladimir (who, nonetheless, tended to idolize his older brother). Vladimir and Olga "were inseparable and played boisterously together." At the same time, Olga was seen as having some of Alexander's qualities: "The depth and strength of character with the prevailing sense of duty, the great evenness and steadiness, the gentleness, and the extraordinary capacity for work." While clever, active and vivacious, it is said Olga's "good example as a conscientious student ... inspired Vladimir to work hard during his last years at school."[4] Their bond, and her influence, would continue into early adulthood.

In the twilight of what Deutscher calls his "buoyant adolescence," however, Vladimir was subjected—due to his father's death, and Alexander being away at university—to the pressure of being "the man of the house." Already at a stage of life when boys "are especially rude and aggressive," according to sister Anna, qualities of "impertinence and sarcasm" became pronounced in him. (Ronald Suny refers to a similar tendency, in Lenin's later years, toward a "reflexive readiness to use the most offensive language to caricature his opponents"—though this could be superseded, in earlier as well as later times, by other, stronger qualities.)[5]

As his 17th year began, a second tragedy hit the family, which catapulted young Vladimir into adulthood and onto the path of becoming an intransigent revolutionary.

REVOLUTIONARY PATHWAY

The policies that had destroyed the progressive educational efforts of Ilya Nikolaevich Ulyanov bore down on the lives of university students, including his son Alexander. These students were quick to see connections between the increasingly intense intellectual-cultural and educational repression they were experiencing and the much deeper oppression and exploitation inherent in the tsarist system. A hybrid of semi-feudal and capitalist economic formations was enhancing the wealth, privilege, and power of arrogant elites at the expense of vast laboring majorities in countryside, village, and city.

Stretching back for more than a hundred years were interweaving critiques and protests and rebellions and insurgencies. These came from relatively privileged intellectuals (often reflected in the poems and novels popular in the Ulyanov household). They also came from impoverished peasants as well as, more recently, from a new, small but growing, sector of wage workers.

A "dual revolution" was sweeping through much of the world. First of all, there was a wave of democratic revolutions—in England of the 1600s, in North America from 1775 to 1783, most radical of all in France of 1789–99, and beyond. No less profound was the Industrial Revolution, beginning in capitalist Britain in the 1770s, transforming more and more of the global economy ever since.

An abundance of ideas and experiences accompanied this dual revolution—in some cases stemming from a variety of intellectuals seeking to comprehend the amazing new realities, while others emerged out of a variety of popular struggles aiming to shape the new world. A few reflected the convergence of both. Since the early nineteenth century, young men and women in Russia from the upper classes were drawn into struggles against the tsarist status quo, forming (as later recounted by Lenin's comrade Gregory Zinoviev) "in the literal sense the cream of the aristocracy, the nobility, the officer caste." They "detached themselves from their class, broke from their families, abandoned their privileges, and joined battle with the autocracy."[6] Humanistic, radical and revolutionary ideas emanated from such people, assuming multiple expressions within the literature and art of their time, and in subterranean and subversive political struggles as well.

Alexander Ulyanov and a circle of friends and associates, influenced by these eclectic currents, blended concepts associated with the revolutionary populist ideas of People's Will with early Marxist insights. Marx had projected a movement of the modern working class to replace an unjust and exploitative capitalism with *socialism*, an economic democracy of the free and equal. Embracing the socialist goal, Alexander and those around him concluded the absence of a modern working class in Russia required them to resort to the individual terrorism of the populists: kill symbols of oppression in order to spark popular resistance to oppression among peasants and others. Well before they were able to implement the plan, the tsarist secret police were on to them—15 were arrested and put on trial in 1887.

During the trial, Alexander sought to protect his comrades by claiming most of the responsibility. He sought to explain the politics behind the plot, with the hope of inspiring and rallying others to take the revolutionary path. "Only the study of social and economic affairs gave me the deep conviction that the existing order of things was not normal," he told the court, with the result that "my vague dreams about freedom, equality, and brotherhood assumed strictly scientific, that is, socialist forms." He emphasized: "I understood that it was not only possible but necessary to change the social order."[7] Alexander and five others paid with their lives for their revolutionary plans. While among small groups of revolutionaries he was seen as a heroic martyr, his actions resulted in the Ulyanov family being shunned by most of their friends and acquaintances in "respectable society." But his siblings heeded his call.

Anna was already acquainted with her brother's beliefs and shared them. For Volodya and Olga it came as a revelation. Over the next few years, they would read everything their brother had been reading to trace his intellectual development, including Marx's *Capital*. When they could, they would have animated discussions, and when separated they would write. "It would be interesting to talk about every 'question,'" Olga wrote to Volodya, "but somehow it doesn't come across well in a letter," adding that she looked forward to seeing him soon so the two like-minded siblings could resume their discussions.[8] To another friend in this period, she reflected:

> The aspiration towards truth and to the ideal is in people's souls … One must always believe in people, in the possibility of something better on earth, despite personal disappointment … If one doesn't believe in people, doesn't love them, then what is one living for?[9]

At the end of 1887, Volodya was briefly arrested for involvement in a peaceful demonstration against the regime. He had just entered the University of Kazan, but his involvement in protest activities resulted in his immediate expulsion and banishment to a small village near Kazan, where he lived under police surveillance. In 1888 he was permitted to return to Kazan, but he was denied entry to any university and therefore embarked on his own rigorous course of study. In 1891 he passed law examinations at the University of St. Petersburg, and for a few months he worked as a lawyer.

Bereavement marred his academic success. That year, Olga died of typhoid fever. Active in revolutionary discussion groups around St. Petersburg State University, she had connected with a Social Democratic group started by M.I. Brusnev, who had been associated with Alexander's circle. "She would certainly have made a revolutionary of great merit and devotion," reflected her sister Anna some years later. At the time of her death one of her classmates lamented to a friend:

> O Arsenii, if only you knew what sort of person Ulyanova was. How much hope was placed in her! It is safe to say that in Ulyanova Russia has lost an honest, tireless activist … She was a person of brilliant mind, intellectual maturity, education, talent … She read the best works on political economy and sociology.[10]

This loss deeply pained Volodya. As was the case with his martyred brother, he absorbed much of his sister's personality into his being. (What her friend had written about Olga would soon match ways Volodya's comrades described Vladimir Ilyich Ulyanov.) Moving to St. Petersburg in 1893, he contacted acquaintances of both, enabling him to connect with the revolutionary underground.

RUSSIAN MARXISM AND VLADIMIR ULYANOV

At this time, impoverished peasants made up about 90 percent of Russia's population. An expanding class of wage workers and their families, created through the country's substantial industrial growth in the late nineteenth century, made up another 7 percent (a percentage that would dramatically rise by the early decades of the twentieth century). At the next level was a small "middle-class" layer of professionals and well-to-do businessmen (the bourgeoisie), and at the very top a landed aristocracy capped by an absolute monarchy. The country was characterized by a complete absence of democracy, limits on freedom of expression, the persecution of religious minorities outside the official Russian Orthodox Church, severe limitations on the rights of women, and oppression of more than a hundred national minorities that inhabited the Russian Empire—a "prison-house of nations." Volatile realities stirred revolutionary sentiments.

Young Ulyanov was especially drawn to the writer Nikolai Chernyshevsky and remnants of revolutionary populism associated with People's Will. Made up of idealistic activists who specialized in clandestine methods and sought to organize a peasant-based revolution, People's Will had hoped to establish a socialist society based largely on traditional communes in peasant villages throughout Russia. One militant, Vera Zasulich, had corresponded with Marx to ask his opinion of this orientation. Marx thought highly of *Narodnaya Volya*, and he devoted much time in his later years to learning Russian and to an intensive study of Russian realities. He thought the People's Will orientation made sense if the hoped-for Russian Revolution sparked and harmonized with revolutionary upheavals among the working classes of the industrial capitalist regions of Western Europe, which would in turn help Russia develop within a global socialist economy replacing world capitalism.

Zasulich would soon leave the ranks of the populists, joining with a handful of other comrades making the same break, particularly the brilliant, imperious George Plekhanov and the thoughtful, dedicated Pavel Axelrod. They formed the explicitly Marxist Emancipation of Labor Group in Swiss exile. Russia was undergoing a capitalist transformation, they argued, and industrialization was creating a factory-based proletariat. This working class would become the most effective force in the struggle to overthrow tsarism. Plekhanov and Axelrod explained in an 1884 article that "our peasantry cannot of its own accord produce from within its own ranks a coherent force of conscious fighters for its own interests," although "it might nonetheless become a significant revolutionary force under the energetic influence of the … working class in the industrial and commercial centers … Our working class has already managed to demonstrate in this short time both its receptivity to the ideas of socialism and its ability to fight for them." They added "the concepts of human well-being, liberty and justice with which the advanced workers and their scholarly representatives are acquainted" were "the fruit of many centuries of difficult experience" pointing the way to successful struggle.[11]

Volodya was part of a growing layer of young activists profoundly attracted to this working-class socialist orientation. They pushed against what seemed to them the ossification of traditional *Narodnaya Volya* perspectives into dogmas inconsistent with modern realities. Those still adhering to the old beliefs would eventually form the Socialist-Revolutionary Party (the Socialist-Revolutionaries, SRs) in 1903. Those converting to Marxism would attempt to launch a Russian Social Democratic Labor Party (RSDLP) in 1898, but the effort stalled because all participants were arrested at the conclusion of the founding congress.

Instead of engaging in terrorist activities (assassinations) against the tsar and his officials, as People's Will had done, the Marxists argued the working class should build trade unions to fight for better working conditions and living standards, should organize mass demonstrations to pressure for broader democratic and social reforms, and should organize their own political party to lead the struggle for a democratic revolution. Such a revolution would clear the way for the economic and political development of Russia (presumably through a capitalist economy and democratic republic). Then, when the working class became the majority, the process would culminate in a second revolution with a socialist character. The workers would take control of the economy and run it for the benefit of all. The Marxists believed workers in other countries would be moving in a similar direction.

As Volodya was becoming a Marxist in 1889, a world network of working-class socialist parties formed, influenced by perspectives outlined by Marx and his co-thinker Frederick Engels in their 1848 classic *The Communist Manifesto* and subsequent writings. This was the Socialist International—known as the Second International because there had been an earlier effort, the International Workingmen's Association (1864–76) with which Marx had been involved.

The most substantial component of the Second International was the massive German Social Democratic Party (SPD), which had developed under the leadership of working-class intellectuals and others close to Marx and Engels. In 1891 it adopted a clear and detailed program for working-class struggle—the Erfurt Program—elaborated upon in Karl Kautsky's classic work *The Class Struggle.* These works influenced and inspired young Marxists throughout the world, including the one who would soon take the name "Lenin," and who would argue that the SPD was the model which Russian revolutionaries should adopt in their efforts to transform Russia.

A comrade of later times, Nikolai Bukharin, added an essential element in understanding Lenin's approach to Marxism. One must embrace not "the entirety of ideas such as existed in the time of Marx," but rather the general approach and "methodology of Marxism," Bukharin argues, concluding:

> It is clear that Leninist Marxism represents quite a particular form of ideological education, for the simple reason that it is itself a child of a somewhat different epoch. It cannot simply be a repetition of the Marxism of Marx, because the epoch in which

> we are living is not a simple repetition of the epoch in which Marx lived.[12]

In the writings of Lenin, this is evident. He complains many calling themselves Marxists have a "conception of Marxism [that] is impossibly pedantic. They have completely failed to understand what is decisive in Marxism, namely, its revolutionary dialectics. They have even failed absolutely to understand Marx's plain statements that in times of revolution the utmost flexibility is demanded." And more:

> "Our theory is not a dogma, but a guide to action," Marx and Engels always said, rightly ridiculing the mere memorizing and repetition of "formulas," that are capable of marking out only *general* tasks, which are necessarily modifiable by the *concrete* economic and political conditions of each particular *period* of the historical process.[13]

It has been asserted "Leninism was Marxism in a hurry," which is perhaps a different way of saying what Hungarian Marxist Georg Lukács once stressed: "*The actuality of the revolution: this is the core of Lenin's thought* and his decisive link with Marx." This didn't mean impatiently flailing about with revolutionary gestures and verbiage, but linking all of one's perceptions, analyses, and activity to the revolutionary commitment. Lenin always saw, Lukács notes, "the problems of the age as a whole: *the onset of the last phase of capitalism and the possibilities of turning the now inevitable final struggle between bourgeoisie and proletariat in favor of the proletariat—of human salvation.*"[14]

Vladimir had no patience if "there was no action, but mostly idle talk and showing off," as his sister Anna put it. "He shrank from all empty talk; he wanted to take his knowledge and his abilities to the class which he knew was destined to accomplish the revolution—the working class." She added: "He was looking for people who, like himself, were convinced that revolution in Russia would be made by the working class or not at all."[15] By 1900, he expressed this in the essay "The Urgent Tasks of Our Movement," just before the 30-year-old Ulyanov adopted the revolutionary pen-name *Lenin.*

> We must train people who will devote the whole of their lives, not only their spare evenings, to the revolution; we must build up an organization large enough to permit the introduction of a strict division of labor in the various forms of our work. ... If we have a strongly organized party, a single strike may turn into a political demonstration, into a political victory over the government. If we have a strongly organized party, a revolt in a single locality may grow into a victorious revolution. We must bear in mind that the struggles with the government for partial demands and the gain of certain concessions are merely light skirmishes with the enemy, encounters between outposts, whereas the decisive battle is still to come. Before us, in all its strength, towers the enemy fortress, which is raining shot and shell upon us, mowing down our best fighters. We must capture this fortress, and we will capture it, if we unite all the forces of the awakening proletariat with all the forces of the Russian revolutionaries into one party which will attract all that is vital and honest in Russia.[16]

This appeal is at the heart of what has been named "Leninist" thought. The political organization, known globally as the Bolshevik party, that Lenin played such a central role in helping to forge, would prove capable of bringing into being the 1917 Revolution that—for many—was seen as an amazing triumph over the enemy fortress of oppression and exploitation.

Yet "the Bolshevik party that emerged by February 1917 was not a personal creation of Lenin," notes the careful scholar Soma Marik. "While he was its foremost theoretician, the party was created by protracted interactions between practical workers and theorists, and repeatedly remodeled."[17] It was the culmination of an interactive process between Ulyanov/Lenin and "people like himself" who shared his commitments. It may be helpful, then, to conclude this initial chapter with further reflections on qualities of the person and relationships from which such perspectives would flow.

LENIN AND HIS COMRADES

In some ways his closest comrade was Nadezhda Krupskaya, a serious-minded young activist he met at a small political meeting in

1894. She was impressed by young Ulyanov's reputation in activist circles as "a very erudite Marxist," but perhaps less impressed by what seemed harsh laughter and sarcasm aimed at someone at the meeting with whom Ulyanov disagreed. Yet she soon found in him more positive qualities: "a scrupulously honest approach to all questions," and a capacity to articulate "the best, the most powerful and complete formulation of the standpoint of revolutionary Social-Democracy."[18]

More than this, Ulyanov showed himself a capable teacher in workers' study circles: for example, in the first half of a class he would provide a presentation of an aspect of Marx's *Capital*, and in the second half of the class he would have the students talk about details from their own work lives, going on to relate this to what Marx had written. He was also in the forefront of those positively responding to a major essay "On Agitation" being circulated in the Marxist underground, which pushed beyond study circles. This method of agitation focused on "the workers' everyday needs," actively assisting workers' struggles for improvements in the workplace, "combining the economic and political struggle." All in all, Ulyanov provided "a brilliant example of how to approach the average worker of that time."[19]

Krupskaya was herself a teacher, popular in the classroom of the local workers' educational institute. She proved to be an extraordinarily diligent and effective organizer, whether in the classroom or in the underground. She would go on to demonstrate a talent in helping draw women workers and youth into the struggle. Keenly aware of the injustices permeating society, she would often comment, almost compulsively, "the Russian worker lives badly" and "our peasants have no rights" and "the autocracy is the enemy of the people" as if to drive herself and others onward to help make things right.[20]

Women like Krupskaya exercised a formative influence upon Vladimir Ulyanov. Throughout his life, outstanding personalities in the socialist movement impacted on him, including some who argued with him, and among these were Rosa Luxemburg, Clara Zetkin, Alexandra Kollontai, Angelica Balabanoff, Inessa Armand. One is reminded of the bond he had with his sister Olga, although in regard to Armand, informed speculation holds that she and

Lenin had a love affair in later years. Setting aside the fiction of a semi-public ménage à trois,[21] there is certainly evidence that Armand and Krupskaya were close, with Krupskaya adopting her daughter after Armand died of cholera in 1920.

When Ulyanov and Krupskaya were both arrested in the late 1890s and sentenced to Siberian exile, they agreed to declare themselves engaged to be married, in order to be confined to the same exile village. This was ostensibly to facilitate political work—but when the request was granted, with the tsarist authorities insisting on a speedy marriage, the two had, for the first time, "a good long talk" in which significant discoveries were made: they both passionately loved Russian literature (Turgenev, Chernyshevsky, Tolstoy, Chekhov, etc.), and they were attracted to each other more than just intellectually. Late in life Krupskaya confided to her secretary what she had discreetly left out of her *Reminiscences of Lenin*: "Just think, we were young then, we had just been married, we were deeply in love with one another. … If I did not write about this in my memoirs, that does not mean that there was neither poetry nor youthful passion in our life."[22]

Also in the late 1890s, however, Krupskaya had contracted Graves' Disease—more popularly known as goiter—for which there was then no known cure. Her youthful beauty gave way to what some termed "rather drab" features[23] and protruding eyes, although the same critical mind and determined commitments from earlier years continued to shine through.

The intimacy of daily life, of comradeship in struggle, and of shared values with Lenin also continued. Krupskaya's contribution in the pre-1917 years was immense. "She was at the very center of all the organizational work," Trotsky wrote of the early 1900s. "She received comrades when they arrived, instructed them when they left, established connections, supplied secret addresses, wrote letters, coded and decoded correspondence."[24] Aside from a pioneering 1899 pamphlet *The Woman Worker* (as well as later educational writings of the 1920s), she left most of the analytical and theoretical labor to other comrades, although such qualities saturate her *Reminiscences of Lenin*.

In charge of their shared household, Krupskaya was little more than a perfunctory housekeeper, and her culinary skills were not judged to be outstanding, but her creative energies found other outlets. During Lenin's early exile, a visiting comrade came upon her "bustling about a Christmas tree, decorating it with absorbing interest, and making toys." While Lenin would have nothing to do with "this religious amusement," the comrade was corralled into helping with "drawing and cutting little animals out of cardboard," and he recalled: "She was as happy as a child thinking of the surprise and delight of the little folk at the magic tree." In fact, Lenin shared his companion's "genuine pleasure from associating with children and entertaining them," though his "love of children was exceeded," according to Isaac Don Levine, "perhaps by his fondness for cats." Krupskaya also seems to have shared Lenin's enjoyment of "being in close touch with nature," and she made it a habit of "gamely joining him on many of his arduous excursions," notes researcher Carter Elwood, which included "swimming, rowing, hunting, skating, gymnastics, cycling, walking and especially mountain climbing."[25]

While Lenin lived, Krupskaya was a sounding-board as he developed his own theoretical, analytical, and polemical works, and she remained his companion at the very end as he was dying. "Everybody has left us—they express sympathy but are afraid to call on us," she wrote in May 1923. "The only thing that keeps me going is that Volodya is glad to see me in the morning, he takes my hand, and sometimes we exchange a few words about things for which however there are no words."[26]

RELATIONSHIPS AND LEADERSHIP

There were also strong intellectual and emotional bonds formed with the older "father of Russian Marxism" George Plekhanov, and with fellow activists and thinkers of Lenin's generation, such as Julius Martov and Alexander Bogdanov. Feelings of warmth and respect persisted toward Plekhanov and Martov, despite the sharp political differences later dividing them. This reality is quite different from the cold and calculating image often used to portray Lenin. After a later political break with Bogdanov, Lenin's feelings of betrayal seem to have gone too deep for him to forgive and forget—but this was unusual for him.

"In his attitude to his enemies there was no feeling of bitterness, but nevertheless he was a cruel political opponent," Anatoly Lunacharsky recounted. Once the debate was over, however, and the disputed issues resolved, Lenin usually was prepared to embrace comrades on the other side of the dispute and draw them into positions of leadership and responsibility—as was the case with Lunacharsky himself, as well as Nikolai Bukharin, Lev Kamenev, Gregory Zinoviev, Leon Trotsky, Nikolai Pokrovsky, and others. Lenin's measuring-stick was what would strengthen the revolutionary organization and enrich the revolutionary struggle. He had little time or inclination to nurse grudges, and he was far from being the grim ascetic that some have portrayed him as being. "Life sparkles and bubbles within him," as Lunacharsky put it, and Trotsky added: "he lived a full life, a wonderfully abundant life, developing, expanding his whole personality, serving a cause which he himself freely chose."[27]

This contributed to what some have seen as Lenin's appeal, which helped ensure his effectiveness as a political leader. One element in this leadership comes through in reflections of Boris I. Nicolaevsky, a Bolshevik-turned-Menshevik, later a prominent archivist and historian. He expressed an enduring admiration for Lenin "as a good *khoziain* or party manager," a "good *Iskra* type of organizer," in contrast to most of the leading Mensheviks. According to Ladis Kristof:

> Boris Ivanovich often wistfully reminisced about how skillfully Lenin generated loyalties by showing, in little things, that he cared for and remembered the services of party activists. For instance, Krupskaya would write a letter to an exile to which Lenin would add a short note, thus forging a lasting bond between the exile and the party leader who remembered him.[28]

Another quality was emphasized by M.N. Pokrovsky who had been involved in more than one factional battle with Lenin. He wrote of Lenin's "colossal insight," explaining: "I often quarreled with him about practical matters, got into a mess each time, and after this operation was repeated about seven times, I stopped arguing and submitted to Ilyich, even when logic was telling me you must not act that way—but, I thought, he understands better."[29]

Writing in 1919 after a stay in Soviet Russia, U.S. journalist Albert Rhys Williams reported similar findings after lengthy discussions with a small cluster of returning Russian-American revolutionaries, whom he described as "free, young, sturdy spirits," who "were neither fools nor imbeciles. Knocking about the world had hammered all of that out of them. Nor were these men hero-worshippers. The Bolshevik movement was elemental and passionate, but it was scientific, realistic, and uncongenial to hero-worship." Nonetheless, regarding Lenin, "on the whole, they trusted him to use his subtle and wide knowledge of Marxist theory, checked against his close knowledge of people, and his genius as a tactician to know the moment when the people were ready to seize power, and to lead the way."[30]

Yet Lenin became increasingly uncomfortable with the implications of this. In 1921, when Adolph Joffe wrote to Lenin that it was the Bolshevik leader who basically called the shots within the organization's Central Committee, Lenin objected. "The old Central Committee (1919–20) defeated me on one gigantically important question, as you know from the discussion. On organizational and personal questions I have been in a minority countless times. You yourself saw many instances when you were a Central Committee member."[31]

Truth was on the side of both Lenin and Joffe. Two opposed tendencies were, in fact, deeply embedded in the Bolshevik experience.

In the first 15 years of that experience, things tilted in the democratic-collective direction. Lenin had committed immense energies to helping create a democratic collective of like-minded (yet critical-minded) comrades who would make use of a Marxist program to help the working class bring a transition from capitalism to socialism. There was need for discussion and debate to determine "what is to be done?"—such a collective process was seen by Lenin as essential in order to actually *do* what must be done.

This was increasingly replaced by a top-down reality in the early Soviet Republic. The political, social, economic, and military cataclysm of foreign invasion and brutal civil war powerfully reinforced an authoritarian trend among the triumphant Bolsheviks. This included an increased deference toward the party's leader—observed by the shrewd Joffe despite Lenin's anxious objection. Ironically, Lenin's strengths worked against what he sought to create: his well-earned authority helped establish a pattern that would undermine the democratic collectivism of his organization. This fatal dynamic persisted and grew stronger after Lenin's life slipped away. Recognition of such ironies contributes to our understanding of what happened—as does a recognition of Lenin's strengths.

2

Theory, Organization, Action (1901–05)

In his 1902 classic *What Is to Be Done?*, Lenin wrote: "Without revolutionary theory, there can be no revolutionary movement."[1] Before we turn to Lenin's explanation, we need to make sense of the actual words—revolutionary, theory, movement.

ESSENTIAL CONCEPTS

As with many important terms, the word *revolutionary* can have more than one meaning, sometimes being little more than flashy rhetoric. But for Lenin and those in his political circle, it has the connotation of genuine and fundamental change in the political and economic structures of society—brought about through the actions and for the benefit of the majority of the population. *Theory* involves sets of ideas one uses to understand and explain aspects of reality. In this case, it involves conceptualizations of realities one finds oppressive and wishes to change, sometimes connecting as well with sets of ideas about the kinds of changes one would like to see, and with the ideas of how such changes could be brought about. Theories that are durable have been tested by practice and are the fruit of an accumulation of experience. *Movement* can refer to motion, activity, action—but it can also refer to sustained, organized activities involving large numbers of people pushing for certain goals.

Wrapping one's mind around all this makes "without revolutionary theory, there can be no revolutionary movement" sound reasonable. Yet in emphasizing this, Lenin explains, he is concerned to challenge what he calls *opportunism.* This term added up to taking advantage of what seem to be opportunities without grounding such action in a deeper understanding that theory provides. (It is important to avoid confusion here: Lenin was always in favor of taking advantage of new opportunities and of "thinking outside the box"—but he consistently sought to do this in ways consistent with, and helping to advance, revolutionary theory and principles.) Within the socialist movement, a "revisionist" current had developed which sought to revise or set aside the revolutionary theories associated with Karl Marx, in order to pursue more modest changes for social or economic improvements (reforms), or as Lenin put it: "fashionable preaching of opportunism goes hand in hand with an infatuation for the narrowest forms of practical activity."[2] Lenin believed the opportunistic approach would be incapable of bringing about a society of the free and the equal in which no person is subjected to oppression, exploitation, or degradation.

BASIC PERSPECTIVES

Lenin linked his nine-word injunction with three additional notions: (1) to find the correct path, the Russian Social Democratic Labor Party (RSDLP)—still in the process of formation—needed to clarify its orientation (including sorting out where it agreed and disagreed with other revolutionary currents, such as the populists); (2) the RSDLP was part of a worldwide movement that was "in its very essence … international," and could "be successful only if it makes use of the experiences of other countries"; and (3) at the same time, the RSDLP faced very specific realities which had "never confronted any other socialist party in the world," which imposed very specific "political and organizational duties which the task of emancipating the whole people from the yoke of autocracy imposes upon us."[3]

Lenin was not developing these ideas on his own. He was part of a significant cluster influenced by such Marxist theorists as Plekhanov, not to mention the writings of Marx and Engels, gathering around the revolutionary paper *Iskra*, and also producing a significant body of literature—for example, Alexander Bogdanov's *Short Course of Economic Science*, published in 1897 and praised by Lenin at the time. "Uniting masses of workers for a single purpose in a single workshop conducted along strictly defined rules," Bogdanov noted, "industrial capitalism trains them to unity and discipline which are necessary pre-requisites for the stability and practical success of any form of organization."[4] Russian Marxists saw this as the wave of the future in their country—but the newly formed organization must make use of revolutionary theory to be coherent and effective.

The revolutionary theories developed by Marx proved most adequate because they were grounded in the social sciences—what we now subdivide into economics, sociology, political science, anthropology, psychology, history. Without the use of such *scientific* socialist theories, Lenin and others felt, the most one can expect to develop among the mass of exploited laborers is an elemental opposition to their oppression and exploitation. Under capitalism, this meant efforts to organize trade unions for limited, achievable improvements at the workplace, *trade union consciousness*. Lenin distinguished this from the more sweeping *class consciousness* he saw as necessary for the working class to free itself both from tsarist oppression and capitalist exploitation.

Some conclude Lenin believed workers need an elite of "vanguard" intellectuals to "literally do their thinking for them" (as anthropologist James C. Scott puts it).[5] But Lenin's actual point is that one cannot assume workers will spontaneously be either pro-socialist or pro-capitalist. They may naturally gravitate toward trade union activity to protect their wages and working conditions, but they may also accept the capitalist reality in which they exist. "Lenin refused to confuse the present with the future," historian Ronald Suny points out, "or to consider the labor movement either one-dimensionally determined by objective economic forces or fated to fall under the sway of the currently hegemonic ideology of the bourgeoisie."[6] He believed the labor movement must move beyond simple trade unionism (focused solely on wages and working conditions) to include socialist ideas and revolutionary politics.

As with Marx and Engels, and with authoritative interpreters Karl Kautsky (in Germany) and George Plekhanov (in Russia), Lenin and his co-thinkers were convinced of the need for both the working class and socialism to merge into a unified entity if either was to triumph. And in all countries—but countries such as Russia most of all—the working-class struggle for socialism was inseparable from the struggle for genuine and thoroughgoing democracy.

Here too, Bogdanov had clearly outlined what Lenin and other Russian Marxists understood:

> In countries that are not free, where the bourgeoisie—and, in the most backward countries, the feudal classes—in their own interests hinder all political life and development of class consciousness among the workers, the trade union economic struggle, the struggle for factory legislation, and the struggle for socialism arouse, as their necessary means and condition, a struggle for civil liberties and a democratic state. In this struggle the workers may find allies among the intelligent peasants, petty artisans, and the badly paid mental workers, generally speaking in the lower classes of bourgeois society, which are economically and politically oppressed by the upper class.[7]

Lenin analyzed the working class—individuals with a variety of occupations, skills, experiences, and psychologies—as crystalizing into different layers. Some would have little interest or inclination to engage with larger social, economic or political issues, while others ("conscious workers") would have greater interest and inclination—and among this latter group is a smaller but vital stratum who were "advanced workers" or "worker-revolutionaries" or "the working-class vanguard."

It is a mistake to define "the party as vanguard," as John Molyneux once put it in his minor classic *Marxism and the Party*. Molyneux himself quickly added this clarification: "the party is a vanguard, but the vanguard is *not* a tiny elite standing outside the main body of the class; it is the hundreds of thousands of workers who actually lead the class in its everyday battles in the factories, the pits, the offices, the housing estates and the streets."[8] This suggests the would-be revolutionary party is *not* "the vanguard." The vanguard is a layer of the working class that has a developed sense of class consciousness and is capable of providing practical leadership in struggles to advance the interests of the working class. A revolutionary party approximates the status of "vanguard party" only if its orientation is embraced by the *broad vanguard layer of the working class* Molyneux describes.

The RSDLP was by no means the only socialist-oriented organization seeking to overthrow tsarism. Deeply rooted in the revolutionary populism of earlier years was the Socialist-Revolutionary Party (the Socialist-Revolutionaries, SRs), reaching out not only to workers and intellectuals, but especially to Russia's vast peasantry. Gregory Zinoviev recalled the SRs were initially able to project "a more revolutionary aura than the Marxists." This was because an essential aspect of their orientation involved a systematic use of individual terrorism. In recruiting activists away from the RSDLP, SRs could say: "There you can see the one who kills the [governmental] minister is the revolutionary, while the one who educates the workers is just a 'high-brow.'" Zinoviev noted that Marxists such as Lenin did not deny the need for revolutionary violence in overthrowing the tsarist order, but Marxists insisted "the assassination of this or that minister does not change things." Instead "we must raise up the masses, organize millions of people, and educate the working class" to bring about the revolutionary overturn.[9]

Such perceptions arose from an immersion of young revolutionaries in the life and struggles of the dynamically growing working class. Some like Nadezhda Krupskaya became night-school teachers to assist workers who spent their off-work hours hungrily pursuing literacy and knowledge. Clusters of workers would sometimes form their own study circles and pitch in to pay a radical student to teach them about *everything*: the natural world, astronomy, history, society and economics, revolutionary theory, and more. Sometimes there were irritated and resentful reactions against what felt like elitism and arrogance from such student-teacher "know-it-alls"—bringing an end to one or another study circle. But the hunger for absorbing and sharing knowledge persisted, and the circles continued to multiply. In factories and communities throughout Russia, a proliferation of self-taught working-class intellectuals challenged growing handfuls of workmates and neighbors to think critically about the world around them for the purpose of *doing something* to change the situation for the better.

In workplaces and working-class communities throughout the Russian Empire, "Marxist concepts passed from visiting *intelligenty* to the 'leading workers,' who in turn influenced other workers' attitudes," as Suny recounts. "The process was tedious and dangerous, but the effects of these discrete contacts with small propaganda circles permanently affected some workers' lives."[10] A proliferation of stories later shared by "conscious" workers emerging from the growing network of informal workers' study and conversation circles give a sense of this development. The reminiscences of Sergei Alliluev (Stalin's future father-in-law) provide one example:

> For the first time doubts crept into my head about the rightness of the order existing on the earth. ... The change in my thinking, the break with old habits and conceptions occurred, understandably, not all at once. Gradually, day by day, under the influence of books and conversations with comrades, under the direct impression of the harsh school of my own life, thoughts began to appear about the need for a struggle against the existing order. From a lone rebel, unable to subordinate his actions to a definite idea, I grew into a conscious participant in the general struggle of the working class.[11]

The role of socialists in helping advance this evolving consciousness was an urgent matter for young activists such as Lenin, and he responded with enthusiasm to ideas put forward in the late 1890s by another youthful theorist and activist who for a time became one of his soulmates, Julius Martov. In a pamphlet written with Arkadi Kremer, "On Agitation," Martov sharply criticized a passive study group mentality prevalent in Social Democratic study circles, observing that "the majority of the worker Social Democrats sympathize with the practical activity that we condemn as useless." Would-be revolutionaries in Russia (the "we" referred to) were getting it wrong: "Scientific socialism appeared in the West [of Europe] as the theoretical expression of the workers' movement; with us it is transformed into abstract theory, unwilling to descend from the transcendental heights of scientific generalization."[12]

Capitalist "entrepreneurs ... strive for an increase in surplus value," which involved "a constant niggling struggle with the proletariat, which defends its existence and cannot but protest against the obvious encroachment on its well-being." As such a dynamic "becomes keener, deeper and more general, this struggle takes on the character of class struggle," which generates working-class consciousness, which increasingly takes on a political character that challenges the tsarist political order. The pamphlet insisted "social democracy can only become the real people's party when it bases its program of activity on the needs that are actually felt by the working class." Two extremes were rejected: (1) "losing touch with the practical basis and only studying" and (2) "agitating among the mass [around practical gains] without at the same time concerning ourselves with theory."[13]

The pamphlet concluded: "We must exert ourselves so that capitalism, in its conquest of one branch of production after another, will not just leave ruination behind it but that following immediately on its heels the ranks of the organized workers' army should rise ... [that] will know how to oppose exploitation with the strength of organization, the strength of class self-consciousness."[14] This became a centerpiece in the orientation of those gathering around *Iskra*.

Iskra adherents argued that such working-class intellectuals, and such non-worker intellectuals as Lenin, Krupskaya, Martov, Plekhanov, Bogdanov, etc. must combine as revolutionary activists, evolving into *professional revolutionaries*. Amateurs, for whom the revolutionary movement was merely a part-time hobby, could not actually do what must be done. What was needed, they believed, were people for whom revolutionary struggle is a central commitment of their lives. Sometimes the term *cadre* has been used to define (as Lenin puts it) someone who becomes, at one and the same time, "a *professional* agitator, organizer, propagandist, literature distributor, etc., etc."[15]

In *What Is to Be Done?* Lenin held up for Russian revolutionaries the ideal of Germany's massive Social Democratic Party (the SPD), then the largest socialist workers' party in the world. He extolled the SPD's example of elevating the professional revolutionary rooted in the advanced layer of the working class, the experienced working-class activist with multifaceted skills, who would

> widen the field of his activity, to spread it from one factory to the whole of the industry, from a single locality to the whole

> country. He acquires experience and dexterity in his profession; he broadens his outlook and increases his knowledge; he observes at close quarters the prominent political leaders from other localities and of other parties; he strives to rise to their level and combine in himself the knowledge of the working-class environment and the freshness of socialist convictions with professional skill, without which the proletariat *cannot* wage a stubborn struggle against its excellently trained enemies.[16]

Lenin emphasized the difference between the very repressive conditions of tsarist Russia and the freer conditions existing in European countries to the West: "what is to a great extent automatic in a politically free country must in Russia be done deliberately and systematically by our organizations." Not indulging in "toy democracy" notions that could get everyone arrested, Lenin insisted the Russian organization must maintain secure underground practices to protect the working-class revolutionary so that "he may go underground in good time," when necessary "change the place of his activity … and be able to hold out for at least a few years in the struggle against the gendarmes." Emphasizing "the fine art of not getting arrested," he projected the development of a network of "an increasing number of talented agitators, but also talented organizers, propagandists, and 'practical workers' in the best sense of the term," intimately connected with "the spontaneous rise of a mass workers' movement [that] becomes broader and deeper." Lenin envisioned the revolutionary party as "a close and compact body of comrades" in which all are infused with "a lively sense of their responsibility." The "forces of specially trained worker-revolutionaries who have gone through extensive preparation," Lenin believed, "boundlessly devoted to the revolution, will enjoy the boundless confidence of the widest masses of the workers."[17]

Lenin and other *Iskra* supporters argued against a trend among Russian Marxists called Economism. The Economists held Marxists should avoid non-economic issues that might be of little interest to the average worker, focusing instead on what they considered more practical questions. Helping to generate immediate trade union activity, they suggested, would do more to generate the mass workers' movement that Russian Marxists believed in. "The Social-Democrat's ideal should not be the trade union secretary, but *the tribune of the people*," Lenin responded, "who is able to react to every manifestation of tyranny and oppression, no matter where it appears, no matter what stratum or class of the people it affects."[18]

This included a long list:

> the rural superintendents and their flogging of peasants, the corruption of the officials and the police treatment of the "common people" in the cities, the fight against the famine-stricken and the suppression of the popular striving towards enlightenment and knowledge, the extortion of taxes and the persecution of the religious sects, the humiliating treatment of soldiers and the barrack methods in the treatment of the students and liberal intellectuals.

A revolutionary tribune of the people would be one

> who is able to generalize all these manifestations and produce a single picture of police violence and capitalist exploitation; who is able to take advantage of every event, however small, in order to set forth *before all* his socialist convictions and his democratic demands, in order to clarify for *all* and everyone the world-historic significance of the struggle for the emancipation of the proletariat.[19]

ACTIVIST MEMBERSHIP, DEMOCRATIC FUNCTIONING, POLITICAL INDEPENDENCE

Theodore Dan (who later became one of Lenin's leading adversaries) smuggled the first copies of this work into Russia in 1902, later noting "the basic objective of *What Is to Be Done?* was the concretization of the organizational ideas formulated in the *Iskra* program." He added that all members of the editorial board and the closest contributors to *Iskra* generally found it to be "superlative."[20] To rebuild the RSDLP around these ideas, they organized a second congress of the RSDLP, this time held in exile (starting in

Brussels, then moving to London) to avoid the calamity of arrests that had undone the work of the 1898 founding congress.

As they gathered for the second congress in 1903, supporters of *Iskra* imagined the outcome would be a more unified, more coherent activist party guided by revolutionary Marxist theory. Instead, there was a stunning eruption of fierce debates. Before the congress ended, there were two distinct factions—the Bolsheviks (from the Russian *bolshe*, meaning "more," since they had gained a plurality of votes) and the Mensheviks (from the Russian word *menshe*, meaning "less"). The Bolsheviks, led by Lenin, insisted on a more disciplined party than was favored by the Mensheviks, who became associated with Martov.

The two major disputes had to do with (1) how to define a member of the RSDLP and (2) how the *Iskra* editorial board should be structured. It was the second dispute that actually resulted in an organizational split.

Lenin's friend Julius Martov proposed the following to define membership: "one who accepts its program and supports it both materially and by regular cooperation under the leadership of one of its organizations." Feeling that was too loose, Lenin proposed this definition: "one who recognizes the Party's program and supports it by material means and by personal participation in one of the Party's organizations."[21]

Martov found Lenin's proposal too restrictive, explaining: "The more widespread the title of Party member the better. We could only rejoice if every striker, every demonstrator, answering for his actions, could proclaim himself a party member. For me a conspiratorial organization only has meaning when it is enveloped by a broad Social-Democratic working-class party."[22]

Lenin argued: "In the period of the Party's life which we are now passing through it is just this 'elasticity' [proposed by Martov] that most certainly opens the door to all the elements of confusion, vacillation and opportunism." He argued for "safeguarding the firmness of the Party's line and the purity of its principles." In the following year, in *One Step Forward, Two Steps Back*, he explained further:

> The stronger our Party organizations, consisting of real Social-Democrats, the less wavering there is within the Party, the more varied, richer, and more fruitful will be the Party's influence on the elements of the masses surrounding it and guided by it. The Party, as the vanguard of the working class, must not be confused, after all, with the entire class.[23]

Lenin lost the vote on this, and he accepted the defeat (although intending to raise the matter again later, perhaps at the next RSDLP congress). Not long afterward, the Mensheviks themselves decided to define membership along the lines of Lenin's wording. In fact, when one looks at Bolshevik and Menshevik ideas and policies on organizational structure and functioning, they seem to be in basic agreement on all essentials—allowing for as much democracy as would be possible, given the constraints of underground functioning under tsarist repression, and within a clearly defined Marxist political framework.

Yet Lenin had a different conception than some of his Menshevik comrades of what inner-party democracy should look like. This comes through in his recounting of a conversation with a comrade taking an "in-between" position at the second RSDLP congress. "How oppressive the atmosphere is at our congress!" the other comrade had complained. "This bitter fighting, this agitation one against the other, this biting controversy, this uncomradely attitude." Lenin felt differently. "What a splendid thing our congress is!" he replied. "A free and open struggle. Opinions have been stated. The shades have been brought out. The groups have taken shape. Hands have been raised. A decision has been taken. A stage has been passed. Forward! That's the stuff for me! That's life!"[24]

Lenin compared this to the "diplomatic" compromises and walking on eggshells that he felt had too often characterized the internal politics of small groups of amateurish would-be revolutionaries—"the endless, tedious word-chopping of intellectuals which terminates not because the question has been settled, but because they are too tired to talk anymore." This brings us to the second controversy splitting Mensheviks from Bolsheviks: the structure of *Iskra*'s editorial board.

The six-person editorial board had proved unwieldy, with three elders (Plekhanov, Axelrod, Zasulich) and three younger activists (Lenin, Martov, Potresov). It generated ongoing collision of egos, much opinionated discussion, too little discipline in doing the work of editing and writing. At the congress Lenin proposed, in the interests of efficiency, a reduction of the editorial board to three: Plekhanov, Lenin, Martov. While Plekhanov supported the measure, Axelrod, Zasulich, and Potresov were insulted, and Martov (who felt his influence would be undermined) was also opposed. Some note that Lenin was concerned to ensure that his own political/organizational approach would dominate—which is obviously the case—but such a desire is hardly inconsistent with a commitment to democratic functioning.

When Lenin's proposal won a majority of votes at the congress, the minority accused Lenin of wanting to be a dictator, furiously denouncing the decision, and refusing to recognize its legitimacy. Lenin was astonished, and Plekhanov—at first siding with Lenin—decided to make his peace with the other side. Lenin resigned from the editorial board, and *Iskra* then waged an open campaign against Lenin's heartlessness and presumed dictatorial intentions. He protested that comrades on the other side of the dispute were the ones violating serious democratic principles.

Pro-*Iskra* working-class militants back in Russia, hearing rumors of the split, suffered "the agony of uncertainty" for many days. "We heard the reports on the Congress from both sides, and immediately each side began agitating for its own line," recalled Osip Piatnitsky. "I was torn between the two." First of all, "I was very sorry that they had offended Zasulich, Potresov … and Axelrod," and on top of this "comrades with whom I had been especially close were in the Menshevik camp"—but on the other hand "I fully endorsed the organizational structure of the Party advocated with Lenin. Logically I was with the majority, but my personal sympathies … were with the minority."[25]

"The comrades grouped around Lenin were far more seriously committed to principles, which they wanted to see applied at all cost and pervading all the practical work," Krupskaya recounted. "The other group had more of the man-in-the-street mentality, were given to compromise and concessions in principle, and had more regard for persons." Some who rallied to Lenin shared Alexander Bogdanov's opinion that "people in a position of leadership in the party and the members of the editorial board of its central organ ... ought not to be for life." Bogdanov agreed with Lenin that "the organization of the RSDLP should be on democratic principles, that there should be majority rule," that there were no "insuperable" divisions between Mensheviks and Bolsheviks, and that "the 'minority' [Mensheviks] have acted reprehensibly in refusing to abide by the decisions of the Second Congress of the party."[26]

As it turned out, more serious differences soon arose. Late in 1904, Pavel Axelrod and other Mensheviks argued that "our attitude towards the liberal bourgeoisie is defined by the task of imbuing it with more courage and impelling it to join in those [democratic] demands being put forward by the proletariat led by the Social-Democracy." Tactical moderation should be adopted so as not to frighten away such liberal allies.[27]

In contrast, Lenin insisted on the need for political independence of the working class from the bourgeois politicians, commenting: "the very notion that 'our' demands, the demands of working-class democracy, should be presented to the government by the liberal democrats is a queer one." There were two reasons:

> On the one hand, the liberal democrats, being bourgeois democrats, can never identify themselves with "our" demands, can never uphold them sincerely, consistently, and resolutely. ... On the other hand, if we should be strong enough to exert serious influence on the bourgeois democrats generally ..., we should be quite strong enough to present our demands to the government ourselves.[28]

Lenin called upon revolutionary socialists to make police stations, censorship offices, and jails holding political prisoners the sites for a "mass demonstration (because demonstrations not of a mass nature are altogether without significance)." He called for an orientation in which

> the workers will rise still more fearlessly in still greater numbers, to finish off the bear, to win by force for themselves what is

> promised as charity to the liberal bourgeois gentry—freedom of assembly, freedom of the workers' press, full political freedom for a broad and open struggle for the complete victory of socialism.[29]

This suggests what would be a great divide between Bolsheviks and Mensheviks. Axelrod's proposal projected a worker-capitalist alliance in the struggle to overthrow tsarism. Lenin envisioned a different alliance, expressed in his 1903 pamphlet *To the Rural Poor*, which noted "the urban workers come out into the streets and squares and publicly demand *freedom*," and went on to forecast the peasants "will rise all over Russia and go to the aid of the urban workers, will fight to the end for the freedom of the workers and peasants."[30]

ACTIVISM VS. SECTARIANISM

There were opposite tendencies arising especially within Bolshevik ranks, however, associated with what is sometimes termed *sectarianism*. This involves a revolutionary group rigidly adhering to abstract "revolutionary principles" (one might say *political correctness*) in ways that only separate it from the actual consciousness and struggles of the oppressed. This also relates to the ability to take advantage of new opportunities and of "thinking outside the box"—the sectarian impulse veers away from such things, in the name of established "revolutionary principles." Lenin's own impulse, generally, was to *engage* with new opportunities in ways consistent with, and helping to advance, revolutionary perspectives.

In late 1904, a mass workers' movement came together around a Russian Orthodox priest, Father Georgi Gapon. He combined an odd blend of Christian Socialist and pro-tsarist notions, involving self-help and mild reform notions, buttressed by a network of workers' tea-rooms and reading rooms whose existence the tsarist authorities facilitated. Attracting far more working-class participants than either the Bolsheviks or Mensheviks were able to rally, sectors of the Gapon movement began to go further than anticipated, organizing militant strikes in the factories of St. Petersburg. Gapon and those around him projected a mass march to the tsar's

Winter Palace to be held in early January of 1905—its purpose being to deliver, respectfully and reverentially, a petition asking the tsar to respond positively to the workers' requests for democratic rights and economic justice.

Many in the RSDLP (Mensheviks as well as Bolsheviks) "strongly insisted that Social Democrats ought to refuse to participate in it in any way," according to the account of Solomon Schwarz, an activist of that time. "It was shameful and unworthy of Social Democrats, they said, to march to the Winter Palace in a religious procession led by a priest, to beg for compassion and pity for workers, especially as it would end only in shooting and beatings." St. Petersburg Bolshevik organizer S.I. Gusev reported to Lenin (then in Switzerland): "Exposing and fighting Gapon will be the basis of the agitation we are hurriedly preparing."[31]

Lenin assessed the Gapon movement differently. He acknowledged Gapon's operations had been "initiated by the police in the interests of the police, in the interests of supporting the autocracy and demoralizing the political consciousness of the workers," but he emphasized that "this movement is turning against the autocracy and is becoming an outbreak of the proletarian class struggle. We are witnessing one of the great clashes between the developing proletarian class and its enemies, clashes that will leave their mark for many years to come."[32]

A similar problem developed in Bolshevik ranks around the question of trade unions. One Bolshevik militant, for example, argued "the trade union struggle … makes bourgeois notions stick to the proletarian's psychology, which obscure his proletarian consciousness or prevent its development." A sectarian Bolshevik resolution warned in 1905 that "in the present period Social-Democracy must not take the initiative in creating unions." St. Petersburg organizer Gusev advanced a resolution which stressed the need "to expose … all the illusions about trade unions," emphasizing "that the most vital, primary task … is to prepare immediately for an armed uprising." The resolution called for "an energetic ideological struggle against the so-called Mensheviks, who are reverting, on the issue of trade unions, to the narrow, erroneous viewpoint of the Economists, which demeans the tasks of Social-Democracy and holds back the thrust of the proletarian movement."[33]

Lenin disagreed. "Generally speaking, I think we should be careful not to exaggerate the struggle against the Mensheviks on this issue," he wrote. "This is probably just the time when trade unions will soon begin to spring up. We must not stand aloof, and above all not give any occasion for thinking that we ought to stand aloof, but endeavor to take part, to influence, etc." He urged "that at the very outset Russian Social-Democrats should strike the right note in regard to the trade unions, and at once create a tradition of Social-Democratic initiative in this matter, of Social-Democratic participation, of Social-Democratic leadership."[34]

The attitude toward the democratic workers' councils—the soviets—that arose in the midst of the revolutionary upsurge of 1905 represents one of the most striking examples of the sectarian impulse. These councils came into being to coordinate working-class action and to oversee the functioning of working-class districts during the insurgency. They were open to all workers, regardless of political affiliation, and there was a strong tendency among the Bolsheviks to see them as a Menshevik maneuver, or at best as "politically amorphous and socialistically immature workers' organizations." The Bolshevik contingent in the St. Petersburg soviet, led by the prestigious co-leader of the Bolsheviks, Alexander Bogdanov, put before the soviet a motion, in the name of the Bolshevik faction, calling for the soviet to commit itself to the RSDLP program and leadership. If this proposal was voted down (as indeed it was), the soviet would be "exposed" as politically inadequate—perhaps justifying a Bolshevik walk-out.[35]

Lenin objected to the stark either/or—Party or Soviet. "I think that … the decision must certainly be: both the Soviet of Workers' Deputies and the Party." He saw the soviets as "representing all occupations" and "should strive to include deputies from all industrial, professional and office workers, domestic servants, farm laborers, etc.," embracing "all who want and are able to fight in common for a better life for the whole working people, from all who have at least an elementary degree of political honesty." It was "inadvisable to demand that the Soviet of Workers' Deputies should accept the Social-Democratic program and join the

Russian Social Democratic Labor Party." Rather than denouncing soviets as "amorphous" and "immature," Lenin suggested they "should be regarded as the embryo of a provisional revolutionary government."[36]

We can draw three conclusions from these events. First, it would be a mistake to see the Bolshevik organization as synonymous with Lenin. It was a revolutionary collective within which he was an active and influential participant. Second, as was the case with Lenin himself, the perceptions and positions of the Bolsheviks as a whole *evolved* through debates between comrades and an interplay with actual struggles and experiences. Third, the Bolshevik organization contained different tendencies and potentialities. We will see that some of these would collide with each other, leading to further factional conflict and the further development of Lenin's thought and Bolshevism's character.

3
The Revolutionary Explosion of 1905

The massive revolutionary upsurge of 1905 has often been tagged a "dress rehearsal" for the revolutionary triumph of 1917. The realities are far more complex than that, but here we can do scant justice to the richness of the upheaval.* Our focus on Lenin's thought in this period must also be limited to several key elements: (1) his conceptualization of links between reform struggles and the revolutionary struggle, and his vision of a mass revolutionary party; (2) his stress on living realities and actual struggles, not abstract revolutionary "correctness"; (3) his orientation toward what came to be labeled the *united front*—its centrality to immediate struggles, and how it fits into the long-term struggle; (4) his view of class alliances in struggles for reform and revolution. A final and somewhat more complex matter involves (5) aspects of Lenin's thinking on armed struggle and revolutionary violence.

BUILDING A MASS REVOLUTIONARY PARTY

Some have inaccurately portrayed Lenin's argument in *What Is to Be Done?* as envisioning a small number of intellectuals organizing themselves as a tightly centralized elite that will somehow lead the workers in making a revolution. Noting that this is not what Lenin ended up doing and saying amid the revolutionary upsurge of 1905, some suggest that the mass actions of the workers, independently

* Informative studies in English include: Abraham Ascher, *The Revolution of 1905*; Laura Engelstein, *Moscow 1905*; Sidney Harcave, *First Blood: The Russian Revolution of 1905*; Solomon Schwarz, *The Russian Revolution of 1905*; Teodor Shanin, *Russia 1905–07*; and Leon Trotsky, *1905*.

of the purported intellectual elite, caused Lenin to change his mind and—at least for a time—to become more democratic.

In fact, we can see an elemental continuity in Lenin's approach. The socialist organizational ideal extolled in *What Is to Be Done?* was, after all, the German Social Democratic Party (SPD)—which Lenin perceived and described as a genuinely revolutionary mass workers' party, profoundly democratic in both its goals and its internal functioning. With the passage of decades, many (including Lenin) would be forced to conclude that the SPD was, in fact, far less democratic and revolutionary, and far more bureaucratic, than seemed evident in 1902. But the model Lenin projected was this radically democratic ideal, modified in Russia only due to the repressive conditions imposed by Tsar Nicholas' police state. Under such conditions, he warned, "broad democracy" in the organization would be "a harmful and useless toy" that would "simply facilitate the work of the police."[1] Instead there must be a network of highly disciplined clandestine committees of activist intellectuals to carry on socialist education contributing to the workers' class consciousness, and to covertly assist workers' struggles.

Just as Lenin and his comrades had been flexible in adapting their ideal to the harsh conditions imposed by tsarist authoritarianism, so did Lenin display an extremely flexible approach as some of those conditions changed for the better.

Disastrous defeat in the Russo-Japanese War of 1904—profoundly undermining the credibility and authority of the autocracy—was followed by a mass march to the Winter Palace in January 1905. As noted in the previous chapter, this was led by a Russian Orthodox priest, Father Georgi Gapon. Peaceful columns of several thousand carried religious icons, sang religious hymns, reverently displayed portraits of Tsar Nicholas II, and carried a petition addressed to him:

> We, workers and residents of the city of St, Petersburg, of various ranks and stations, our wives, children, and helpless old parents, have come to Thee, Sire, to seek justice and protection. We have become beggars; we are oppressed and burdened by labor beyond our strength; we are humiliated; we are regarded, not as human beings, but as slaves who must endure their bitter fate in

> silence. … Is it better to die—for all of us, the toiling people of all Russia, to die, allowing the capitalists (the exploiters of the working class) and the bureaucrats (who rob the government and plunder the Russian people) to live and enjoy themselves? … Do not deny Thy people help; lead them out of the depths of injustice, poverty, and ignorance; give them the chance to direct their own fate and rid themselves of the unbearable bureaucratic yoke, tear down the wall between Thyself and Thy people and let them rule together with Thee.[2]

When the tsar's troops opened fire on the crowds, a popular uprising was generated among broadening sectors of the working class. The horrified Father Gapon voiced the rage of many when he proclaimed: "We have no Tsar!" The urban insurgency helped unleash rebellion among land-hungry peasants in the countryside as tsarist authority began to crumble.

In a panic to stabilize the situation, the tsarist regime promised a new day for the people of Russia—embracing freedom of speech, freedom of press, freedom of assembly, freedom of organization (including the legalization of trade unions and the variety of liberal and socialist parties), and elections to a new parliament, the Duma. Of course, the regime had no intention of relinquishing power and would, as soon as possible, restrict what it had felt compelled to concede. At the same time, the popular mood among workers, peasants, and others remained volatile.

New opportunities called for new measures, and—as we saw in the previous chapter—Lenin was in the forefront of pushing to open up the Russian Social Democratic Labor Party's (RSDLP) functioning, bringing it more in line with the ideal of a democratic mass workers' party. The party's committee structure should be opened to an influx of newly radicalized workers, and the democratic principle should animate its functioning. This collided with more cautious inclinations of some stalwarts in Bolshevik ranks, but Lenin was insistent: "The workers have a class instinct, and given a little political experience they fairly quickly become staunch Social Democrats. I would strongly be in favor of having eight workers on our committees to every two intellectuals."[3] Soon he was calling for several hundred workers for every two intellectuals!

We have noted that Lenin also pushed for active participation of the RSDLP Bolsheviks in mass organizations and struggles *not under their control*—the democratic councils (soviets), trade unions, etc. Functioning intelligently, sharing their ideas, and helping to win victories in these broader contexts would enhance their influence and authority, contributing to an increasingly expansive class consciousness and revolutionary struggle.

This could not be advanced simply by militant pronouncements and abstract appeals, however, but must—as Krupskaya later explained—be grounded in specific demands around urgent needs. Among factory workers this had not begun with demands of workers' control of industry, but "with a campaign for tea service, for reducing working hours, and paying wages punctually."[4] Only in successful struggles for reforms, connecting with people's actual levels of consciousness and enhancing their sense of dignity and their capacity to change things for the better, could the pathway to revolution be found.

LIVING REALITY VS "POLITICAL CORRECTNESS"

Late in 1905, Lenin published an often-cited article "Party Organization and Party Literature," which many have claimed elevates "political correctness" (to be defined and controlled by Lenin's party) over the living reality and vibrant creativity essential to serious literature. He wrote that "party literature ... cannot, in fact, be an individual undertaking, independent of the common cause of the proletariat." Denouncing "non-partisan writers" and "literary supermen," he explained that "literature must become part of the common cause of the proletariat, 'a cog and a screw' of one singe great ... mechanism set in motion by the entire politically conscious vanguard of the entire working class."[5] This has often been interpreted as justifying censorship.

Two of the more careful scholars dealing with Lenin's thought, Robert C. Tucker and Christopher Read (neither of whom can be tagged as a Leninist, and both of whom could be quite critical of Lenin), have pointed out that the article in question does not have anything to do with creative literature or art. Instead, it deals with political writing published under the auspices of the RSDLP, which should be consistent with the organization's agreed-upon political orientation.[6]

As Lenin himself explained, "we are discussing party literature and its subordination to party control," adding that, independently of the revolutionary party, "everyone is free to write and say whatever he likes, without any restrictions." He concluded: "Freedom of speech and the press must be complete. But then freedom of association must be complete too."[7] Which meant that an organization must be free to decide upon what literature it shall publish to advance its own perspectives.

Lenin's actual approach to creative literature was highlighted in the years after the Russian Revolution through his close association with Alexander Voronsky's journal *Red Virgin Soil*, which pushed against those pseudo-revolutionary literary critics who maintained a presumably *politically correct* stance which feared looking too closely at life, instead "demanding propaganda" portrayals populated by "wooden, stilted figures, written according to stereotypes." As Voronsky stressed, "art is the cognition of life in the form of the sensual, imaginative contemplation," and "we must not fear differences, deviations or ideological quirks" as the artist seeks to give expression to the actualities of human life and experience.[8]

Serious political analysis and engagement, no less than serious literature, must avoid any rigid "political correctness" that obliterates the vibrant reality and creativity of life itself. This open approach can be seen in Lenin's eagerness to meet, get to know, and learn from the strange Russian Orthodox priest who had led the workers' procession to the Winter Palace, Father Gapon. Krupskaya notes that many in the revolutionary movement were inclined simply to dismiss him, "deciding beforehand that nothing good could ever be expected from a priest. … But Lenin's strength lay in the fact that to him the revolution is a living thing, like a face that one could study in all its varied features." Gapon, "still red hot from the breath of the revolution," was "closely bound up with the working-class masses who implicitly believed in him." The son of Ukrainian peasants, he knew the villages intimately, "and his speech was simple and familiar to the uneducated working masses."[9]

At one point, Gapon passionately recited to Lenin his draft of an appeal for revolutionary insurrection, declaiming: "We want no tsar. Let there be one master over the land—God, with all of you his tenants!" Taken aback by Lenin's involuntary laughter, he asked what should be changed. Krupskaya later explained that Gapon's phrasing "revealed most strikingly the very traits that made Gapon stand so close to the masses: himself a peasant, he had stirred up in the workers, who were still half connected with the village, their age-old land hunger." At the time, Lenin responded to Gapon that it wouldn't make sense for him to offer corrections. "My whole train of thought is different," he concluded. "Write it in your own way, in your own style."[10]

When Gapon issued "An Open Letter to the Socialist Parties of Russia," Lenin duplicated it in an article he wrote that polemicized against the peasant-based Socialist-Revolutionary Party while embracing Gapon's call, at the same time developing a key conceptualization—the united front.

UNITED FRONT: MARCH SEPARATELY, STRIKE TOGETHER

The term "united front" did not exist in this period, but Lenin clearly advanced the concept in February in response to Father Gapon's appeal to "all the socialist parties of Russia to enter immediately into an agreement among themselves and to proceed to the armed uprising against tsarism."[11]

Of "all the socialist parties of Russia," the two most substantial were the Russian Social Democratic Labor Party (RSDLP, with its contending Bolshevik and Menshevik factions) and the Socialist-Revolutionary Party (the Socialist-Revolutionaries, SRs).

The RSDLP adhered closely to Marxist perspectives, with an insistence that capitalism was inevitably becoming dominant in the Russian economy. The forward movement toward democracy and socialism would be dependent on struggles of the working class, growing stronger and building a mass base through winning reforms. The resulting experience and self-confidence would pave the way for the future revolutionary transformation.

The SRs were inclined to dismiss such "narrow dogma" with a very different emphasis on Russia's vast peasantry, whose traditional village communes were seen as providing a possible shortcut to a socialist future. Workers were certainly viewed as part of the impending popular insurgencies, but the peasants represented the mass wave destined to transform Russia. SRs believed that individual terrorism would help generate that wave, through the assassination of prominent individuals associated with the tsarist order.

Lenin wrote:

> We consider that the "agreement" ... is possible, useful, and essential. We welcome the fact that Gapon speaks explicitly of an "agreement", since only through the preservation of complete independence by each separate party on points of principle and organization can the efforts at a fighting unity of these parties rest on hope.[12]

In this unified struggle, Lenin believed, it would be important for the Bolsheviks to demonstrate their abilities in effectively advancing the common effort, at the same time allowing others to consider and be persuaded by the superior revolutionary Marxist orientation, which should never be compromised or muted. "We must be very careful, in making these endeavors, not to spoil things by vainly trying to lump together heterogeneous elements," he emphasized. A key element of success would involve organizations with diverse orientations agreeing to disagree on matters going beyond the specific common actions. "We shall inevitably have to ... march separately, but we can ... strike together more than once and particularly now."[13]

There was another point Lenin went on to make. He shared with all members of the RSDLP a conviction that backward Russia was not yet ready for socialism. There would be a need for a period of industrialization, modernization, and relative democratization of Russian society, allowing for the creation of a *working-class majority* organized into a powerful labor movement. The immediate revolutionary goal, therefore, was not socialism but replacing the tsarist order with a democratic republic. This particular united front should not be restricted to socialist organizations.

> It would be desirable, from our point of view, to have this agreement embrace the revolutionary as well as the socialist parties, for there is nothing socialistic in the immediate aim of the struggle, and we must not confound or allow anyone ever to confound the immediate democratic aims with our ultimate aims of socialist revolution.[14]

This added to his conviction that "complete clarity and definiteness in the relations between parties, trends, and shades are absolutely necessary if a temporary agreement among them is to be in any way successful." He elaborated:

> In the interests of the revolution our ideal should by no means be that all parties, all trends and shades of opinion fuse in a revolutionary chaos. On the contrary, the growth and spread of the revolutionary movement, its constantly deeper penetration among the various classes and strata of the people, will inevitably give rise (all to the good) to constantly newer trends and shades.[15]

The purpose of the united front was to win victory for specific goals through the unity of diverse forces. But its purpose was also to enable revolutionary Marxists to grow in experience, effectiveness, and influence. For this they needed to preserve their organizational and political integrity. "Only full clarity and definite-ness in their mutual relations and in their attitude towards the position of the revolutionary proletariat can guarantee maximum success for the revolutionary movement. Only full clarity in mutual relations can guarantee the success of an agreement to achieve a common immediate aim."[16]

CLASS ALLIANCES AND DEMOCRATIC DICTATORSHIPS

A key text that Lenin wrote in this period was the book-length polemic *Two Tactics of Social Democracy in the Democratic Revolution*. The word "tactics" here actually added up to what would later be understood as *strategic orientation*. It referred to what would become the central political difference between the Bolsheviks and the Mensheviks.

It was necessary for Russia's relatively small working class to ally itself with other forces in the struggle to overthrow the tsarist autocracy. The Mensheviks saw the obvious and primary ally as the democratic liberals associated with the capitalist class. The Bolsheviks saw the primary ally as the vast Russian peasantry. The Mensheviks believed the peasants were too backward to be a reliable ally. The Bolsheviks believed the capitalists were too hostile to working-class rights, too frightened of mass insurgency, and too inclined to make deals with authoritarian elites to be a reliable ally.

Lenin argued that the Bolshevik strategic orientation should, with the overthrow of tsarism, culminate in what he called a *democratic dictatorship of proletariat and peasantry*. It is worth lingering over this odd-sounding phrase to grasp its meaning.

An obvious first question is how a dictatorship can be genuinely democratic. Here we are helped by the work of such scholars as Hal Draper and Richard N. Hunt, explicating what Marx and Engels (who in the *Communist Manifesto* had exhorted the workers to "win the battle of democracy") actually meant by the term *dictatorship of the proletariat*. Draper and Hunt note that the latter-day connotation of the word "dictatorship" as being the opposite of democracy is relatively new. In ancient Rome dictatorship was consistent with the existence of a republic (government by elected representatives), often referring to a benign form of *crisis government*. In the time of Karl Marx and Frederick Engels it had a similar connotation, consistent with a democratically elected assembly—as Hunt puts it "the large-scale replacement of officials necessary in any democratic revolution that overthrows an old, established authoritarian regime."[17]

Marx and Engels believed that the demands of the Chartist movement of England, fighting for the right to vote for the electorally excluded working class, would amount, in Hunt's words, to "the revolutionary rule of the working-class majority in England," and was therefore consistent "with proletarian dictatorship." He cites Engels' reference to a situation in which "one part of the population imposes its will upon the other part." The two revolutionaries therefore viewed political domination by the capitalist class in society—even with the existence of democratic political structures —as a "dictatorship of the bourgeoisie," which they wanted to replace by a *dictatorship of the proletariat.*[18]

The word "democratic" in the *democratic dictatorship of the proletariat and the peasantry* had a dual meaning. It coincides with the outlook of Marx and Engels, except instead of referring to political domination by the working class alone, it referred to *majority* domination by the alliance of workers and peasants. Related to that, it means that Lenin saw the upcoming revolution not as a socialist revolution, but as a democratic revolution to overthrow the tsar—not a transition to socialism, but a transition to a capitalist social and political order.

A decisive question for Lenin, however, was the actual nature of the new capitalist order. As he put it, "there are bourgeois-democratic regimes like the one in Germany and also in England, like the one in Austria and also like those in America or Switzerland." The Austrian, English, and German variants had evolved, through compromises between capitalists and feudal landowners, as profoundly less democratic than outcomes realized in the United States and Switzerland. Lenin warned that Russian capitalists would be inclined toward a similar orientation (which would amount to *the persistence of the old order*, as historian Arno Mayer put it). "We know that owing to their class position they are incapable of waging a decisive struggle against tsarism; they are too heavily fettered by private property, capital and land to enter into a decisive struggle," he wrote. "They need tsarism with its bureaucratic, police and military forces for use against the proletariat and the peasantry too much to be able to strive for its destruction." He warned that if "the bourgeoisie will be at the head of the democratic revolution" then it "will impart to it an inconsistent and self-seeking nature."[19]

"A decisive victory over tsarism" would require a worker-peasant alliance to push forward to a more thoroughgoing democratic outcome. "Only the proletariat can be a consistent fighter for democracy," he wrote. "It may become a victorious fighter for democracy only if the peasant masses join its revolutionary struggle." A victory must culminate in a *revolutionary-democratic dictatorship of the proletariat and the peasantry* to overcome "desperate resistance from the landlords, the big bourgeoisie, and tsarism," Lenin insisted. "Without a dictatorship it is impossible to break down that resistance and repel counter-revolutionary attempts." The positive program of the democratic dictatorship was no less essential in Lenin's thinking:

> At best it may bring about a radical redistribution of landed property in favor of the peasantry, establish consistent and full democracy including the formation of a republic, eradicate all the oppressive features of Asiatic bondage, not only in village but also in factory life, lay the foundation for a thorough improvement in the position of the workers and for a rise in their standard of living, and—last but not least—carry the revolutionary conflagration into Europe.[20]

This spread of "revolutionary conflagration" into Europe, Lenin speculated, might generate socialist revolutions in advanced industrial countries, which could, in turn, create socialist workers' regimes that would assist the Russian working class in moving forward to its own socialist transformation.

In light of all this, it is understandable that the prominent Menshevik Raphael Abramovitch accused Lenin of wanting "a bourgeois revolution without the bourgeoisie." It seems clear that a genuine ambiguity was embedded in what Lenin was saying. "Marxists are absolutely convinced of the bourgeois character of the Russian revolution," he emphasized in *Two Tactics*. He elaborated:

> What does this mean? It means that the democratic reforms in the political system and the social and economic reforms, which have become a necessity for Russia, do not in themselves imply the undermining of capitalism, the undermining of bourgeois rule; on the contrary, they will, for the first time, really clear the ground for a wide and rapid, European, and not Asiatic, development of capitalism; they will, for the first time, make it possible for the bourgeoisie to rule as a class.[21]

Yet we have seen that implications in other passages of the same pamphlet appear to be going far beyond this. Later that year, he seemed to make explicit how far: "from the democratic revolution we shall at once, and precisely in accordance with the measure of our strength, the strength of the class-conscious and organized proletariat, begin to pass to the socialist revolution. We stand for uninterrupted revolution. We shall not stop half-way."[22]

This very real ambiguity may indicate an uncertainty in Lenin's thinking, or perhaps his characteristic openness and flexibility. It certainly suggests a powerful underlying impulse in his thinking, which resurfaced and became dominant in 1917. It was an ambiguity that fueled a dispute among the Bolsheviks themselves in that revolutionary year.

THE ARMED UPRISING

Lenin was alert to the dynamics of the 1905 upsurge, but this was a learning experience for all of the revolutionaries. A blend of insights and miscalculations is evident in the circumstances and the aftermath of the December 1905 revolutionary rising in Moscow.

We can see, in what Lenin said and did, his typically practical approach to theory and to the actual dynamics of workers' consciousness and struggle. The exhilarating turbulence of 1905 had shown that "the working class is instinctively, spontaneously Social Democratic," he noted, "and the more than ten years of work of Social Democracy has done a great deal to turn this spontaneity into consciousness." At the same time, with brutal realism, he observed that "major questions in the life of nations are settled only by force," adding that "the reactionary classes themselves are usually the first to resort to violence, to civil war," and pointing out that this had been the Russian autocracy's approach at the start of 1905. It backed off—but only temporarily—with the massive insurgent reaction (which he called "mass terror," in contrast to the "individual terror" of the SRs).[23]

The tsarist regime sought to quell the insurgency with the promise of concessions. Working-class activists, in turn, sought to make the concessions real and to push forward to genuine democracy and economic justice. Their demonstrations and strikes were not effective. Instead, tsarist forces were in motion to erode and liquidate the concessions. This also impacted on the perceptions and mood of masses of workers. As Lenin later noted, "they asked: What is to be done next? And they demanded more resolute action."[24] Krupskaya's reminiscences are relevant here:

> Ilyich knew that the workers were already determined to fight to the bitter end. And he was with them. He knew that there could be no stopping halfway, that this would so demoralize the working class, so weaken the impetus of their struggle and do such tremendous damage to the cause, that it was not to be thought of under any circumstances. History showed that in the Revolution of 1905 the working class was defeated but not vanquished. Its will to fight was not broken. This is what some people failed to understand, people who had attacked Lenin for his "extreme views" and who had had nothing better to say after the defeat than that "they should not have taken to arms." If one was to remain true to one's class, it was impossible not to take to arms, it was impossible for the vanguard to leave its fighting class in the lurch.[25]

Apparently, this mood was most advanced in Moscow, and that is where the rising was organized by Bolsheviks and others in the thick of events. Keenly aware of how poorly armed the militants were, some of Lenin's most frantic and even blood-curdling appeals can be found in this period, urging the acquisition of guns and bombs and other possible implements of violence—"knives, knuckledusters, sticks, rags coated with kerosene …, barbed wire, nails (against cavalry), etc., etc."[26] Several hundred people were formed into fighting squads armed with revolvers and some rifles. The fighting was over quickly.

If the Moscow workers had been joined by those in St. Petersburg, and if some of the tsarist troops had been won over (which Lenin and others believed was necessary for victory), the outcome might have been different. But any soldiers who mutinied under the actual circumstances would have been committing suicide. And according to Krupskaya, "the St. Petersburg workers were worn out by previous strikes, and most important of all, they realized how badly organized and poorly armed they were for a decisive struggle with tsarism. And that would be a struggle to death, they had the example of Moscow to tell them."[27]

Analyzing what had happened, Plekhanov in early 1906 bluntly commented it was obvious beforehand that the working class was too weak to triumph in an armed conflict with the regime, "and therefore it was wrong to take up arms." Lenin responded that "it was necessary to take up arms, for otherwise the movement would not have risen to a higher plane, it would not have obtained the necessary practical experience of insurrection nor freed itself from the narrow limits of the peaceful strike alone, which had spent itself as a weapon in the struggle." He added that "on the basis of the practical experience which has been acquired, which has proved that it is quite possible to fight against regular troops, and which has suggested the immediate task of a more persevering and more patient preparation for the next outbreak."[28]

The next outbreak, in the opinion of the Bolsheviks, was only months away. It was time to "more perseveringly and patiently" acquire arms, organize volunteer fighting units and urban guerrilla detachments, forge links with the rebellious peasantry. All ideas of participating in Duma elections should be discarded, and trade union work should be allowed to draw on only a modest amount of revolutionaries' energies. "Let us remember that a great mass struggle is approaching," Lenin emphasized. "It will be an armed uprising. It must, as far as possible, be simultaneous. The masses must know that they are entering upon an armed, bloody and desperate struggle. … And in this momentous struggle, the party of the class-conscious proletariat must discharge its duty to the full."[29]

From the Bolshevik standpoint, revolutionary victory might be won by 1907. And yet, it turned out that this was not the case.

Much had been gained and learned in 1905, including in the failed Moscow rising. All of this contributed essential elements to Lenin's developing perspectives. But his insurrectionary expectations were off by roughly a decade. Several years later, however, Lenin's evaluation remained a positive, optimistic vindication of the revolutionary outlook:

> Wait, we will have another 1905. That is how the workers look at it. To the workers that year of struggle provided an example of *what is to be done*. To the intelligentsia and the renegade petty-bourgeois it was a "mad year," an example of *what is not to be done*. To the proletariat, the study and critical assimilation of the experience of the revolution means learning to apply the methods of struggle of *that time more effectually*, learning to convert that October strike movement and December armed struggle into something broader, more concentrated and more class-conscious.[30]

An essential aspect of Lenin's orientation can be found in his mistakes and defeats. As he put it more than a decade later, in the summer of 1917, "those who don't take risks never win; without defeats there are no victories."[31]

Further adjustments and political development would be required, however, before the victory Lenin anticipated could be realized.

4

Comrades and Coherence (1905–14)

One of the problems with uncritically accepting the 1905 upsurge as "the dress rehearsal" for Russia's 1917 Revolution is that what happened in 1905 did not fully prepare the revolutionaries for the actual revolution's Opening Night. An additional decade of both painful and exhilarating experiences and "practice sessions," and also the gathering of a number of additional "cast members," would be required for the revolutionaries to be capable of making the revolution. Nor was there a single "script" to be memorized by the participants. There were multiple "scripts" from which the revolutionaries were "learning their lines"—and new "lines" were being composed as they found themselves engaging with new and evolving scenarios.

In speaking of *the revolutionaries*, it is necessary to look beyond Lenin and his Bolshevik comrades. Much larger and more diverse gatherings of workers, peasants, intellectuals and others, coming together in a variety of organizations and factions, provided the interactive context out of which an adequately coherent revolutionary outcome could be generated. A swirl of ideas could be found in this insurgent milieu—the Menshevik and Bolshevik factions of the Russian Social Democratic Labor Party (RSDLP), different currents associated with the Socialist-Revolutionaries (SRs), different points of view among the liberal Constitutional Democrats (the Russian acronym, KDs, pronounced as Kadets), various anarchists, and more. Despite significant points of agreement, there were often profound points of disagreement—and the debates could help to clarify major issues among these diverse revolutionary currents.

Some of the debates and polemics could also be disorienting or even toxic. Despite pulls toward RSDLP unity, the fierce factional struggle still flared. One on-the-ground Menshevik won support from some workers by saying the Bolsheviks "are against workers being in the party. The Bolsheviks want to command us like [tsar] Nicholas." In reaction, as a crude "joke," an on-the-ground Bolshevik (in this case Stalin), dismissing Menshevik leaders as "cowards and petty tradesmen," elaborated: "Martov, Dan, Axelrod—circumcised Yids. Yes, and that old grandma Vera Zasulich. Go and try to work with them. You can't go into the struggle with them ..."[1]

Stalin was not expressing the actual Bolshevik position here, since what Eric Blanc would later characterize as "ballpark Bolshevism" left plenty of room for individual idiosyncrasies. On the other hand, Mensheviks as well as Bolsheviks would probably have agreed with Anatoly Lunacharsky (in an article Lenin edited for the Bolshevik paper *Vpered*) that "conscious" workers and revolutionary intellectuals should together build "a solid but centralized party, closely connected with the proletarian mass, aspiring to enlighten and organize it by revolutionary action to its true interests."[2] The question was how to actualize this shared goal.

REVOLUTIONARY ORGANIZATION

What became an influential concept, *democratic centralism*, arose within the RSDLP. As 1905 began to blend into 1906, despite theoretical and analytical disagreements among some of their leading personalities, the Bolshevik and Menshevik factions drew closer together—a result of the fact that activists of both currents found themselves animated by similar hopes and perceptions, and they were very much on the same side of the barricades.

The factions continued to exist, but both were now inclined to function more harmoniously together within the common framework of the RSDLP. In discussions and resolutions dealing with the matter of organizational functioning, the Mensheviks introduced the term *democratic centralism*, which seems to have first arisen in the German socialist labor movement in the late 1860s. The Bolsheviks also embraced the term. In later years it was incorrectly assumed to be an invention of Lenin himself, developed to ensure "complete inner unity of outlook," as a Stalinist educator once put it.[3]

Critics commonly described it as a Leninist mechanism far more centralist than democratic, requiring, on the one hand, "a strong leader" and, on the other hand, a rank-and-file membership "consciously and joyfully submitting to the leadership imposed on it by senior members."[4] But this is not how the term was understood by the Russian revolutionaries.

According to the Mensheviks, in addition to democratic decision-making and democratic elections within all party organizations, "decisions of the guiding organizations are binding on the members of those organizations of which the collective is the organ," and "decisions of lower-level organizations are not to be implemented if they contradict decisions of higher organizations." The Bolsheviks agreed, while emphasizing that "while granting elected centers full powers in matters of ideological and practical leadership, they are at the same time subject to recall, their actions are given wide publicity, and they are to be strictly accountable for these activities."[5]

In line with this, Bolshevik leader Alexander Bogdanov stressed that "a party which espoused the comradely principle was alien to naked centralization and blind discipline," which meant the need for "free and conscious comradely connection" and "democratic forms of organization." Lenin concurred that the health of the revolutionary organization required "that the ideological struggle in the Party on the question of theory and tactics … [be] conducted as openly, widely and freely as possible," just so long as this not "disturb or hamper the unity of revolutionary action." Lenin also underscored the necessity for "the rights of all minorities and for all loyal opposition" as well as for the relative autonomy of local organizations. He summarized: "Freedom of discussion, unity of action—this is what we must achieve."[6]

The highest decision-making body in the party was not a central committee or political committee but rather the party congress (or convention). The central committee was elected by and answerable to the party congress. The congress was to be held every year or two, consisting of elected delegates from every local branch of the party. These elections were to take place after a period of written and oral discussion and debate on the issues facing the party, and the decisions considered "binding" on the members and lower-level organizations were those made by the party congress. Lenin "always, as long as he lived, attached tremendous importance to Party congresses," recalled Krupskaya. "He held the Party congress to be the highest authority, where all things personal had to be cast aside, where nothing was to be concealed, and everything was to be open and above board."[7]

CONFUSIONS, SPLITS, FUSIONS, PRACTICAL WORK

When one studies the development of the organization (more accurately, the organizations) that Lenin helped to lead, in the almost two-decade preparation for the Revolution's "Opening Night" in 1917, one finds what can be seen as a confusing accumulation of debates, polemics, splits, and fusions. Some analysts have interpreted all of this as stemming from Lenin's craziness—stemming from his impatience (one biographer termed him "a Marxist in a hurry")[8] or from his insatiable lust for power. Others see Lenin as being *crazy like a fox*, cleverly manipulating people and events in order to concentrate power in his own hands—for either evil or altruistic purposes.

Yet there is another way of interpreting events that is more consistent with what we know of Lenin and his political orientation. It is also consistent with what we know of the social, political, and psychological dynamics of our own life experiences.

Amid the complex multiple swirls of the perpetually interactive realms of political, social, economic, cultural, and psychological dynamics, a would-be revolutionary organization can remain coherent (true to its guiding principles) by sealing itself off from contamination—and then it becomes irrelevant, fails to grow, withers, finally passes out of existence. An alternative course of development involves an organization's openness and adaptation to the swirl of realities in part by letting go of its guiding principles. It then either becomes incoherent and passes out of existence or it comes to adhere to different guiding principles, and it becomes something other than what it initially sought to be. It transforms into an organization that is no longer revolutionary.

Lenin adhered to a different method. He was incredibly flexible, engaging with and adapting to complex and ever-changing situations, but he was inflexible in regard to revolutionary principles. Such situations and principles proved to be inseparable elements in his conception of the revolutionary program. He was absolutely unwilling to set aside the revolutionary goal, but he was always seeking ways to develop practical activity in the here-and-now in ways that would bring the goal closer to realization. This approach generated two major conflicts.

In the period from 1907 to 1912, the controversies in which Lenin was engaged had to do with a substantial grouping among the Mensheviks who were tagged "Liquidators" and a substantial grouping within the Bolshevik faction, led by Alexander Bogdanov, who were later sometimes tagged as "Ultra-Left."

The dissipation and defeat of the 1905–06 revolutionary upsurge, and the systematic shoring up of the tsarist order, resulted in a widespread demoralization among revolutionary activists. Nor was this all. Modest reforms became possible, but with narrowed scope and firm tsarist controls. This combined with an increase of governmental repression, further impacted by a substantial influx into the industrial centers of less politicized laborers fresh from the peasant villages. The RSDLP seemed to melt away throughout much of the Russian Empire. Its remaining activists responded to this situation in very different ways.

Among the Mensheviks, a substantial current arose favoring liquidation of the underground in order to focus exclusively on legal work—electoral efforts in the recently created Duma, trade union efforts, action to advance social reforms, etc. Marxists naturally favored such activity as essential in building the revolutionary movement, but liquidation of underground work in such a country as tsarist Russia smacked of severing reform work from the revolutionary goal. All Bolsheviks and many Mensheviks opposed such a Liquidator orientation as inconsistent with the program of the RSDLP. At more than one gathering of the unified RSDLP (consisting of representatives of Bolshevik and Menshevik factions), resolutions were passed saying as much. On the other hand, the divergence between Bolsheviks and Mensheviks had widened. After the partial convergence in 1905, differences on the question of worker-peasant alliance versus worker-capitalist alliance became more pronounced. In part because of this, the non-Liquidator Mensheviks around Martov—to secure a majority in the RSDLP—refused to allow the actual implementation of the anti-Liquidator resolutions.

Another sharp difference between Bolsheviks and Mensheviks was the fact that those around Martov, while not favoring the liquidation of underground work, did very much favor the stress on participating in elections for the Duma, building trade unions, helping to generate movements for social reforms, etc. We have seen that the Bolsheviks, anticipating an imminent resurgence of mass revolutionary activity, insisted on an emphasis of acquiring arms, organizing volunteer fighting units and urban guerrilla detachments, and agitating for insurrection. They insisted:

> At the present time armed uprising is not only the necessary means of fighting for freedom, but a stage actually reached by the movement, a step which, in view of the growth and intensification of a new political crisis, begins the transition from defensive to offensive forms of armed struggle.[9]

Lenin, Bogdanov, and Leonid Krasin formed a special Bolshevik troika to focus on such matters: securing, storing, and distributing guns, ammunition, explosives; organizing armed units and urban guerilla detachments; carrying out small-scale armed actions, including "expropriations" in the form of bank robberies to fund revolutionary activity.

Yet Lenin soon came to the conclusion that the Mensheviks were right and the Bolsheviks wrong: the revolutionary wave had, in fact, subsided. The armed struggle orientation no longer made practical sense and was proving to be counterproductive and self-destructive. The need under the new conditions was to focus on building working-class struggles and consciousness through serious electoral work, committing to reform struggles. If one was serious about building a powerful revolutionary capacity of the working class to overthrow tsarism, he was convinced, it was necessary to break sharply from what had become identified as the Bolshevik orientation. And that is what he did—not only arguing the point within his own faction, but at party-wide assemblies voting with the Mensheviks.

Krupskaya later described Lenin's battle with comrades, led by the truly brilliant Bogdanov, who continued to adhere to what had become the Bolshevik orientation in 1905:

> A Bolshevik, they declared, should be hard and unyielding. Lenin considered this view fallacious. It would mean giving up all practical work, standing aside from the masses instead of organizing them on real-life issues. Prior to the Revolution of 1905 the Bolsheviks showed themselves capable of making good use of every legal possibility, of forging ahead and rallying the masses behind them under the most adverse conditions. Step by step, beginning with the campaign for tea service and ventilation, they had led the masses up to the national armed insurrection. The ability to adjust oneself to the most adverse conditions and at the same time to stand out and maintain one's high-principled positions—such were the traditions of Leninism.[10]

M.N. Pokrovsky, at the time aligned with Bogdanov, later recalled the response of many Bolsheviks—"the man who had sounded the call for armed revolt began to urge us to read ... stenographic reports on the sessions of the State Duma." The reaction was "a hail of ridicule," jeering and baiting. "The man had lost his fire, nothing of the revolutionary was left in him."[11]

Bogdanov noted that Lenin had "come to the conclusion that we must radically change the previous Bolshevik evaluation of the present historical moment and hold a course not toward a new revolutionary wave, but toward a long period of peaceful, constitutional development." He saw this as representing a convergence with "the right wing of our party, the Menshevik comrades." He concluded:

> Bolshevism continues to exist as before. ... Comrades, a glorious cause—political, cultural, social—stands before us. It would be shameful for us if leaders who have outlived their times, overcome by adversity, should prevent us from fulfilling it. ... We will proceed on our way according to the old slogan—with

> our leaders, if they wish; without them if they do not; against them, if they oppose us.[12]

There was a devastating quality to this dispute. "For about three years prior to this we had been working with Bogdanov and the Bogdanovites hand in hand, and not just working, but fighting side by side," Krupskaya recalled. "Fighting for a common cause draws people together more than anything." The conflict with these comrades was "a nerve-wracking business," as she put it. She remembered Lenin once coming home after a debate with his Bolshevik comrades. "He looked awful, and even his tongue seemed to have turned grey."[13]

The dispute also spilled over into the terrain of philosophy—with Lenin writing *Materialism and Empirio-Criticism*, which sharply took issue with Bogdanov's efforts to update Marxism's philosophy. The sense of close comradeship turning into the deepest animosity was incredibly profound. Lenin had once been personally close to Martov, and despite their sharp differences and polemics, Lenin always hoped for eventual reconciliation. Neither Lenin nor Bogdanov had such feelings about each other after their own break.

Yet the dispute went far beyond personalities and emotions, which is why Lenin was finally able to win a majority in the Bolshevik faction by 1909–10, with a new leadership team in which increasingly important roles were played by Zinoviev, Kamenev, Stalin, Jacob Sverdlov, Alexei Rykov, and others—including a very capable working-class leader who famously turned out to be a spy for the tsarist secret police, Roman Malinovsky. The Leninist-Bolsheviks went on to become a powerful revolutionary force. In contrast, those gathered around Bogdanov—despite impressive advantages and resources—soon suffered decline and fragmentation. Zinoviev later elaborated on the essential political issues:

> Comrade Lenin's main idea was that we had to remain with the working class and be a mass party and not to coop ourselves up exclusively in the underground and turn into a narrow circle. If the workers are in the trade unions, then we must be there too; if we can send just one man into the Tsar's Duma, then we shall: let

him tell the workers the truth and we can publish his speeches as leaflets. If something can be done for the workers in the workers' clubs, then we shall be there. We have to use every legal opportunity, so as not to divorce ourselves from the masses.[14]

CONSOLIDATING A REVOLUTIONARY PARTY

With the internal conflict within the Bolshevik faction resolved, Lenin was hopeful that forces in the RSDLP might overcome the Bolshevik-Menshevik divide and move forward to transform the RSDLP into an effective revolutionary party. Yet he insisted that this must be done in a clear, honest, principled manner. If the primary goal was to reconcile different political tendencies, and therefore submerge the differences, it would not be possible to build a serious organization. It would mean that "differences of opinion must be hushed up, their causes, their significance, their objective conditions should not be elucidated." In that case, if divergent tendencies "do not agree upon the carrying out of a common policy, that policy must be interpreted in such a way as to be acceptable to all. Live and let live."[15]

In contrast to this, Lenin insisted on what he considered a principled revolutionary approach to party unity: "the unification of the Party may proceed slowly, with difficulties, vacillations, waverings and relapses, but proceed it must." This would mean "the process of unification does not necessarily take place among 'given persons, groups and institutions,' but irrespective of given persons." All members would be subordinated to the democratic collective process of developing an agreed-upon revolutionary program. Those not wishing to be part of such a collective process would simply not be part of the organization. At the same time, new people—not members of the old tendencies—would be recruited and promoted, and among veteran members there would be "changes, reshufflings and regroupings within the old factions, trends and divisions. From this point of view, unity is inseparable from its ideological foundation, it can grow only on the basis of an ideological rapprochement."[16]

In Lenin's view, this rapprochement must take place through an adherence to the traditional Marxist orientation: immersion in the actual struggles of the working class, particularly struggles for reforms in the here-and-now, while explicitly and practically adhering to perspectives, dynamics, and commitments of revolutionary transformation. This precluded both Liquidator and Ultra-Left perspectives. Among the Mensheviks, the one current that represented a principled and uncompromising rejection of the Liquidators was the so-called "party Menshevik" group associated with Lenin's old mentor Georgi Plekhanov. He hoped a cohesive RSDLP could be constituted around a unified center of Leninist-Bolsheviks and party Mensheviks, animated by "changes, reshufflings and regroupings," in this revitalized RSDLP.

Bogdanov would later shrewdly describe and assess how this orientation turned out:

> Lenin's attempt in 1909 to split the Bolshevik fraction and ally with Plekhanov's supporters among the Mensheviks was doomed to failure. The maneuver involved the Leninists getting rid of the left wing of the Bolsheviks, while Plekhanov detached his group from the "liquidationist" right wing of the Mensheviks. The Leninist Bolsheviks and the "party Mensheviks" would then be required to form a coherent center organization. However, the two fractions had become so distant that the desired merger was impossible, and the organization collapsed at its point of least resistance. No center grouping of Lenin's and Plekhanov's forces gelled, and instead of two factions there were now four.[17]

Three points should be made here.

First, there were not four but no less than six groupings: (1) Leninist Bolsheviks; (2) "Ultra-Left" Bolsheviks; (3) Liquidator-Mensheviks working with (4) Martov's non-Liquidator Mensheviks; (5) Plekhanov's party Mensheviks; and (6) a "non-faction" faction led by Trotsky. There were other currents as well, including a clutch of pro-unity Bolshevik "conciliators," plus affiliates from other Social Democratic groups within the Russian Empire, such as the Jewish Labor Bund and the Social Democracy of the Kingdom of Poland and Lithuania (which included Rosa Luxemburg, Leo Jogiches, Felix Dzerzhinsky, and Karl Radek).

Second, it is obvious that Lenin was not motivated by a desire to create a monolithic party under his personal control. The centrality of Plekhanov to his vision of a unified party precluded such a notion. The old Marxist war-horse had sharply disagreed with Lenin on questions of class alliances and armed uprising. More than this, Lenin's notion of "changes, reshufflings and regroupings" among the revolutionaries mirrored his own experience over the past 15 years, and it seems obvious that he envisioned a continuation of this collective process into the future. It should be added that even Lenin's new leadership team among the Bolsheviks—in contrast to some latter-day accounts by hostile commentators—did not consist of "yes-men" simply carrying out the boss's orders. They were capable and critical-minded individuals who would disagree with Lenin and sometimes vote him down. Editors of the Bolshevik paper *Pravda*, for example, could sometimes lecture him that his "strong language and sharpness go too far," and—to his chagrin—they could actually turn down some of his articles (a total of 47 between 1912 and 1914).

Third, Lenin's effort to build a coherent version of the RSDLP with at least a few "party Mensheviks" moved forward even without Plekhanov (who shied away from merging with Lenin's faction). Lenin was not bound by Bogdanov's schema, worked with what he had, and with like-minded comrades forged a cohesive organization that was able to connect with local organizations throughout Russia.

Lenin and his Bolshevik comrades worked from 1910 to 1912 to build an "authoritative" RSDLP conference in Prague that would draw together the kind of organization they were reaching for. Most of those invited refused to attend, instead organizing an alternative conference in Vienna, involving a bloc of non-Bolshevik RSDLP groupings that were hostile to what Lenin was trying to do. Although a few "party Mensheviks" attended the Prague conference, Plekhanov himself stayed away. Even though the Vienna conference was broader, its diverse participants proved incapable of producing anything durable. The 1912 Prague conference, on the other hand, provided a coherent orientation that sustained a well-organized revolutionary collective that caught wind in its sails from the working-class radicalization and upsurge that swept through the Russian Empire in 1912–14. As Osip Piatnitsky later noted, the Prague conference "reorganized the central Party organizations, which remained in existence until the Party Conference of April 1917."[18] Krupskaya elaborated:

> The Prague Conference was the first conference with Party workers from Russia which we succeeded in calling after 1908 and at which we were able in a businesslike manner to discuss questions relating to the work in Russia and frame a clear line for this work. Resolutions were adopted on the issues of the moment and the tasks of the Party, on the elections to the Fourth Duma, on the Social-Democratic group in the Duma, on the character and organizational forms of Party work, on the tasks of the Social Democrats in the anti-famine campaign, on the attitude toward the State Insurance for Workers' bill before the Duma, and on the petition campaign [calling for freedom of trade union organization, assembly, and strikes]. The results of the Prague Conference were a clearly defined Party line on questions of work in Russia, and real leadership of practical work … A unity was achieved on the [Central Committee] without which it would have been impossible to carry on the work at such a difficult time.[19]

The result, for all practical purposes, was a Bolshevik-dominated incarnation of the RSDLP, sometimes referred to as the Russian Social Democratic Labor Party (Bolsheviks). "The only well-organized and cohesive faction in the RSDLP at the present time is the Bolshevik-Leninist faction," according to a 1912 report of the Okhrana, the tsarist secret police. "They established their 'all-Russian Conference', they have their Central Committee, their illegal organs abroad and legal ones in Russia, they have their committees."[20]

Historian Pierre Broué, in his study *Le Parti Bolchévique*, gives a partial sense of this vibrant revolutionary collective—with a helpful identification of some of its leading personalities' ages, occupations, and social backgrounds:

> A Mikhail Tomsky, lithographer, who enters the party at twenty-five years of age, is an exceptional figure, despite his earlier years passed as a non-party fighter. At his age, in fact, the majority of the others have behind them years of political militancy. The student Piatakov, son of a great bourgeois family in the Ukraine, becomes a Bolshevik at twenty, previously having been an anarchist militant. The student Rosenfeld, whose party name was Kamenev, is nineteen when he joins, as is the metalworker Schmidt and the skilled mechanic I.N. Smirnov. It is at the age of eighteen that there enter into the party the metalworker Bakaiev, the students Bukharin and Krestinski, the shoemaker Kaganovitch. The clerk Zinoviev, the metalworkers Serebriakov and Lutovinov are Bolsheviks at seventeen. Sverdlov works in a pharmacists' shop when he enters the struggle at sixteen, as does the student Kuibyshev. The shoemaker Drobnis and the student Smilga enter the party at fifteen and Piatnitski at fourteen. These young men haven't left the age of adolescence when they are already old militants and cadres. Sverdlov, at the age of seventeen, directs the Social Democratic organization in Sormovo, and the tsarist police look for him under the nickname "Tiny." Sokolnikov is eighteen when he is secretary of one of the Moscow districts. Rykov is twenty-four when, as a spokesman for the "committeemen," he enters the Central Committee in London [at the conference of 1905]. Zinoviev is already known as a leading Petersburg Bolshevik and writer for Proletary when at the age of twenty-four he begins his residence on the Central Committee. Kamenev is twenty-two when he is a delegate to London, Sverdlov twenty at the Tammerfors conference [1906]. Serebriakov is the organizer and one of the delegates of the Russian underground organizations, at the age of twenty, at the Prague conference of 1912.[21]

REVOLUTIONARY ACTIVISM

The Bolshevik party was hardly monolithic, but it was cohesive and was able to rebuild a revolutionary workers' organization inside Russia through the combination of legal and illegal methods. Lenin's description of what this looked like is worth considering.

"The exceptional and unique feature of our position … is that our illegal Social-Democratic Labor Party consists of illegal workers' organizations (often called 'cells') which are surrounded by a more or less dense network of legal workers' associations (such as sick insurance societies, trade unions, educational associations, athletic clubs, temperance societies, and so forth)," he wrote in a report to the leaders of the Socialist International. "Most of these legal associations exist in the metropolis; in many parts of the provinces there are none at all," he added. "Some of the illegal organizations are fairly large, others are quite small and in some cases they consist only of trusted agents." He explained that these "trusted agents" were leading workers who were chosen to maintain contact between the RSDLP central committee and the local groups. Their function was also "to create flexible forms of leadership for local activities in the large centers of the labor movement."[22]

The "dense network" of legal associations had an essential interrelationship with the illegal organizations: "The legal associations serve to some extent as a screen for the illegal organizations and for the extensive, legal advocacy of the idea of working-class solidarity among the masses." More than this, "nation-wide contacts between the leading working-class organizations, the maintenance of a center (the Central Committee) and the passing of precise Party resolutions on all questions—all these are of course carried out quite illegally and call for the utmost secrecy and trustworthiness on the part of advanced and tested workers." Lenin also commented on the interplay of reform struggles and revolutionary perspectives. "We make use of every reform (insurance, for example) and of every legal society," he wrote. "But we use them to develop the revolutionary consciousness and the revolutionary struggle of the masses."[23]

In order to advance this goal, Lenin stressed, workers were encouraged to conduct political strikes, meetings, and street demonstrations in order to draw more forces into the struggle to advance workers' interests and challenge established authority. This was linked to the publication and circulation of revolutionary leaflets and an illegal newspaper. He added: "The ideological unification of all these propaganda and agitation activities among the masses is achieved by the slogans adopted by the supreme bodies of our Party, namely: (1) an eight-hour day; (2) confiscation of the landed estates, and (3) a democratic republic."[24] This third goal was advanced through the insistent demand (embraced by most of Russia's revolutionaries) for a Constituent Assembly.

These demands were related to the Bolsheviks' fundamental strategic orientation—a worker-peasant alliance to carry out the democratic revolution. Incessantly put forward and popularized by the Bolshevik party, they became known as *the three whales of Bolshevism* (derived from a fable picturing the world as balanced on the backs of three whales).

The underground RSDLP, under Bolshevik leadership, began to revive dramatically on the basis of this orientation. "The sudden growth of the illegal Bolshevik nuclei," recalled prominent Menshevik Theodore Dan, "was an unpleasant surprise for those Mensheviks who regarded these nuclei as a product of the disintegration of the old pre-revolutionary Party organization and doomed to inevitable extinction."[25] At the same time, Bolsheviks also gained predominance in the legal work—trade unions, electoral campaigns, insurance societies, workers' clubs, etc.—which the Mensheviks had considered their own turf.

In the wake of government violence against workers in the Lena goldfields, during a 1912 strike, a nationwide upsurge of labor militancy provided the context for an intense escalation of Bolshevik influenced actions. Historian Leopold Haimson has remarked on the Bolsheviks' ability "to strike a note of militance, and yet seemingly a note of realism; to appeal to anger, and also to make its expression appear eminently reasonable, if not practical." The upsurge was interrupted only by the explosion of the First World War. Some have speculated that it could well have escalated into a full-scale revolution. "It is because of this multiplicity of the notes they strike, and the varying ways in which they harmonize them," according to Haimson, "that Bolshevik propaganda and agitation prove so successful by the eve of the war, not only among the explosive strata of the Petersburg working class, but also among the 'less advanced' workers of the more isolated industrial towns and villages."[26] Haimson's rich elaboration gives a vivid sense of Bolshevik-Leninist triumph:

> By 1914 the Bolshevik platform variously offers the workers the promise of the eventual overthrow of the bourgeoisie and establishment of a proletarian dictatorship; the more ambiguous, if less distant, promise of the establishment of a "firm democratic regime," in which the masses of workers and peasants will already hold the upper hand over the privileged elements of "census" society; and most literally the political objective of a democratic republic, under which the workers will gain civic and political rights equal to those of more privileged elements, as well as a better opportunity to pursue their struggle against their employers. Even more strikingly, Bolshevik slogans emphasize the need for workers to unite, not only in pursuit of these (varyingly distant) political objectives, but also to achieve more immediate improvements in their lives. And even the definition of these ostensibly more tangible objectives, particularly in the workers' economic struggle with their employers, are subtly adjusted to the differences in the mood and expectations of the various working-class groups to which they are presented.[27]

The triumph was brutally cut short by the First World War, but the war also helped set the stage for a resumption of the revolutionary upsurge and the Bolshevik triumph.

5
Engaging with Catastrophe (1914–17)

The fictionalized film *Reds* attempts to give a sense of the period of war and revolution in which John Reed produced his journalistic classic about the 1917 Russian Revolution, *Ten Days That Shook the World*. The massive 1981 film is interspersed with snippets from interviews of aging survivors who had been young men and women six decades before. The now-grizzled American Communist William Weinstone summarizes the First World War and its consequences:

> Sixty-five million go to war, right? Ten million die, ten million become orphans, twenty million become maimed, crippled, or wounded. You had *catastrophe* in Europe, you had a holocaust in Europe. You had a desire for change. Who can stop 'em when there was such a revolutionary sentiment, huh? Who can stop 'em?

IMPACTS OF THE GREAT WAR

Weinstone's emphatic assertions are, if anything, understated. Among the 65 million fighting men in the conflict, there were about nine million documented combat deaths (one soldier out of seven), with an additional five million reported missing, and seven million suffering permanent disabilities (out of approximately 21 million wounded). The estimated civilian deaths in the war exceeded the number of military casualties. Costs of the war totaled $208 billion according to 1920 estimates (approximating $3 trillion in 2022 values). Such calculations understate the disruptive and destructive economic realities, which translated into multiple catastrophes in the quality of life for many millions who survived.

The First World War was like a convergence of mighty tempests and tidal waves and earthquakes, whose horrors changed everything. Technology and modernizing "progress" turned lethal. Competitive nationalisms and imperialisms unleashed a backdraft from the murderous firestorms of conquest and subordination of the colonies, suddenly exploding throughout the lands of the conquerors. It was devastating for the peoples, as well as the social and political structures of Europe and other parts of the world, and certainly for Russia.

It also had a devastating impact on the global working-class movement. Angelica Balabanoff later recalled the mighty Socialist International on the eve of the war, embracing "millions of men and women in every nation of the world," including "the most advanced and articulate workers, the most influential leaders of labor, many of the ablest journalists and foremost intellectuals of the day." A bulwark of working-class consciousness and socialist commitment, "its leaders sat in parliaments and trade union councils," and "its hundreds of newspapers were daily fare of the European masses, animated by a common faith."[1]

In a 1912 manifesto on war and militarism, the International had proclaimed: "Proletarians consider it a crime to shoot each other down in the interests of and for the profit of the capitalists, for the sake of dynastic honor and secret diplomatic treaties." Lenin, Rosa Luxemburg, and Julius Martov had closely collaborated in helping draft a similar document adopted in Stuttgart at the International's 1907 conference, promising that "in case war should break out," socialists "shall be bound to intervene for its speedy termination, and to employ all their forces to utilize the economic and political crisis created by the war in order to rouse the masses of the people and thereby hasten the downfall of capitalist class rule."[2]

Yet when war came at last, leaders of the Second International's affiliates—in their great majority—reneged, giving full-throated support to the war effort, collaborating with their wartime governments, encouraging workers to enlist in the military to shoot down workers in the opposing army.

A common orientation among parties of the Second International contributed to this shocking turnaround. A seemingly quite reasonable separation had been made between a *minimum program* (reforms that could actually be achieved under capitalism) and a *maximum program* (the replacement of capitalism with socialism, when the time was right). The crystallization of a bureaucratic apparatus evolved to ensure the practical functioning of the party. This included avoiding moves toward revolutionary socialism when the time was deemed (by the bureaucracy) not to be right. There was a keen sense of the need to prevent revolutionary goals from undermining the reformist goals of the minimum program. There was also a powerful inclination to avoid the fierce repression that would be unleashed upon socialist parties seeking to block "patriotic" policies on behalf of imperialism and war. Such dynamics contributed to the pro-war orientations of many socialists.

The complexities of global politics intertwined with such practical pressures in ways that impacted on those who sought to remain true to left-wing commitments. Among pro-war socialists were the most orthodox of theorists, drawing from the writings of Marx and Engels to justify their positions. This included the prestigious "party Menshevik" Georgi Plekhanov, who was joined in his patriotic enthusiasm by the venerable anarchist icon Peter Kropotkin. There were others who justified—in the manner of Benito Mussolini in Italy and Józef Piłsudski in Poland—their transition from revolutionary socialism to strident nationalism with calls to shed "stale dogmas" and embrace bold new thinking and decisive action, carrying them far to the political Right. Socialist-Revolutionary terrorist Boris Savinkov and "Ultra-Left" Bolshevik Gregor Alexinsky were among these.

Within the radicalized sectors of the Russian working class—fresh from an upwelling of militant demonstrations and clashes with authorities for economic demands and democratic rights—there was a loss of balance. "Events developed so rapidly that organized workers were caught off guard," recalled Alexander Shlyapnikov. "Newspaper articles spoke about the leaders of German social democracy justifying the war and voting for war credits," he noted. "Our first thought was that the government wire-services were false and that they wanted to whip us Russian social democrats into line." But the reports proved to be true. "Workers showered us with questions as to the meaning of the behavior of the German socialists, whom we had always presented as models for ourselves. Where was all that world solidarity?"[3]

While Shlyapnikov and those around him in the Bolshevik underground were able to draw together an anti-war cohort, they had to contend with a fierce governmental repression of those challenging the war effort, and a powerful wave of patriotic sentiment among broad sectors of the population. The war's beginning, as Krupskaya later recalled, "temporarily checked the rising revolutionary movement in Russia, turned the whole world upside down, precipitated a number of grave crises," and "gave new and much sharper emphasis to vital issues of the revolutionary struggle." She added that "although war had been in the air for a long time it came as a shock to all of us." Many around the Bolshevik organization, she commented, "were not clear on the question, and spoke mostly about which side was the attacking side."[4]

CONTINUITIES AND TRANSFORMATIONS

Lenin confronted George Plekhanov at a forum in Switzerland, when his old mentor presented a Marxist-inflected defense of the Russian war effort to the exile community. He was given ten minutes to outline what was becoming the Bolshevik position. According to Krupskaya:

> He went up to the speaker's table with a pot of beer in his hand. He spoke calmly and only the pallor of his face betrayed his agitation. He said in effect that the war was not an accidental occurrence, that the way for it had been paved by the whole nature of the development of bourgeois society. The International congresses at Stuttgart, Copenhagen and Basle had defined what the attitude of the Socialists should be towards the impending war. Only by combatting the chauvinist intoxication in their countries would the Social-Democrats be fulfilling their duty. The war, which had just begun, ought to be converted into a decisive fight against the ruling classes on the part of the proletariat.[5]

Years after she had broken decisively from Lenin, Angelica Balabanoff recalled Lenin when, in the early days of the war, she was beginning to draw closer to him. "Lenin was the strategist of the workers' movement," she wrote. "The world was a chessboard to him on which the two opponents were represented by two social classes, the exploited and the exploiters, both vying for power." She observed: "Lenin was the first to recover from the terrible shock which the war and the failure and capitulation of the Socialist International had caused in all of us. … Lenin had already started his game of chess." For him, Balabanoff commented severely, "military clashes, deaths, defeats, and victories paid for with the existence of an immense number of human beings, incalculable struggles, physical and mental disease—all this was reduced to numbers, exemplified on the chessboard." Refusing to be immobilized, he was wrestling with how to move forward. "While we were still stunned by the blow of the disaster and had not yet got used to the idea that it had really happened, Lenin was already forging ahead with his plans."[6]

Out of catastrophe comes the impetus for intensified struggles—and also new possibilities for moving such struggles forward.

Another revolutionary strategist, no less horrified than Balabanoff by the impacts of the war, was also pushing forward. For Rosa Luxemburg, as was the case with Krupskaya and Lenin, "war had been in the air for a long time." (The careful scholar Georges Haupt tells us that in Lenin's case, "he was aware of that probability from 1911.") Luxemburg's 1913 anti-imperialist classic, *The Accumulation of Capital*, is infused with its imminence. "Out of the world war which, sooner or later, is unavoidable," she emphasized in her May Day speech of the same year, "will come forth a definite and victorious struggle between the world of labor and the world of capital."[7]

Lenin's own major work on imperialism was only written while the First World War was in full swing. Before its eruption, Lenin "remained preoccupied to the point of obsession with the contradictions of Russian society and with the struggle to build a revolutionary party capable of exploiting these contradictions when they finally exploded." Or so argues Alex Callinicos in an interesting essay on Lenin and imperialism, which poses the question of "why did Lenin come so late to the subject of imperialism." Callinicos goes on to suggest that with the coming of the global conflict, Lenin can be seen urgently "playing catch-up" around questions of imperialism and nationalism.[8]

This point can be overstated. As Callinicos himself acknowledges, the young Ulyanov who transformed himself into the Marxist *Lenin* was from the start identifying with a Socialist International animated by conceptualizations emanating from far beyond Russia and spanning the world. More than this, in 1913 we find Lenin mentoring his younger comrade Joseph Stalin in developing an analysis of nationalism. He himself—in a brief essay on "The Historical Destiny of the Doctrine of Karl Marx"—expressed a premonition similar to that of Luxemburg in the same year: "We see a political crisis brewing" in which "frenzied arming and the policy of imperialism are turning modern Europe into a 'social peace' which is more like a barrel of gun powder than anything else." More than this, he posited a shift in the development of Marxism shaped by "a new source of great world storms" opening up in Asia—with the Russian revolutionary upsurge of 1905 "followed by revolutions in Turkey, Persia and China."[9] At the same time, there is something to what Callinicos has to say, and this will absorb much of our attention later in this chapter.

There are two additional overstatements, related to G.W.F. Hegel's dialectical philosophy. Complex and contradictory catastrophes of 1914 sent Lenin reeling, forcing him to re-examine his Marxism, in part through the study of Hegel. This is simply a well-documented statement of fact, but there are two counterposed interpretations. One overstatement is that Lenin's Marxism was utterly transformed, with sharp philosophical and political breaks from previous conceptions. The other overstatement is that Lenin's Marxism basically remained as it had been before his study of Hegel, suggesting a disconnect between his intense philosophical studies and the rest of his politics. In fact, both continuity and transformation can be found in Lenin's pre-1914 and post-1914 thought. Conceptualizations in Lenin's post-1914 writings—his study of imperialism and engagement with "the national question," and his *State and Revolution*—were certainly influenced by his immersion in Hegel's thought as reflected in *The Philosophical Notebooks* of 1914–16.

Dialectics was described in Lenin's philosophical notebooks in 1915 as "*living*, many-sided knowledge (with the number of sides eternally increasing), with an infinite number of shades of every approach and approximation to reality (with a philosophical system growing into a whole out of each shade)—here we have an immeasurably rich content as compared with 'metaphysical' materialism ..." We can certainly find such dialectical qualities in much of what Lenin thought and said in earlier years. Nor can we see the abandonment of basic political conceptualizations Lenin had developed since the late 1890s. But we can find aspects of these conceptualizations developed in fresh ways as he engaged with Hegel's writings. More than one analyst has noted a new stress on breaks in continuity, highlighting "leaps, catastrophes, and revolutions."[10]

In his outstanding 1914 summary of Marx's life and ideas for *Granat* encyclopedia, Lenin did something unusual for Marxists of that time—placing an explication of dialectical philosophy (rather than historical materialism or economic analysis) at the beginning of his discussion of Marx's thought:

> In our times, the idea of development, of evolution, has almost completely penetrated social consciousness, only in other ways, and not through Hegelian philosophy. Still, this idea, as formulated by Marx and Engels on the basis of Hegel's philosophy, is far more comprehensive and far richer in content than the current idea of evolution is. A development that repeats, as it were, stages that have already been passed, but repeats them in a different way, on a higher basis ("the negation of the negation"), a development, so to speak, that proceeds in spirals, not in a straight line; a development by leaps, catastrophes, and revolutions; "breaks in continuity"; the transformation of quantity into quality; inner impulses towards development, imparted by the contradiction and conflict of the various forces and tendencies acting on a given body, or within a given phenomenon, or within a given society; the interdependence and the closest and indissoluble connection between *all* aspects of any phenomenon (history constantly revealing ever new aspects), a connection

that provides a uniform, and universal process of motion, one that follows definite laws—these are some of the features of dialectics as a doctrine of development that is richer than the conventional one.[11]

Such notions found their way into what Lenin wrote, said, and did as he engaged in what Balabanoff terms his chessboard strategy. Actually, in the war years we can trace multiple strategies, which Lenin sought to advance (though sometimes unsuccessfully) through a variety of theorizations and tactical maneuvers. Here we can focus on only several key elements in his thinking of this period: approaches to imperialism, nationalism, democracy, the state and revolution.

IMPERIALISM

Lenin's 1916 work *Imperialism, the Highest Stage of Capitalism* is presented as a popularization, or popular outline. As will be highlighted in Chapter 7, it became a cornerstone of an internationalist strategic orientation guiding revolutionaries in the wake of the First World War. But it was grounded in a body of research and analysis throwing light on economic causes of the war's horrific explosion. It drew from liberal John A. Hobson's 1902 classic *Imperialism: A Study*, and the work of two Marxists: Rudolf Hilferding's *Finance Capital* (1910) and Nikolai Bukharin's *Imperialism and the World Economy* (1915). Lenin was certainly influenced as well by Rosa Luxemburg's *The Accumulation of Capital* 1913, even if he had sharp differences with aspects of her analysis, and his theorizations were formulated independently from hers.

Lenin's popularization would captivate many, especially with his heightened prestige in the wake of the Russian Revolution of 1917. "The world hastened along a clearly marked out path toward war," Victor Serge later recalled in his post-war review of Lenin's book. "The majority of those who held themselves to be revolutionists were in reality carelessly and blindly drifting toward it. They were lacking in a scientific method of research and thought." That, in his opinion, is what Lenin's *Imperialism, the Highest Stage of Capitalism* provided, deftly employing the method of revolutionary Marxism:

> That great things may be accomplished by its aid is clearly and indisputably shown by this little work of Lenin's on imperialism. The first thing which this work accomplishes is immensely to broaden and expand the horizon of all events. The petty happenings of daily life, the drama of your personal life, comrade, the ministerial crises—all these are doubtless of great significance, but they depend on infinitely greater things. The capitalist world is a whole, and in this whole the ministers and all individuals are like infinitesimally small protozoa of the ocean. Everything becomes and passes away. We are no revolutionists if we cannot recognize at one glance the great main ruling factors ruling all the others, if we are not thoroughly permeated with the feeling of mighty changes.[12]

A common but inadequate understanding of imperialism, according to a more recent economist John Weeks, sees it as an "economic and political relationship between advanced capitalist countries and backward countries" which is simply defined as "the oppression and 'exploitation' of weak, impoverished countries by powerful ones."[13] Lenin's conception was broader than this. For him, imperialism involved neither a policy of capitalism (as Karl Kautsky argued) nor a permanent feature of capitalism (as Rosa Luxemburg indicated), but a *new stage of capitalism*, the transformation of its very structure.

According to Lenin, Marx's analysis held that under capitalist development "free competition gives way to the concentration of production, which, in turn, at a certain stage of development, leads to monopoly" in the twentieth century. "Although commodity production still 'reigns' and continues to be regarded as the basis of economic life, it has in reality been undermined and the bulk of the profits go to the 'geniuses' of financial manipulation." This meant "the 20th century marks the turning-point from the old capitalism to the new, from the domination of capital in general to the domination of finance capital."[14]

Finance capital referred to "the concentration of production; the monopolies arising therefrom; the merging or coalescence of the banks with industry." He identified this period as one in which a monopoly "inevitably penetrates into every sphere of public life, regardless of the form of government and all other 'details,'" with a tendency by the state to identify the needs of the massive firms with the national interest. Financial-managerial interests assume heightened importance. While under the old capitalism, the export of goods was typical, under the new capitalism the more important dynamic is the export of capital to invest in the enterprises of other lands.[15]

The logic of the capital accumulation process would mean

> surplus capital will be utilized not for the purpose of raising the standard of living of the masses in a given country, for this would mean a decline of profits for the capitalists, but for the purpose of increasing profits by exporting capital abroad to the backward countries. In these backward countries profits are usually high, for capital is scarce, the price of land is relatively low, wages are low, raw materials are cheap.[16]

According to Lenin, the new capitalism continued to increase and intensify "the anarchy inherent in capitalist production as a whole," certainly for workers affected by capital flight to far-off lands. Yet imperialism involved not simply the quest for profits in formally colonized areas (such as the case of the British Empire), but also the drive to invest in independent countries, sometimes "semi-colonies" for all practical purposes, but sometimes enjoying even greater autonomy than that—creating "diverse forms of dependent countries which, politically, are formally independent, but in fact, are enmeshed in the net of financial and diplomatic dependence." While this might "to a certain extent ... arrest development in the capital-exporting countries, it can only do so by expanding and deepening the further development of capitalism throughout the world."[17]

In contrast to Rosa Luxemburg's theory of imperialism, Lenin argued expanding capital sought entry into "not only agrarian territories, but even most highly industrialized regions." This was true because "the world is already partitioned," compelling investors of capital "to reach out for every kind of territory." According to Lenin, another "essential feature of imperialism is the rivalry between several great powers in the striving for hegemony." He elaborated:

> The epoch of the latest stage of capitalism shows us that certain relations between capitalist associations grow up, based on the economic division of the world; while parallel to and in connection with it, certain relations grow up between political alliances, between states, on the basis of the territorial division of the world, of the struggle for colonies, of the "struggle for spheres of influence."[18]

The result of all this, for Lenin no less than for Luxemburg, was what she had called the *chain of catastrophes*: world crises, wars, revolutions—and the ultimate intensification of struggles by oppressed working people throughout the world. Lenin cautioned, however, that the process was complex because divisions could be created between workers—not simply along national lines but even within countries: "Imperialism has the tendency to create privileged sections also among the workers, and to detach them from the broad masses of the proletariat."[19]

From this analysis flowed several practical conclusions.

Given the nature and actual dynamics of imperialism, its permeation of the political and economic life of all the world's dominant countries, it made no sense to try to determine which one made the first aggressive move—because all were poised for what was, in fact, an inevitable conflict. The duty of revolutionaries, Lenin concluded, was not to "take sides" with whomever did not fire the first shot, but instead "transformation of the imperialist war into a civil war." Social revolution within each warring country would involve the working class overturning the capitalist regimes responsible for the catastrophic turn of events.

This also amounted to a policy in each country of "revolutionary defeatism"—*not* hoping for the victory of the war effort of one's own country but instead hoping for the defeat of war efforts in all countries. For this, Lenin's erstwhile comrade Gregor Alexinsky, now a pro-war patriot, attacked him by referring to "the hysterical conduct of those few irresponsible intellectuals who are ready to rejoice in the defeat of their country when attacked by a cowardly and brutal enemy."[20] Alexinsky later famously accused Lenin of being a paid agent of Imperial Germany.

Embedded in Lenin's analysis was also a key to the betrayals by the leaderships of the various socialist parties, described by Victor Serge as pursuing "a miserable policy of vote catching." Serge commented that "party functionaries and deputies capable of seeing beyond the narrow limits of their constituencies or of parliamentary intrigue were few and far between." The social base of such practical opportunists consisted of the "privileged sections among the workers" that had become dis-attached from the broader working masses.[21] (Contrary to what some have claimed, Lenin did not see the development of such a "labor aristocracy" as inevitable—more "privileged" skilled workers had also shown themselves in Russia and elsewhere as being essential elements in the vanguard of "conscious workers" of the revolutionary movement.)

Lenin's analysis of imperialism also had implications for understanding what many have seen as a "secular faith" constituting the great rival of socialism—*nationalism.*

THE NATIONAL QUESTION

Lenin sharply distinguished between "national wars" of the late eighteenth and early nineteenth centuries and the modern imperialist war. The old national wars were struggles "for the self-determination of the nation, for its independence, for the freedom of its language, for popular representation [through] the creation of national states, which were, at a certain stage of capitalism, indispensable soil for the growth of productive forces." Imperialism "impresses a quite specific stamp on the present war, distinguishing it from all its predecessors. Only by examining this war in its distinctive historical environment … can we clarify our attitude to it. Otherwise, we shall be operating with old conceptions … applied to a different, an old situation." Among the outdated conceptions are "the fatherland idea" and "the division … of wars into defensive and aggressive." This dovetailed with Lenin's rejection of all capitalist war efforts, regardless of who "fired the first shot."[22]

In this "special epoch ... a struggle is on for a division of the remaining portions" of the world. "We cannot say how long this epoch will last. There may well be several such wars, but there must be a clear understanding that these are quite different wars from those waged earlier, and that, accordingly, the tasks facing socialists have changed."[23]

Operating within a similar framework of understanding, some revolutionaries—including Rosa Luxemburg and some comrades in the Bolshevik party—argued all forms of nationalism were incompatible with working-class internationalism. Lenin sharply took issue with this conclusion. There were different forms of nationalism—some worthy of support, others worthy of denunciation. A distinction must be made between the nationalism (to be opposed) of the imperialist nations and the nationalism (to be supported) of those countries oppressed by imperialism. He insisted that, in regard to colonial oppression, revolutionaries must therefore "unequivocally demand that the Social Democrats of the oppressing countries (of the so-called 'great' nations in particular) should recognize and defend the right of the oppressed nations to self-determination."[24]

REVOLUTIONARY DEMOCRACY

We can also see a spill-over and interplay between Lenin's evolving thought on "the national question" and his thinking about the question of democracy. Lenin was always a fierce partisan of genuine democracy—which he saw as rule by the laboring majority—and in his 1905 work *Two Tactics of Social-Democracy in the Democratic Revolution* he emphasized: "Whoever wants to reach socialism by any other path than that of political democracy will inevitably arrive at conclusions that are absurd and reactionary both in the economic and the political sense." Yet in the war years, Krupskaya notes in her *Reminiscences of Lenin*, the nature and role of democracy was a key question animating Lenin's thinking, and he arrived at "a very clear and definite view of the relationship between economics and politics in the epoch of struggle for socialism."[25]

Stressing that "the role of democracy in the struggle for socialism could not be ignored," Krupskaya quotes Lenin as insisting that democracy is necessary for the achievement of socialism in two respects: first, the working class cannot carry out a socialist revolution unless it is prepared for that through struggles for democracy; and second, "socialism cannot maintain its victory and bring humanity to the time when the state will wither away unless democracy is fully achieved."[26]

Lenin's linkage of the socialist goal with "the withering away of the state" is a matter to which we will return at the end of this chapter. Yet he sees the existence of genuine democracy, to the extent that it becomes *a habit in the way people function* as decision-makers, as inseparable from achieving the desired goal of a stateless socialism. But he also saw it as an essential element in the political strategy to replace capitalism with socialism. This is detailed in a lengthy quotation from "The Revolutionary Proletariat and the Right of Nations to Self-Determination":

> We must *combine* the revolutionary struggle against capitalism with a revolutionary program and tactics in respect of *all* democratic demands, including a republic, a militia, election of government officials by the people, equal rights for women, self-determination of nations, etc. So long as capitalism exists all these demands are capable of realization only as an exception, and in incomplete, distorted form. Basing ourselves on democracy as already achieved, and showing up its deficiency under capitalism, we demand the overthrow of capitalism and expropriation of the bourgeoisie as an essential basis both for abolishing the poverty of the masses and for *fully and thoroughly* implementing *all* democratic transformations. Some of those transformations will be started before the overthrow of the bourgeoisie, others *in the course of* this overthrow, and still others after it. The social revolution is not a single battle but an epoch of a series of battles on all and every problem of economic and democratic transformations, whose completion will be effected only with the expropriation of the bourgeoisie. It is for the sake of this ultimate goal that we must formulate *every one* of our democratic demands in a consistently revolutionary manner.[27]

This approach was translated into vibrant reality in the revolutionary year of 1917—in actual events unfolding in Russia, but also in Lenin's theorizations written down in the late summer of that year, in his classic study, *The State and Revolution.*

THE STATE AND REVOLUTION

In 1915 and 1916, Lenin found himself in polemical conflict with a rising young Bolshevik theorist named Nikolai Bukharin. Influenced by "Ultra-Left" currents (including Lenin's old Bolshevik adversary Alexander Bogdanov), Bukharin was developing an interpretation of the Marxist theory of the state that Lenin at first dismissed as "semi-anarchism"; by 1917, however, he was to conclude Bukharin's interpretation had merit. It would coincide with the analysis offered in *The State and Revolution*, as Lenin sought to excavate Marx's actual views on the state and revolution, which he concluded had been diluted and distorted by prominent figures in the now-discredited Second International.

Following Marx and Engels, Lenin viewed the state in any society as reflecting the power relations between social-economic classes, seeing "the modern representative state" (even the most democratic of republics) in capitalist society as being under the domination of the capitalist class, and this added up to the dictatorship (political domination) of the bourgeoisie. "The executive of the modern state," they had written in the *Communist Manifesto*, "is but a committee for managing the common affairs of the whole bourgeoisie." Lenin added: "Marx grasped the essence of capitalist democracy splendidly when, in analyzing the experience of the Commune, he said that the oppressed are allowed once every few years to decide which particular representatives of the oppressing class shall represent and repress them in parliament."[28]

Influenced by the experience of the 1871 Paris Commune (in which the working class "for the first time in history held political power for two whole months"), Marx and Engels had added in an 1872 preface to the *Communist Manifesto* that "the working class cannot simply lay hold of the ready-made state machinery and wield it for its own purposes."[29] Political domination by the working class (dictatorship of the proletariat) would require a new, radically democratized state machinery.

Lenin believed a genuine democracy could only exist under the political rule of the proletariat: "The dictatorship of the proletariat, the period of transition to communism, will for the first time create democracy for the people, the majority, along with the necessary suppression of the exploiters, the minority." This would amount to "the proletariat organized as the ruling class."

As Lenin put it, there would be "an immense expansion of democracy, which for the first time becomes democracy for the poor, democracy for the people, and not democracy for the money-bags."[30]

This radicalized democracy would lead to an even more radical transformation. "The more complete the democracy, the nearer the moment when it becomes unnecessary," Lenin wrote. "The more democratic the 'state' which consists of the armed workers, and which is 'no longer a state in the proper sense of the word,' the more rapidly *every form* of state begins to wither away."[31]

Following Marx, Lenin turns anarchist:

> From the moment all members of society, or at least the vast majority, have learned to administer the state *themselves*, have taken this work into their own hands, have organized control over the insignificant capitalist minority, over the gentry who wish to preserve their capitalist habits and over the workers who have been thoroughly corrupted by capitalism—from this moment the need for government of any kind begins to disappear altogether.

Even democracy *as a form of governmental* institution "will *wither away* in the process of changing and becoming a habit."[32]

Lenin himself had been inclined to dismiss such "semi-anarchism," and he was now scathing in his criticism of onetime mentors whom he felt had disoriented him.

> The proletariat needs the state—this is repeated by all the opportunists, social-chauvinists and Kautskyites, who assure us that this is what Marx taught. But they "forget" to add that, in the

> first place, according to Marx, the proletariat needs only a state which is withering away, i.e., a state so constituted that it begins to wither away immediately, and cannot but wither away.[33]

Lenin never completed the writing of *The State and Revolution.* Instead he composed this November postscript:

> This pamphlet was written in August and September 1917. I had already drawn up the plan for the next, the seventh chapter, "The Experience of the Russian Revolutions of 1905 and 1917." Apart from the title, however, I had no time to write a single line of the chapter; I was "interrupted" by a political crisis—the eve of the October revolution of 1917. Such an "interruption" can only be welcomed; but the writing of the second part of this pamphlet ("The Experience of the Russian Revolutions of 1905 and 1917") will probably have to be put off for a long time. It is more pleasant and useful to go through the "experience of revolution" than to write about it.[34]

Lev Kamenev elaborated on the question of dictatorship in 1920: "During several years, before the eyes of the whole human race, a picture of the practice of dictatorship is unrolled—a dictatorship ruling over the whole world, determining everything, regulating everything, penetrating everything, and confirming its existence by 20 million corpses on the fields of Europe and Asia."

Kamenev continued: "Open your eyes and you will see before you a splendidly elaborated system of bourgeois dictatorship, which has achieved its object: for it has given that concentration of power into the hands of a small group of world imperialists which allowed them to conduct their war and attain their peace."

In 1914–18 this "bourgeois dictatorship showed itself to be "the most bloody, most tyrannical, most pitiless, cynical and hypocritical of all forms of power that ever existed." The alternative to this, Kamenev argued, was the organized working class taking political power—which is what he and his Bolshevik comrades referred to as the dictatorship of the proletariat.[35]

6
The 1917 Revolution

In January 1917, an exiled Lenin wrapped up a lecture to a Swiss audience on the 1905 revolution: "We of the older generation may not live to see the decisive battles of this coming revolution." This rhetorical device emphasized the need for "a long view of history" and set up his concluding line, with young activist listeners in mind: "I can, I believe, express the confident hope that the youth which is working so splendidly in the socialist movement of Switzerland, and of the whole world, will be fortunate enough not only to fight, but also to win, in the coming proletarian revolution."[1]

Based on this thin reed, it has been said: "It is easy to see that Russia was ripe for revolt, though no one realized it at the time, not even the Bolsheviks." In fact, astute observers of the time clearly saw Russia was ripe for revolt. A private memorandum (highlighted by historian Dominic Lieven) was given to the tsar, for example, in the summer of 1914, warning him against launching Russia's participation in what would erupt as the Great War. The memorandum foretold that the war would bring revolution in its wake—inevitably originating either in a defeated Germany or a defeated Russia, either way threatening to overturn all "European values" rooted in private property. The author of this memorandum was Pyotr Durnovo, a conservative traditionalist and the tsar's former minister of internal affairs who had helped crush the 1905 revolution.[2]

Revolutionaries in the period immediately preceding the February Revolution were saying that "the revolution is growing," that "Europe is pregnant with revolution," that "our day will come." Krupskaya writes: "Never before had Vladimir Ilyich been in such an uncompromising mood as he was during the last months of 1916 and the early months of 1917. He was positively certain that the revolution was imminent." Historian Georges Haupt concurs that "the February Revolution did not take him unawares."[3]

THE FEBRUARY REVOLUTION*

The war did not go well for the tsar's army or for the Russian people, adding new grievances to old. Yet another wave of working-class radicalization was generated. The tsarist system was beginning to collapse and an ever-deeper crisis was overtaking Russian society under the impact of the First World War, which was greatly intensifying the immense problems already created by the processes of industrialization and "modernization."

Historian Allan Wildman writes that "the soldiers felt they were being used and recklessly expended by the rich and powerful, of whom their officers were the most visible, immediate representatives." Roy Medvedev adds: "By drafting millions of peasants and workers into the army and training them to handle weapons, the tsarist regime, without intending to, provided military and technical training. ... The likely allies of the working class, the peasants, were armed and organized in military garrisons in every major city, with especially large garrisons in Moscow and Petrograd."[4]

Journalist-historian William Henry Chamberlin once commented "the collapse of the Romanov autocracy in March 1917 was one of the most leaderless, spontaneous, anonymous revolutions of all time."[5] This is both true and false—a paradox shedding light on the role of the revolutionary party.

Historians have noted the growth of war-weariness, despair, and exasperation with the old system throughout Russian society. The only hope for a better life seemed either in a Russian victory in the First World War (which seemed increasingly illusory or even irrelevant) or in some kind of radical social change. These moods and feelings and beliefs, "spontaneously" generated by objective conditions, were certainly the source of the uprising, but the revolutionary parties played an essential role in offering coherent conceptual alternatives to the status quo. Only the orga-

* Portions of this section are drawn from my books *Lenin and the Revolutionary Party* and *October Song*.

nized socialists—both those who had supported and those who had opposed the war effort—articulated such alternatives, and their appeals were yielding an increasingly visible response among the Russian workers as 1916 faded into 1917. Trotsky's description merits attention:

> In every factory, in each guild, in each company, in each tavern, in the military hospital, at the transfer stations, even in the depopulated villages, the molecular work of revolutionary thought was in progress. Everywhere were to be found the interpreters of events, chiefly from among the workers, from whom one inquired, "What's the news?" and from whom one awaited the needed words. These leaders had often been left to themselves, and nourished themselves upon fragments of revolutionary generalizations arriving in their hands by various routes, had studied out by themselves between the lines of the liberal papers what they needed. Their class instinct was refined by a political criterion, and though they did not think all their ideas through to the end, nevertheless their thought ceaselessly and stubbornly worked its way in a single direction.[6]

There was a proliferation of protest actions organized by such people, including on the socialist-inspired holiday, International Women's Day of March 8, 1917 (February 23, according to the old Russian calendar). In earlier years, there had traditionally been a relative political "backwardness" and passivity among unskilled workers—such as female textile workers—in contrast to the militant activism of the "conscious workers" among the more skilled laboring strata, such as those predominating in the heavily Bolshevik-influenced metal trades. Now, in a number of instances, it was metalworkers who were inspired to take to the streets in response to the appeals of militant textile workers, women who marched through the factory districts on International Women's Day chanting: "Down with the war! Down with high prices! Down with hunger! Bread for the workers!"

An up-to-the-minute account written by Lenin's sisters, Anna and Maria Ulyanov (both experienced revolutionary militants) appeared in the Bolshevik paper *Pravda*:

> On Women's Day, February 23, a strike was declared at the majority of factories and plants. The women were in a very militant mood—not only the women workers, but the masses of women queuing for bread and kerosene. They held political meetings, they predominated in the streets, they moved to the city duma with a demand for bread, they stopped trams. "Comrades, come out!" they shouted enthusiastically. They went to the factories and plants and summoned workers to [put] down tools. All in all, Women's Day was a tremendous success and gave rise to the revolutionary spirit.[7]

Even as the revolution was getting underway, a "progressive" industrialist (Alexis Meshchersky) confided to Menshevik acquaintance Simon Liberman: "It's too bad the authorities are acting with such caution, afraid to shed blood. We need a real bloodletting, to put a quick end to all these disorders." Liberman, whose bourgeois origins gave him access, could later report: "The industrialists were afraid of the workers and also of the peasants. They declared openly that they were ready and willing to make their peace with the tsarist regime in order to withstand the desires and demands of the working class and, in part, of the peasantry too."[8]

On the following day demonstrations and strikes spread throughout Petrograd, with a proliferation of anti-war and anti-government banners. The military units of the city for the most part refused to take action against the insurgents, and in some cases even joined them. More and more workers were responding to an appeal issued by an on-the-ground united front:

> We Bolsheviks, Menshevik SDs [Social Democrats], and SRs [Socialist-Revolutionaries] summon the proletariat of Petersburg and all Russia to organization and feverish mobilization of our forces. Comrades! In the factories organize illegal strike committees. Link one district to another. Organize collections for the illegal press and for arms. Prepare yourselves, comrades. The hour of decisive struggle is nearing![9]

Days of street fighting saw the police take the offensive, fire into the crowds, and then be routed as the workers fought back with growing confidence. As a general strike paralyzed the city, the overwhelming majority of the working class seemed alive with enthusiasm for revolutionary change. Historian Michael Melancon has emphasized the interplay between the socialist groups and radicalized working-class layers that were coming into the streets. "Direct and organized socialist involvement and intervention occurred at every single stage."[10]

The 1917 reports from knowledgeable *New York Tribune* foreign correspondent Isaac Don Levine give a sense of the events. While the "mainstream" politicians in the Duma reared back in fear (with prominent liberal Pavel Miliukov predicting "the revolution will be crushed in fifteen minutes" by tsarist troops), "the leaders of the socialistic, revolutionary, and labor elements organized for a general attack … against the old regime." Forming democratic-activist councils (soviets), they mobilized

> a revolutionary army, composed of soldiers, armed students, and workers. Red flags were now waving in the air everywhere, and, singing the songs of freedom and revolution, the masses continued their victorious fight. The leaders of the movement commandeered every motorcar they could get, armed it with a machine-gun and a gun crew, and set it free to tour the city and round up agents of the Government.[11]

By the fourth day of the insurgency, the troops were disobeying the commands of tsarist officers, openly joining the workers in massive numbers, firing on the police stations, helping to free all political prisoners. The tsarist autocracy collapsed. The revolution was triumphant. Traditional liberal and conservative politicians, with support from moderate socialists, hastily composed a Provisional Government, but its power was limited. "It was the workmen and soldiers that actually fought and shed their blood for the freedom of Russia. The Duma took a hand in the situation only after the revolution had achieved its main success," Levine reported at the time.[12]

"The gulf between the Provisional Government and the Council of Deputies is as wide as between the United States Government and socialism," Levine explained to his readers. "Only such an upheaval as the revolution could have bridged this chasm between the two extremes." While the Provisional Government "represents … business and commerce," he noted, "the ultimate aim of the Workmen's Council is social revolution. To achieve this revolution it is necessary to de-throne the political autocrats first, they say. Then the capitalistic system must be attacked by the working classes of all nations as their common enemy." This was in June 1917. Ronald Suny aptly summarizes: "To put it simply, the top of society was moving to the right, while the bottom was moving to the left."[13]

FROM APRIL TO JULY

When he returned to Russia from revolutionary exile, Lenin came into conflict with some of his comrades who were in the leading circles of the Bolshevik party. Before his return, he had already written to them about some disagreements, and these became further clarified after he presented to a Bolshevik meeting (and then to a larger gathering of Russian Social Democrats) his April Theses.

The theses asserted Russia was "*passing* from the first stage of the revolution which … placed power in the hands of the bourgeoisie to its *second stage*, which must place power in the hands of the proletariat and the poorest sections of the peasants." They denounced "unreasoning trust" in the Provisional Government, which he termed a "government of capitalists, those worst enemies of peace and socialism." Instead, the theses insisted, the Soviets of Workers' Deputies (or Soviets of Workers', Agricultural Laborers' and Peasants' Deputies) "are the *only possible* form of revolutionary government." There should not be a parliamentary republic, but instead a soviet republic "throughout the country, from top to bottom." The theses called for abolition of the police, the army and the bureaucracy—Lenin believed the organized workers and peasants should take over the functions of these entities, with "salaries of all officials, all of whom are elective and displaceable at any time, not to exceed the average wage of a competent worker." The theses also emphasized that "it is not our *immediate* task to 'introduce' socialism, but only to bring social production and the distribution of products at once under the *control* of the Soviets of Workers' Deputies."[14]

It appeared that Lenin's 1905 option of "uninterrupted revolution" (from bourgeois-democratic to proletarian-socialist revolution) was now on the table. "The comrades were somewhat taken aback for the moment," according to Krupskaya. "Many of them thought that Ilyich was presenting the case in much too blunt a manner, and that it was too early yet to speak of a socialist revolution." The same April Theses were then shared at a joint meeting of Bolsheviks and Mensheviks—and they caused an uproar. Lenin was accused of raising "the banner of civil war in the midst of the revolutionary democrats." Alexandra Kollontai "warmly defended Lenin's theses," but other Bolsheviks present were not prepared to do so.[15] It was obvious that the theses would mean a sharp break with many of the Mensheviks and Socialist-Revolutionaries with whom the Bolsheviks had been working.

Lenin's theses were printed in *Pravda*, three days later, on April 7. The editor of the Bolshevik paper was Lev Kamenev, and on the following day Kamenev published an article, "Our Disagreements," not only dissociating himself from the April Theses but noting they represented Lenin's private views, shared by neither *Pravda* nor the Bolshevik Central Committee Bureau.

In a recent reinterpretation of 1917 events, Eric Blanc has offered an excellent explanation of why, in order to understand what Lenin's party was doing in 1917, one cannot afford to restrict oneself to examining Lenin's writings. "These were undoubtedly important," he has argued, "but it is hardly the case that Lenin's approach (which itself was in flux, both strategically and tactically) can be equated with that of the Bolshevik leadership or ranks in 1917." Instead, we "must broaden our source base to include other Bolshevik leaders, local and regional party bodies, public speeches, and mass leaflets." And further broadening our scope beyond Petrograd "to include the Russian empire's periphery and provinces provides a better sense of what we might call 'ballpark Bolshevism,' i.e., the core political stances generally shared by all levels of Bolshevik cadres and projected by them to working people across the empire."[16]

Within this "ballpark Bolshevism" there was general agreement with the 1905 orientation—favoring a radical worker-peasant alliance to push through (against the resistance of capitalists and big landowners) a thoroughgoing democratic revolution. There was also agreement on the need for a "democratic dictatorship of the proletariat and the peasantry" to replace any vacillating regime of conservative and liberal moderates. "The Bolshevik label for the Russian revolution was far from a straightforward application of the traditional Marxist binary framework," as Lars Lih has emphasized. "When talking about the bourgeois-democratic revolution, the Bolsheviks put the emphasis heavily on 'democratic', aiming at a democracy of a radical kind."[17] Yet the "uninterrupted revolution" thrust of Lenin's new position (only hinted at late in 1905) threatened to alienate united front partners among the Mensheviks and Socialist-Revolutionaries (SRs). Kamenev wasn't the only Bolshevik not inclined to do that. Bolshevik isolation seemed a recipe for disaster. Lenin saw it differently: "All the oppressed will come to us, because the war will bring them to us. They have no other way out."[18]

"A struggle started within the Bolshevik organization," Krupskaya wrote. "It did not last long."[19] Before the end of April, a general city conference of the Bolsheviks of Petrograd took place, upholding Lenin's position after extensive discussion and debate. The considerable common ground shared by those debating the question facilitated Lenin's victory among his Bolshevik comrades. There was another important factor preserving Bolshevik unity. Lenin was insistent that what he was proposing in the April Theses could not become reality until majorities in the soviets agreed. There had to be majority agreement within the working class for the demand of "all power to the soviets." This spoke to the concern over Bolshevik isolation.

Mensheviks and SRs were in control of the soviets. The Bolsheviks had not yet recovered the hegemony they had gained in the workers' movement before the wartime repression of 1914. Despite growing frustration with the Provisional Government, the moderate socialist leaders insisted the soviets should support the Provisional Government to help establish a capitalist democracy, which they saw as a lengthy but necessary prelude to eventual socialist transition.

Alexander Kerensky, on the periphery of the SRs, had put himself forward as a bridge between the soviets and the Provisional Government. He was ultimately selected by others in the Provisional Government as President. Though many believed Kerensky was destined to build a democratic Russia, those who knew him well had doubts. "In Kerensky everything was illogical, contradictory, changing, often capricious, imagined, or feigned," wrote SR leader Victor Chernov, who served as Kerensky's minister of agriculture. "Kerensky," he went on, "was tormented by the need to believe in himself, and was always winning or losing that faith."[20]

While still claiming to represent the soviets' interests within the Provisional Government, Kerensky began to side with other establishment politicians against the councils, which were undermining his government's authority. More and more frustrated workers were joining the Bolsheviks—even the SR and Menshevik left wings found Bolshevik arguments convincing. Leon Trotsky, a brilliant leader in the 1905 revolutionary upsurge, became the Bolsheviks' most famous recruit.

The popular aspirations animating the February Revolution had been peace, bread, and land: an end to the mass slaughter of Russians in the imperialist war; the end of bread shortages caused by the impact of the war; and sweeping reforms to transfer land from the thin layer of aristocrats to the masses of land-hungry peasants. The Provisional Government balked at all these aspirations, and it was especially committed to continuing the war effort.

A crescendo of working-class anger in July culminated in a revolutionary demonstration. Militants in Petrograd, not under party control but with Bolshevik support, initiated what verged on a spontaneous uprising. The ensuing violence gave the government a pretext for large-scale repression. As Left SR Isaac Steinberg recounted, "troops of officers, students, Cossacks came out on the streets, searched passers-by for weapons and evidence of 'Bolshevism,' committed atrocities."[21] Lenin was publicly accused of being a treasonous agent of Imperial Germany. The Provisional Government outlawed the Bolshevik party, raided and wrecked its headquarters, arresting or driving underground its leaders and most visible militants.

FROM AUGUST TO OCTOBER*

In the wake of "the July Days" (as this upheaval came to be known), Kerensky appointed right-wing general Lavr Kornilov commander-in-chief of the Russian army. Both hoped to counter the pressure from "unreasonable" workers, who were setting up factory committees to take control of workplaces and organizing their own "red guard" paramilitary groups to maintain public order and protect the revolution against reactionary violence. Kerensky found such radicalism disturbing, but right-wingers like General Kornilov thought moderates like Kerensky were just as distasteful. Traditional politicians—liberals as well as conservatives—began viewing military dictatorship as the only way to stabilize the nation.

In his memoirs, Kerensky quotes this message from Kornilov, which displays Kornilov's contempt for all socialists, even the moderates:

> I feel sure … that the spineless weaklings who form the Provisional Government will be swept away. If by some miracle they should remain in power, the leaders of the Bolsheviks and the Soviet will go unpunished through the connivance of such men as Chernov. It is time to put an end to all of this. It is time to hang the German spies led by Lenin, to break up the Soviet, and to break it up in such a way that it will never meet again anywhere![22]

Kerensky suddenly realized he was in danger. With the soviets out of the way, why would the general bother deferring to the moderate leftist president? As Kornilov marched his troops toward Petrograd to "save Russia," the president tried to dismiss

* Portions of this are drawn from my online article "The Kornilov Coup," *Jacobin*, September 2017 (with a correction regarding the degree of Kerensky's complicity in the projected coup).

the general and appealed to the workers' organizations—including the Bolsheviks, to whom he granted full legal recognition—to rally to the revolution's defense. Kerensky later wrote:

> The first news of the approach of general Kornilov's troops had much the same effect on the people of Petrograd as a lighted match on a powder keg. Soldiers, sailors, and workers were all seized with a sudden fit of paranoid suspicion. They fancied they saw counterrevolution everywhere. Panic-stricken that they might lose the rights they had only just gained, they vented their rage against all the generals, landed proprietors, bankers and other "bourgeois' groups."[23]

The "paranoid suspicion" Kerensky attributes to the insurgent masses was, in fact, their recognition of the grim realities they faced.

"The news of Kornilov's revolt electrified the nation, and especially the left," recalled prominent Menshevik Raphael Abramovitch. "The Soviets and their affiliated organizations, the railroad workers and some sections of the army, declared themselves ready to resist Kornilov by force if necessary." Another Menshevik eyewitness, N.N. Sukhanov, noted the Bolsheviks had "the only organization that was large, welded together by an elementary discipline, and linked with the democratic lowest levels of the capital." He emphasized: "The masses, insofar as they were organized, were organized by the Bolsheviks."[24]

Though Lenin's party had certainly gained support since February, the insurgents still identified with a variety of socialist currents. As Abramovitch explained, "the threat of a counterrevolutionary revolt roused and united the entire left, including the Bolsheviks, who still exerted considerable influence in the Soviets. It seemed impossible to reject their offers of co-operation at such a dangerous moment." Trotsky later recalled "the Bolsheviks proposed the united front struggle to the Mensheviks and Socialist Revolutionaries and created with them joint organizations of struggle."[25]

U.S. Ambassador to Russia, David Francis, blamed Kerensky for the fiasco. He had decided not "to execute as traitors Lenin and

Trotsky" in July, he had "failed to conciliate General Kornilov, and instead he had turned to the Council of Workmen's and Soldiers' Deputies and distributed arms and ammunition among the workingmen of Petrograd." Kerensky himself mused many years later: "How could Lenin fail to take advantage of this?"[26]

Lenin took full advantage. "*Even now* we must not support Kerensky's government. This is unprincipled," he emphasized. "We shall fight, we are fighting against Kornilov, *just as* Kerensky's *troops do*, but we do not support Kerensky. *On the contrary*, we expose his weakness." The Bolshevik leader explained: "Now is the time for *action*; the war against Kornilov must be conducted in a revolutionary way, by drawing the masses in, by arousing them, by inflaming them (Kerensky is *afraid* of the masses, *afraid* of the people)."[27] Mobilizing against the counter-revolutionary forces, the Bolsheviks won immense authority in the soviets and greater support from workers.

Trotsky, who helped manage these practical efforts and became president of the Petrograd Soviet, later recalled: "The Bolsheviks were in the front ranks; they smashed down the barriers blocking them from the Menshevik workers and especially from the Social Revolutionary soldiers, and carried them along in their wake."[28]

The right-wing military offensive disintegrated before it could reach Petrograd. "The hundreds of agitators—workers, soldiers, members of the Soviets—who infiltrated Kornilov's camp … encountered little resistance," wrote Abramovitch. Kornilov's troops, workers, and peasants in uniform responded to the Bolshevik, SR, and Left-Menshevik agitators' appeals by turning against their officers and rallying to the soviets.

In the wake of Kornilov's failed coup, the Bolsheviks won decisive majorities in the soviets and secured overwhelming support among the working class as a whole. A majority of the Socialist-Revolutionary Party split to the Left, as did a significant Menshevik current, aligning with Lenin and Trotsky. This united front set the stage for revolutionary triumph in October. A majority was won for the demands: "Down with the Provisional Government, All Power to the Soviets!"

SHAKING THE WORLD

There are multiple accounts of the October Revolution, and the details need not be elaborated here.* Only a few key points can be offered.

Eyewitness John Reed offered this judgment:

> Not by compromise with the propertied classes, or with the other political leaders; not by conciliating the old Government mechanism, did the Bolsheviki conquer the power. Nor by the organized violence of a small clique. If the masses all over Russia had not been ready for insurrection it must have failed. The only reason for Bolshevik success lay in their accomplishing the vast and simple desires of the most profound strata of the people, calling them to the work of tearing down and destroying the old, and afterward, in the smoke of falling ruins, cooperating with them to erect the framework of the new.[29]

This is consistent with a consensus among historians seriously studying the matter. The revolutionary majority soon crumbled amid the terrible difficulties that overwhelmed Russia in 1918–21. But if we restrict ourselves to 1917, what Reed says is true. The spirit of this reality can be found in Lenin's proclamation to the Russian population immediately after the triumph of the Bolsheviks and their allies:

> Comrades—workers, soldiers, peasants and all working people!
>
> The workers' and peasants' revolution has definitely triumphed in Petrograd, having dispersed or arrested the last remnants of the small number of Cossacks deceived by Kerensky. The revo-

* Relevant works, cited in the bibliography, include two incredible page-turners: John Reed's *Ten Days That Shook the World* and, more recently, China Miéville's *October*. Among the many other substantial and informative accounts are: William H. Chamberlain, *The Russian Revolution*; Leon Trotsky, *The History of the Russian Revolution*; Victor Serge, *Year One of the Russian Revolution*; Alexander Rabinowitch, *The Bolsheviks Come to Power*; David Mandel, *The Petrograd Workers in the Russian Revolution*; Rex Wade, The *Russian Revolution 1917*; Stephen A. Smith, *Revolution in Russia.*

lution has triumphed in Moscow too. Even before the arrival of a number of troop trains dispatched from Petrograd, the officer cadets and other Kornilovites in Moscow signed peace terms—the disarming of the cadets and the dissolution of the Committee of Salvation.

Daily and hourly reports are coming in from the front and from the villages announcing the support of the overwhelming majority of the soldiers in the trenches and the peasants in the *uyezds* [administrative districts] for the new government and its decrees on peace and the immediate transfer of the land to the peasants. The victory of the workers' and peasants' revolution is assured because the majority of the people have already sided with it. …

Comrades, working people! Remember that now you yourselves are at the helm of state. No one will help you if you yourselves do not unite and take into *your* hands *all affairs* of the state. *Your* Soviets are from now on the organs of state authority, legislative bodies with full powers.

Rally around your Soviets. Strengthen them. Get on with the job yourselves; begin right at the bottom, do not wait for anyone. Establish the strictest revolutionary law and order, mercilessly suppress any attempts to create anarchy by drunkards, hooligans, counter-revolutionary officer cadets, Kornilovites and their like.

Ensure the strictest control over production and accounting of products. Arrest and hand over to the revolutionary courts all who dare to injure the people's cause, irrespective of whether the injury is manifested in sabotaging production (damage, delay and subversion), or in hoarding grain and products or holding up shipments of grain, disorganizing the railways and the postal, telegraph and telephone services, or any resistance whatever to the great cause of peace, the cause of transferring the land to the peasants, of ensuring workers' control over the production and distribution of products.

Comrades, workers, soldiers, peasants and all working people! Take all power into the hands of your Soviets. Be watchful and guard like the apple of your eye your land, grain, factories, equipment, products, transport—all that from now onwards will be entirely your property, public property. Gradually, with the consent and approval of the majority of the peasants, in keeping with their *practical* experience and that of the workers, we shall go forward firmly and unswervingly to the victory of socialism—a victory that will be sealed by the advanced workers of the most civilized countries, bring the peoples lasting peace and liberate them from all oppression and exploitation.[30]

It is worth giving attention to certain key formulations in this final paragraph. Lenin is not proclaiming the existence of socialism in Russia. He is saying:

- socialism is dependent on the Russian working people taking power into their own hands;
- it will come into being gradually;
- it must take place with the consent and approval of a majority of peasants;
- it must be in keeping with practical experience of the workers as well as of the peasants;
- it must be sealed by the advanced workers of the most modernized and industrialized countries.

Another useful insight has recently been emphasized by Eric Blanc, who notes "the party that led the October Revolution ... was not simply the product of the numeric expansion of the Bolshevik current." Rather, "Bolshevism itself contained a wide variation of tendencies" but also "underwent a fundamental transformation in 1917 due to ... unification with other Marxist currents," including left-wing Mensheviks, some who had been aligned with the Bogdanov wing of the Bolshevik faction, an anti-factional "Inter-District" grouping associated with Trotsky and others, veterans of the Jewish Bund, militants of the Social Democracy of the Kingdom of Poland and Lithuania, and more. "An ability to avoid the crystallization of a rigid, self-perpetuating leadership team was one of the secrets of Bolshevik success."[31]

What is provided here is quite inadequate as an account of the 1917 Russian Revolution. The actual complexity and richness of the Russian Revolution are suggested in Rex Wade's splendid summary:

> The Russian revolution of 1917 was a series of concurrent and overlapping revolutions: the popular revolt against the old regime; the workers' revolution against the hardships of the old industrial and social order; the revolt of the soldiers against the old system of military service and then against the war itself [i.e., against the First World War]; the peasants' revolution for land and for control of their own lives; the striving of middle class elements for civil rights and a constitutional parliamentary system; the revolution of the non-Russian nationalities for rights and self-determination; the revolt of most of the population against the war and its seemingly endless slaughter. People also struggled over differing cultural visions, over women's rights, between nationalities, for domination within ethnic or religious groups and among and within political parties, and for fulfillment of a multitude of aspirations large and small. These various revolutions and group struggles played out within the general context of political realignments and instability, growing social anarchy, economic collapse, and ongoing world war. They contributed to both the revolution's vitality and the sense of chaos that so often overwhelmed people in 1917. The revolution of 1917 propelled Russia with blinding speed through liberal, moderate socialist and then radical socialist phases, at the end bringing to power the extreme left wing of Russian, even European, politics. an equally sweeping social revolution accompanied the rapid political movement. and all this occurred within a remarkably compressed time period—less than a year.[32]

The purpose of this book is to provide a survey of Lenin's basic ideas. But to have an adequate sense of those ideas, we must have some sense of the contexts within which the ideas took shape, and how those ideas, in turn, helped to shape the contexts.

DEMOCRACY

A clash of opinions and tilt toward majority rule is suggested in Ronald Suny's point: "much of the revolution took place in meetings of one sort or another—committees, soviets, conferences, and congresses—punctuated by demonstrations and the occasional armed clashes."[33]

This was inseparable from a frame of mind among his circle of youthful friends described by a young participant, Mikhail Baitalsky, who recalled "our exhilaration with the ideas of the revolution," which "came from the depths of our soul." He explained:

> We were sincere above all because we formulated our views in absolute freedom. ... It was based on a Communist faith—pure and unsullied—probably much like the faith of the first pre-Christian societies on the shores of the Dead Sea, with their doctrine of justice and their sacred writings that they read many hours each day.

Engaged in similar reading, discussions, meetings, Baitalsky and his young comrades "were never bored." This was living democracy. "Democracy is directly related to sincerity in human relations. I speak not about democracy as a social institution but about democracy as an element of social norms." He concluded: "For us, a commitment to democracy was like being aware of having a kind of mission—a marvelous mission for universal human equality."[34]

The question of democracy is worth considering from a different vantage-point. How serious was Lenin himself about democracy? Shortly after the Bolshevik Revolution, a democratically elected Constituent Assembly was dissolved by Lenin's government after the Bolsheviks secured only a minority of the delegates. This has been seen by many as revealing an authoritarian essence at the core of Lenin's outlook.

The Bolsheviks had for many years—along with all Russian revolutionaries—called for an elected Constituent Assembly, to replace tsarism with a parliamentary democracy. It was essential to the bourgeois-democratic revolution they advocated. It was one of the famous *three whales of Bolshevism*! The Provisional Government had planned for elections to establish just such a Constituent Assembly. After the October Revolution, the Bolsheviks—as head of the new Soviet Republic—helped to finish organizing those elections.

When the election returns came in, the Bolsheviks received 23.4 percent of the vote, winning overwhelmingly in working-class districts (the Mensheviks only got 3 percent). But the great majority of voters were peasants, and a majority of their votes went to the Socialist-Revolutionaries—50.3 percent. Most of the elected SR candidates were in the Right faction of their party (the candidate lists had been drawn up before the split), fiercely opposed the October Revolution, refusing to recognize the legitimacy of the Soviet Republic.

With their allies (Left Socialist-Revolutionaries and anarchists), the Bolsheviks closed down the Constituent Assembly after its first day of existence. It would be interesting to sit in on the stormy session of the Central Executive Committee of the All-Russian Soviet where Lenin justified this action. And thanks to Bessie Beatty, we can.

Beatty was a left-wing journalist from the United States who—along with John Reed, Louise Bryant, and Albert Rhys Williams—was an eyewitness to the 1917 Revolution and its aftermath. In her 1918 eyewitness account *The Red Heart of Russia*, she provides a vivid portrait of Lenin speaking at the contentious meeting of the Central Executive Committee of the All-Russian Soviet. It was composed of delegates from a number of working-class parties, among which Lenin's party had become the dominant force only three months earlier—at which point the soviet had set up a military committee (under Trotsky's leadership) to overthrow Kerensky's Provisional Government under the slogan of "all power to the soviets."

At this meeting Lenin had come to defend the decision to dissolve the recently elected Constituent Assembly. A member of the body, upon Lenin's arrival, angrily jeered: "Long live the dictator!" This set off a commotion of insults and counter-insults among the delegates. Beatty offers a vibrant description of this historic moment.

> When the chairman had calmed them, Lenin took his place. He stood quietly for a moment, surveying his audience, with his hands in his pockets and an appraising expression in his brown eyes. He knew what was expected of him. He must win the wavering members of his own flock. He must reach out to

> the larger audience spread over the vast areas of Russia. He must speak so that he would be heard beyond the confines of his country, in that world whose attention was focused for the time on this group of strange new actors in the international drama.[35]

Lenin began quietly tracing the historical developments of the soviet as an institution. He made a critical analysis of the workings of various parliaments—they had become merely a sparring-place for the verbal contests of politicians.

"In Russia," he said,

> the workers have developed organizations, which give them power to execute their aspirations. You are told that we ask you to jump a hundred years. We do not ask you to do anything. We did not organize the soviets. They were not organized in 1917: they were created in the revolution of 1905. The people organized the soviets. When I tell you that the government of the soviets is superior to the Constituent Assembly, that it is more fundamentally representative of the will of the mass, I do not tell you anything new.

Making reference to his April Theses, he said, "As long ago as April 4, I told you that the soviets were more representative of the people than this Constituent Assembly which you wanted to organize."[36]

Explaining in detail the political break within the Socialist-Revolutionary Party—in which a left-wing majority, before the elections, abandoned their less radical comrades and allied with the Bolsheviks to help make the October Revolution—Lenin noted:

> When the people voted for delegates of the Constituent Assembly, they did not know the difference between the Right SR's and the Left. They did not know that when they voted for the Right Social Revolutionists they voted for the bourgeoisie, and when they voted for the Left they voted for socialism.

Beatty observed: "At first he spoke quietly, but before long his hands had come out of his pockets. These, and his brown eyes alternately snapping and smiling, and his eyebrows humorously expressive, all vigorously emphasized his phrases."[37] His presentation was effectively connecting with a majority of his listeners.

"The February revolution was a political bourgeois revolution overthrowing Tsarism," Lenin continued. And then he got to the crux of the matter:

> In November a social revolution occurred, and the working masses became the sovereign authority. The workers' and soldiers' delegates are not bound by any rules or traditions to the old bourgeois society. Their government has taken all the power and rights into its own hands. The Constituent Assembly is the highest expression of the political ideals of bourgeois society, which are no longer necessary in a socialist state. The Constituent Assembly will be dissolved.[38]

Lenin's emphasis was on what form of government would be most genuinely democratic. "If the Constituent Assembly represented the will of the people, we would shout: 'Long live the Constituent Assembly!' Instead, we shout: 'Down with the Constituent Assembly!'" With this conclusion, Beatty observed, Lenin won a decisive majority of the vote when the question was called. "He's such a wise man!" an exuberant delegate said to her.[39]

While not everyone agreed with this exuberant delegate, many revolutionaries in Russia who were committed to socialist democracy fully agreed with Lenin that democratic soviets provided the best governmental form through which this could be realized. "In the era which we are now entering the old standards no longer suffice," proclaimed the leading Left SR Maria Spiridonova, whose party initially worked in coalition with the Bolsheviks to help make the October Revolution and participate in the Soviet regime. "Until recently the phrase Constituent Assembly spelled revolution," she acknowledged. "It is only recently, when the character of the revolution has made itself more and more clearly felt, that parliamentary illusions began to be dispelled from our minds." Lenin's choice was also her own:

> It is the people themselves, not parliaments, that can bring about the social release of man. Yes, when the people discovers the

> secret of its own power, when it recognizes the soviets as its best social stronghold, let it then proclaim a real national assembly. Let that national assembly be the only one invested with legislative and executive functions.[40]

After the dissolution of the Constituent Assembly, many Right SRs and even a few Mensheviks joined with pro-tsarist and pro-capitalist forces who were already launching a bloody civil war, supplemented by military interventions from major capitalist powers and an economic blockade, designed to bring down the Soviet regime.

Lenin and his comrades had anticipated some of these possibilities. But they were banking on the revolutionary-internationalist factor: the spread of the revolution, particularly in more advanced capitalist countries, to save the Russian Revolution and to bring a global victory for a new socialist order.

7
Revolutionary Internationalism (1882–1922)

A serious consideration of Lenin's ideas must ultimately bring us into the realm of International Relations: a dynamic "cluster-concept" involving the interplay of different countries and regions, and also of political science, economics, sociology, history, and political action. For Lenin, it blended understandings of the way the world is, the way the world could be, and the way the world should be. It added up to a variant of internationalism associated, as Fred Halliday once noted, with "the radical and Marxist traditions, from Tom Paine, Saint-Simon and Flora Tristan to Marx, Lenin, Rosa Luxemburg and Trotsky."[1]

Lenin's basic orientation was grounded in the traditions of Russian revolutionaries evolving in symbiotic interaction with revolutionaries of other lands. Powerful influences from "the West" impacted on Russia's intellectual elites and growing numbers of others: Enlightenment ideas and Romanticism, with science, philosophy, art, music, literature, richly supplemented by ideas and examples of the American and French revolutions, not to mention the spread of capitalist industrialization and the examples of growing labor and socialist movements. Even those insisting on the superiority of Slavic traditions could not avoid such influences and impacts from other lands, particularly given the economic interdependence fostered by global capitalism and the inexorably growing dynamics of world politics.

"The most consistently espoused and theoretically elaborated version of this form of internationalism," as Halliday put it, "was and is the proletarian internationalism of Marxist theory: in Lenin's formula, *Weltklasse, Weltpartei, Weltrevolution* (world class, world party, world revolutionary movement)."[2] This was essential to Lenin's understanding and definition of the revolution he was helping to make. It was also inseparable from the rise of modern Communism in the wake of the 1917 Revolution.

MARX AND RUSSIA

"Western" impacts on Russia were most vibrantly combined in the intellectual synthesis of Karl Marx. The interaction is nicely summarized by historian James White:

> The history of Marxism in Russia begins with Marx himself. At the start of the 1870s Marx began an intensive study of Russia, its economy and its society, which led him to modify his conceptions in the light of what he found. Simultaneously, to understand the economic processes taking place in their country following the liberation of the serfs in 1861, the Russians began to take an interest in Marx and his economic doctrines. It is this mutual relationship that provides an insight both into Marx's thought in the last years of his life and the direction taken by the development of Marxism in Russia.[3]

Scholars and commentators have, over the years, argued that economically backward Russia was "the last place" where Marx's revolutionary program—designed for a working-class majority in an advanced industrial capitalist economy—could be expected to take root. "Lenin changed this concept fundamentally," according, for example, to Wolfgang Leonhard. "In his view the prerequisites listed by Marx and Engels were no longer decisive; instead, a socialist revolution would take place at 'the weakest link of the chain'" of *the global capitalist system.*[4]

Lenin would have responded with impatience: this gave him too much credit, and Marx not enough. Nor was Lenin alone among his contemporaries. Eric Blanc emphasizes that Karl Kautsky, in his most radical period of 1903–06, had theorized "proletarian revolution would likely break out in world capitalism's weakest link, the Tsarist Empire."[5] Lenin, Kautsky and others had access to Marx's correspondence with Vera Zasulich (the People's Will veteran who became an early Russian Marxist), as well as to the 1882 preface

Marx and Engels wrote for the Russian edition of their *Communist Manifesto.*

"The *Communist Manifesto* had as its object," they acknowledged, "the proclamation of the inevitable impending dissolution of modern bourgeois property. But in Russia we find, face-to-face with the rapidly flowering capitalist swindle and bourgeois property, just beginning to develop, more than half the land owned in common by the peasants." The militants of People's Will were hopeful that a peasant revolution (which they hoped to spark) might enable these communes to provide the basis for a distinctively Russian form of socialism. Marx and Engels speculated: "If the Russian Revolution becomes the signal for a proletarian revolution in the West, so that both complement each other, the present Russian common ownership of land may serve as the starting point for a communist development."[6]

As we have already seen, Russian revolutionaries would eventually pull apart onto different pathways—the Socialist-Revolutionaries continuing to place hopes in a peasant revolution and the peasant communes, the Social Democrats concluding that the capitalist erosion of the peasant communes and the growth of a Russian industrial working class dictated the need for a different road to socialism. The spirit of People's Will remained vibrant in both, however, as did the fact that Russia's fate remained inseparable from an internationalist framework.

INTERNATIONAL SOLIDARITY AND REVOLUTIONARY RUSSIA

Simon Liberman, a Menshevik who worked closely with Lenin on economic matters after the establishment of Soviet power, highlights in his memoirs two quite different ways Lenin viewed the internationalist dimension of revolutionary Russia. One involved a minimal expectation, and the other a far more expansive hope.

"In 1917–18, the Bolsheviks believed no more than their opponents did that the Soviet government would actually last," Liberman reflected. Lenin told him in their first interview: "Our government may not last long, but these decrees [of the new Soviet regime] will be part of history. Future revolutionaries will learn from them." He drew a parallel with the Paris Commune of 1871, the first workers' government which lasted less than three months. "We ourselves keep the decrees of the Paris Commune before our eyes as a model."[7] What the Russian revolutionaries would be able to accomplish before defeat would be helpful to revolutionaries of the future around the world.

Of course, Lenin was also taken with the French adage "*On s'engage et puis ... on voit*"—commit yourself and then see. By the end of 1918, with the conclusion of the First World War, Liberman notes, "central Europe was in the throes of revolution," and now "Lenin and his party were afire with the high hope of a quick success for Communism all over Europe." One of the many texts in which Lenin expressed this was his "Letter to American Workers," written eight months after the October Revolution. "We are now, as it were, in a besieged fortress, waiting for the other detachments of the world socialist revolution to come to our relief," he explained. "These detachments *exist*, they are *more numerous* than ours, they are maturing, growing, gaining more strength the longer the brutalities of imperialism continue."[8]

Lenin's optimism was related to the strength of Europe's left-wing workers' movement of that time. Historian Arno J. Mayer notes that "the Socialist parties were by far the largest numerical component of the forces inside each of the major European nations." Mayer adds (as we saw in Chapter 5) that "very few nationally and internationally recognized leaders had the courage to proclaim that their own country was partly at fault, that a campaign to stop the war should immediately be launched, or that every effort should be made to transform the war into a proletarian revolution." Only when "the Bolsheviks began to preach and practice successfully their revolutionary defeatism in crisis-torn Russia did the Leninist anti-war theses begin to affect the other sectors of the Socialist movement." Mayer tells us that Lenin believed "the impending Socialist revolution 'must not be looked at as one single act, but must be considered as an epoch, a number of stormy political and economic upheavals, a most sharpened class struggle, civil war, revolutions, and counter-revolutions,'" which would grow "out of the multiplicity of diverse phenomena, phases, traits, characteristic, consequences of the imperialist war." Lenin and his comrades

> were convinced that since "an overwhelming majority of the workers and the laboring classes of all the belligerent countries" were longing for an immediate peace, all the belligerent governments would be subjected to irresistible pressure for negotiation. In turn, like in Russia, this peace issue would be instrumental in paving the way for the equalitarian revolution in Western Europe."[9]

Lenin's revolutionary internationalism was also informed, to a significant degree, by his close study of Marx's political writings. The *Communist Manifesto* was addressed, of course, to "workers of all countries," although the membership of the early Communist League was made up only of militants from various European countries. This was also the case, to a large extent, with the International Workingmen's Association, the First International, that Marx helped to create in 1864, at least at the start.

But revolutionary internationalism was not restricted to which nationalities were represented. In his inaugural address at the launching of the International, Marx insisted the workers of different countries must "stand firmly by each other in all their struggles for emancipation," developing a working-class foreign policy to stand in opposition to the capitalists' "foreign policy in pursuit of criminal designs, playing upon national prejudices, and squandering in piratical wars the people's blood and treasure." The preamble to the International's Provisional Rules warned of the need for "a fraternal bond of union between the working classes of different countries," emphasizing that "the emancipation of labor is neither a local nor a national, but a social problem, embracing all countries in which modern society exists."[10]

In an 1868 report, basing himself on experiences of U.S. workers struggling for an eight-hour workday, Marx emphasized: "nothing but an international bond of the working classes can ever ensure their definitive triumph." In 1872, after the short-lived working-class government was drowned in blood the previous year, he made the decisive point in a new way: "The revolution requires solidarity, as the great example of the Paris Commune teaches us, for this most powerful uprising of the Parisian proletariat failed because no great revolutionary movements equal in stature arose in any of the other centers such as Berlin, Madrid, etc."[11]

In 1889, a Second International—the great Socialist International—coalesced largely around ideas of Marx and Engels, based on the mass workers' organizations rapidly crystallizing in Europe, although also drawing in militants from the Americas and beyond. A resolution on "International Solidarity," adopted in 1910, harked back to the "traditions of active solidarity which owe their origins to the First International." Specific strategic conceptualizations (in line with those of Marx) were advanced by representatives of the revolutionary Left within the ranks of the International, some with specific reference to Russia. For example, Karl Kautsky in 1906, seeking to "do justice to the Russian revolution and the tasks that it sets us," saw the 1905 revolutionary upsurge revealing "a completely unique process that is happening on the borderline between bourgeois and socialist society ... one that is bringing all of humanity living within capitalist civilization a powerful stage further in its development." He added suggestively that it was still unclear "what influence it will exert on Western Europe and how it will stimulate the proletarian movement there." The Russian Revolution's promise was "the ushering in of an era of European revolutions that will end with the *dictatorship* [dominance] *of the socialist society*."[12]

In later years Kautsky would back away from this, but the orientation endured among those who remained true to the revolutionary orientation. In 1917, Rosa Luxemburg, from her prison cell in Germany, hailed the overthrow of Russian tsarism as an "invigorating gust of air"—showing "the revolutionary action of the proletariat" could bring liberation from "the choking noose" of world war. She added that "even with the greatest heroism the proletariat of one single country cannot loosen this noose. The Russian revolution is growing of its own accord into an international problem."[13]

The Russian workers' "aspirations for peace come into the harshest conflict not only with their own bourgeoisie, but also with the English, French, and Italian bourgeoisie," Luxemburg noted. To the extent that the Russian Revolution turned "logically against war and imperialism, then its cherished allies would bare their teeth and attempt to curb it by all possible means." This would mean "the socialist proletariat of England, France and Italy" would need to "raise the banner of revolt against war ... through vigorous mass action in their own countries, against their own ruling classes." More than this, "the awakening of the German proletariat" would be on the agenda. Even before the Bolshevik triumph, Luxemburg's strategic and tactical orientation in relation to both the Russian and German Revolutions was framed by this internationalist analysis: "Imperialism or Socialism! War or Revolution! There is no third way!"[14]

Lenin's orientation was much the same. While he and his comrades had special hopes for Germany, however, the openness and breadth of his outlook comes through in his "Letter to American Workers":

> We know that help from you will probably not come soon, comrade American workers, for the revolution is developing in different countries in different forms and at different tempos (and it cannot be otherwise). We know that although the European proletarian revolution has been maturing very rapidly lately, it may, after all, not flare up within the next few weeks. We are banking on the inevitability of the world revolution, but this does not mean that we are such fools as to bank on the revolution inevitably coming on a definite and early date. We have seen two great revolutions in our country, 1905 and 1917, and we know revolutions are not made to order, or by agreement. We know that circumstances brought our Russian detachment of the socialist proletariat to the fore not because of our merits, but because of the exceptional backwardness of Russia, and that before the world revolution breaks out a number of separate revolutions may be defeated.[15]

GLOBAL CHESS GAME

Of course, policymakers and their expert advisors in the major capitalist powers were well aware of the very same dynamics identified by Luxemburg and Lenin. The Russian Revolution, notes Jonathan Haslam, "threatened chaos to an international system already shaken by an unexpectedly long and destructive war." The leaders of Britain, France, and the United States (Lloyd George, Clemenceau, Wilson), as well as others at the Versailles peace conference at the conclusion of the First World War, were busy designing—as an essential component of the post-war world—a *cordon sanitaire* (sanitary barrier), designed to isolate and thereby strangle the Soviet Republic. An economic blockade plus aid to counter-revolutionary forces inside the former Russian Empire were bolstered by a ring of right-wing dictatorships around Russia. This was designed to "stem the tide of Bolshevism" by savagely repressing working-class radicalization in those areas, also blocking off revolutionary Russia from Germany and Western Europe. As Arno Mayer documents, this broadened into an "anti-Bolshevik freedom fight" embracing ferociously anti-democratic elements, with a "drift toward conservatism, reaction, counter-revolution, and proto-fascism" out of which such figures as Mussolini and Hitler rose to power.[16]

In the early years of this global chess game, Lenin's focus pushed well beyond Europe and North America. Victor Serge describes a lengthy presentation Lenin made at the Second World Congress of the Communist International in 1920. Serge tells us that he spoke not in the formal manner of a public speaker, "but like someone who talked easily on a subject with which he was perfectly familiar," with no oratorical flourishes, but simply analyzing, describing, presenting facts, appealing to reason and "sound ordinary common sense." Serge adds: "He spoke with humor and frequently concluded his demonstrations by expressive gestures of both hands. 'Do you understand?'"[17]

The understanding Lenin sought to convey was consistent with his exposition in *Imperialism, the Highest Stage of Capitalism*. Serge summarizes it in this way:

> In a few brief strokes, Lenin outlined truly colossal pictures. The word "millions" was on his lips oftener than any other. … He calculated with millions and again with millions of human beings, with worldwide humanity, with the mighty *social* reality. He spoke constantly of the masses and brought the different races before our mental vision. … He showed the surging up of

> new forms of social life of the races of Asia: 330 million Chinese, 320 million Hindus, 80 million Japanese, 45 million Malays … millions and again millions of human beings, impelled forward by the lash of plantation owner, the whip of the slaveholder, the machine gun of the agents of "civilization" … masses of human beings slowly setting themselves into motion. …[18]

Karl Kautsky's 1909 classic *The Road to Power* (of which Lenin thought highly) had made similar points: "Everywhere in Asia and Africa, the spirit of rebellion is spreading. … Capitalist exploitation cannot be transplanted into a country without the seed of rebellion against this exploitation also being sown there."[19] Yet far greater stress was now given to this expanding insurgency. Masses of laboring people not only of Europe and the Americas, but of Asia and Africa as well, were part of the mighty force that Lenin envisioned overwhelming whatever *cordon sanitaire* the enemies of revolution might construct.

While things turned out quite differently than Lenin hoped, what he and his comrades sought to accomplish powerfully impacted on international affairs during the final decade of his life, and for decades afterward. Enzo Traverso suggests the years 1914–45 can be seen as constituting a European civil war, defined by the confrontation of Communism and fascism, inseparable as well from the violence inherent in modern capitalism. Such dynamics have also been capably traced in a recent study by Jonathan Haslam, documenting the centrality of the conflict between international Communism and anti-Communism in the origins of the Second World War. This conflict was "a multifarious affair," argued Ernest Mandel, a combination of different conflicts involving "revolutionary class struggle from below; revolution from above; national liberation movements under bourgeois and working-class leaderships; reform of the old order; and violent counter-revolution." The meaning of the Cold War, blossoming as the Second World War was ending and concluding almost five decades later, has been described by yet another scholar, Odd Arne Westad, as "the (slow) defeat of the socialist Left, especially in the form espoused by Lenin."[20]

This defeat to Lenin's expansive hope was actually inflicted in the 1920s, when the world socialist revolution was blocked, and when Russia's soviet democracy was decisively overwhelmed, internally, by a repressive bureaucratic dictatorship. At the same time, a variety of positive and negative lessons could certainly be said to have met Lenin's minimal expectation—providing much from which future revolutionaries could learn.

Much can be learned from the Communist International, commonly ignored, belittled, and mocked. For all its undoubted limitations, its early years demonstrated heroic and impressive qualities, crackling with insights. Lenin's contributions were essential in making it so.

COMMUNIST INTERNATIONAL

Given the centrality of revolutionary internationalism to the Marxism which Lenin and his comrades embraced, and given the necessity of spreading socialist revolutions for the survival of revolutionary Russia and achievement of its goals, and—finally—given the demonstrated inadequacy of the Second International, it was a foregone conclusion that the creation of a Third International, the Communist International, would be a priority for Lenin and his co-thinkers around the world. The founding manifesto described its continuity with previous internationals and its fundamental purpose in this way:

> If the First International presaged the future course of development and indicated its paths; if the Second International gathered and organized millions of workers; then the Third International is the International of open mass action, the International of revolutionary realization, the International of the deed.
>
> Bourgeois world order has been sufficiently lashed by Socialist criticism. The task of the International Communist Party consists in overthrowing this order and erecting in its place the edifice of the socialist order. We summon the working men and women of all countries to unite under the Communist banner which is already the banner of the first great victories.

> *Workers of the World*—in the struggle against imperialist barbarism, against monarchy, against the privileged estates, against the bourgeois state and bourgeois property, against all kinds and forms of class or national oppression—*Unite!*
>
> Under the banner of Workers' Soviets, under the banner of revolutionary struggle for power and the dictatorship of the proletariat, under the banner of the Third International—*Workers of the World Unite!*[21]

"The first days of the International were days of heroic camaraderie," Victor Serge later recalled. "We lived in boundless hope. There were rumblings of revolution in the whole of Europe." It was "a great moral and political force, not only because following the war the workers' revolution was on the ascendant in Europe and was very nearly victorious in several countries, but because it brought together a multitude of passionate, sincere, devoted minds determined to live and die for communism."[22]

The origins and early history of the Communist International—subjects of various conflicting interpretations—fall beyond the framework of this book.* Here we restrict ourselves to several key ideas Lenin advanced as a leader of this revolutionary "world party." After that, we will briefly address the question of how the Third International changed after Lenin's death. A key concern animating Lenin was that would-be revolutionaries around the world could be misled by stilted understandings of the Bolshevik experience. In arguing with Italian, German and other comrades against the "theory of the offensive," for example, he insisted small parties could not win if trying to seize power without majority support:

> Terracini says that we were victorious in Russia although the Party was very small. ... Comrade Terracini has understood very little of the Russian revolution. In Russia, we were a small party, but we had with us in addition the majority of the Soviets

* The most substantial one-volume histories in English are: C.L.R. James, *World Revolution 1917–1936*; Franz Borkenau, *World Communism*; Kevin McDermott and Jeremy Agnew, *The Comintern*. John Riddell's remarkable multi-volume collection on the first four congresses of the Communist International suggests the need for an updated history.

> of Workers' and Peasants' Deputies throughout the country. … We were victorious in Russia not only because the undisputed majority of the working class was on our side (during the elections in 1917 the overwhelming majority of the workers were with us against the Mensheviks), but also because half the army, immediately after our seizure of power, and nine-tenths of the peasants, in the course of some weeks, came over to our side …[23]

Related to this was the question of how an effective revolutionary party can be created, a matter addressed in Lenin's 1920 pamphlet *Left-Wing Communism, an Infantile Disorder*, which pointed to three key elements in maintaining, testing, and reinforcing such a disciplined party:

> First, by the class-consciousness of the proletarian vanguard and by its devotion to the revolution, by its tenacity, self-sacrifice and heroism. Second, by its ability to link up, maintain the closest contact, and—if you wish—merge, in certain measure, with the broadest masses of the working people—primarily with the proletariat, *but also with the non-proletarian* masses of working people. Third, by the correctness of the political leadership exercised by this vanguard, by the correctness of its political strategy and tactics, provided the broad masses have seen, *from their own experience*, that they are correct.[24]

None of this can be automatically claimed or grandly proclaimed by a party wishing to be genuinely revolutionary. The first element exists independently—a class-conscious vanguard layer of the working class, which must be the base of a would-be vanguard party. The second element, the intimate connection of this organized vanguard layer to the broader working class, was no less essential. To achieve the desired goal, he acknowledged, there must be a leadership with correct political strategy and tactics—but again this could not be proclaimed, but must be the conclusion drawn by "the broad masses" based on their own experience.

Lenin went on to describe the consequences if a party sought to short-circuit this process. "Without these conditions, discipline in a revolutionary party really capable of being the party of the advanced class, whose mission it is to overthrow the bourgeoisie and transform the whole of society, cannot be achieved," he wrote, following that up with a devastating observation: "Without these conditions, all attempts to establish discipline inevitably fall flat and end up in phrase-mongering and clowning." In fact, "these conditions cannot emerge at once. They are created only by prolonged effort and hard-won experience." It is important to make use of "a correct revolutionary theory" (implying not every "revolutionary theory" is correct). Lenin's next point is that such theory "is not a dogma, but assumes final shape only in close connection with the practical activity of a truly mass and truly revolutionary movement."[25]

In the course of the pamphlet, Lenin briefly reviewed the history of Bolshevism in its various phases, to indicate what this "prolonged effort and hard-won experience" actually looked like. This included a variety of qualities: adherence to basic revolutionary conceptions combined with the struggle for more modest reforms, knowing the difference between revolutionary practice and revolutionary phrase-mongering, the interplay of democracy and class-consciousness, being able to push forward against opponents on the Left, flexibility to compromise and form a united front, knowing when to attack and when to retreat, always learning from experience.

Over the next few years, as delays in the advance of the world revolution became evident, special emphasis would be placed on the united front tactic. This was described as "an initiative of the Communists with all workers who belong to other parties and groups, with all unaligned workers, to defend the most basic vital interests of the working class against the bourgeoisie." While the revolution might not be about to break out in one or another particular country, "every struggle for the most limited immediate demand is a source of revolutionary education, for it is the experiences of struggle that will convince working people of the inevitability of revolution and the significance of communism."[26]

Flexibility was key to Lenin's orientation. "History as a whole, and the history of revolutions in particular," Lenin emphasized, "is always richer in content, more varied, more multiform, more lively and ingenious than is imagined by even the best parties, the most class-conscious vanguards of the most advanced classes." This was an essential proposition in his *Left-Wing Communism* pamphlet. Lenin asserted that serious revolutionaries, while they must not lose sight of the objectives they share with comrades around the world, should quite consciously take into account "the *concrete features* which this struggle assumes and must inevitably assume in each country, in conformity with the specific character of its economics, politics, culture, and national composition, its colonies, religious divisions, and so on and so forth."[27]

An effective Communist International "can never be built up on stereotyped, mechanically equated, and identical tactical rules of struggle." Dismissing as "a pipe dream" the notion that there can be "the elimination of variety or the suppression of national distinctions," Lenin urged his comrades of different countries "to seek out, investigate, predict, and grasp that which is nationally specific and nationally distinctive," to correctly adapt and apply revolutionary perspectives to their specific contexts. "The revolution in Italy will run a different course than that in Russia," he commented to his Italian comrades. "How? Neither you nor we know." He rejected as "stupid" the notion that the Communist International would ever call upon revolutionaries of other lands "slavishly to imitate the Russians."[28]

It is worth considering the broader context of the Second Congress of the Third International, within which Lenin was advancing his views. "There was something intoxicating about the atmosphere of Moscow in that month of June 1920," recalled Alfred Rosmer. "The quiver of the armed revolution could still be felt," he added. Although "among the delegates who had come from every country and every political tendency, some already knew each other," a majority were new to each other. "The discussions were heated, for there was no shortage of points of disagreement, but what overrode everything was an unshakable attachment to the revolution and to the new-born communist movement."[29]

There were more than two hundred delegates representing substantial organizations from more than 35 countries. In addition, an enormous number of supporters and participants were present from around the world. "For the first time at an international labor congress, the peoples of the far east were represented—

China, Korea, Indo-China, India," wrote two participants (Julian Gumperz and Karl Volk), and "with them the Mohammedan tribes of Middle Asia, the Persians and the Turks, all following the lead of the Indian, Manabendranath Roy."[30] At this congress M.N. Roy challenged Lenin himself on strategic perspectives regarding anti-colonial and anti-imperialist struggles—and Lenin listened. Both perspectives were put into resolutions of the congress proceedings, paving the way for further discussion and clarification.

Lenin's influence on national liberation and anti-colonial struggles across the world would be immense throughout the twentieth century—particularly his conceptualization of, and his uncompromising support for, the nationalism of the oppressed in opposition to the nationalism of the oppressor nations. His politics had a huge influence on movements across the Global South.

"The imperialist war of 1914–18 has very clearly revealed to all nations and to the oppressed classes of the whole world the falseness of bourgeois-democratic phrases," Lenin argued. The "peace treaty" of Versailles, condoning colonial empires of the "Western democracies," represented a "brutal and foul act of violence against weak nations." This called for "intensifying the revolutionary struggle both of the proletariat in the advanced countries and of the toiling masses in the colonial and dependent countries." He insisted: "Only when the Indian, Chinese, Korean, Japanese, Persian, and Turkish workers and peasants join hands and march together in the common cause of liberation—only then will decisive victory over the exploiters be ensured."[31]

At the third Comintern congress the following year, Lenin again stressed the centrality of revolutionary internationalism to the Russian Revolution:

> We thought: either the international revolution comes to our assistance, and in that case our victory will be fully assured, or we shall do our modest revolutionary work in the conviction that even in the event of defeat we shall have served the cause of the revolution and that our experience will benefit other revolutions. It was clear to us that without the support of the international world revolution the victory of the proletarian revolution was impossible. Before the revolution, and even after it,

> we thought: either revolution breaks out in the other countries, in the capitalistically more developed countries, immediately, or at least very quickly, or we must perish. In spite of this conviction, we did all we possibly could to preserve the soviet system under all circumstances, come what may, because we knew that we were not only working for ourselves, but also for the international revolution.[32]

In the same year, Lenin wrote that the Soviet Republic could survive capitalist encirclement—"but not for very long, of course."[33]

SURVIVAL AND DEFEAT

Despite impressive achievements, the Communist International was never able to bring an end to capitalist encirclement. This failure would have grim consequences for the revolution that Lenin and his comrades had made. The Soviet Union was able to endure longer than Lenin might have expected under those circumstances, and here too one can find impressive achievements. "Contrary to the claim made by pure universalism, that a revolution has to be global in order to survive," scholar Fred Halliday observed near the twentieth century's conclusion, "it is the case that revolutions have survived in specific states without either spreading or being overthrown." Yet he immediately felt compelled to add a caveat:

> But as the history of the Russian revolution shows so clearly, embattled and protracted relations with the outside world are inimical to post-revolutionary development and encourage the waste of resources, loss of life, and internal repression that may well traduce the initial hopes of the revolutionaries. ... It is not that a revolution is nothing if it is not international, but it is certainly bound to be a lot less than the makers of the revolution intended.[34]

8
Besieged Fortress (1918–22)

The revolution that Lenin led was in response to multiple catastrophes—some already unfolding, some impending—flowing from the crises of tsarism, the dynamics of capitalism, and the horrific impacts of the First World War. Lenin's wager was that the Russian Revolution could help spark revolutions in other, more economically advanced countries, and the assistance and resources generated by the expanding socialist revolutions would help revolutionary Russia overcome its problems—problems made worse by powerful forces inside and outside of Russia that were hostile to the revolutionary goals.

The anticipation of the Russian Revolution being joined by similar revolutions in Europe and elsewhere flowed into the expectation of an unfolding socialist order of radical democracy and freedom, and found reflection in the brief "honeymoon period" described by Alfred G. Meyer, a Cold War anti-Communist scholar:

> The October Revolution brought about the overthrow of all remnants of the old order. It radically destroyed the last shreds of tsarism and the old bureaucracy and relegated the landowner to the realm of dead institutions. The distribution of all gentry land among the peasants, which the Leninist seizure of power guaranteed, was as thorough as it could possibly have been. This was indeed the "bourgeois revolution" of which Lenin had spoken. It carried with it all those changes usually attributed to the complete abolition of the precapitalist order. National self-determination of Russia's many nationalities was, at least for the moment, carried to its logical conclusion. … Legal separation of church and state, removal of the old judiciary, reform of the calendar—all these measures were within the European liberal tradition, as part of the "bourgeois revolution." This revolution

> was also expressed in the social institutions, in science, art, and education—in virtually all functions of public and private life. Everywhere ... the revolution carried with it maximum freedom of expression and experimentation. Even where political liberties were soon curtailed, a certain degree of personal freedom was not extinguished for several years.[1]

But the new Soviet Republic was quickly engulfed by the fierce reaction of a hostile capitalist world, generating an increasingly brutal civil war, foreign invasion, and economic collapse. The "delay" of socialist revolutions spreading to other countries meant the catastrophes already afflicting revolutionary Russia widened and deepened. As Lenin noted, the Soviet Republic became a "besieged fortress." We need to give attention to the abuses that resulted, commonly associated with the terms *war communism* and *Red Terror.**

ESSENTIAL AND NON-ESSENTIAL

The harmony between the revolutionary-democratic strategy and radical democratic goals was wrecked. In the face of escalating assaults by external and internal enemies, the new Communist regime responded with "emergency measures" including one-party dictatorship, the "Red Terror" and hyper-centralized economic policies of "war communism," the 1921 banning of factions in the Bolshevik party, and persecution of party dissidents.

"The Bolshevism of 1917–1927 wanted a socialist regime founded on the democracy of labor and international solidar-

* There are also bogus allegations—for example, that the deadly forced labor camps, the dreaded gulags, for which the Stalin era became infamous, were actually set up by Lenin, and on the cultural front that 2000 "politically incorrect" treasures were purged from early Soviet libraries by Lenin's companion Nadezhda Krupskaya. The first allegation is deflated if one consults Dallin and Nicolaevsky, *Forced Labor in Soviet Russia* and the more recent study by Khlevniak, *The History of the Gulag* (documenting that prison camp populations under Lenin did not exceed those under the tsar, in contrast to Stalin's skyrocketing incarcerations of the 1930s). The second allegation is deflated by the online "Seeds of Evil" review by David Bruce (who shows that Krupskaya's ineffectual efforts to reorganize Russia's run-down libraries were far from the sinister cultural purge falsely attributed to her). Setting aside such allegations, we will focus here on actual abuses.

ity," Victor Serge recalled in his notebooks of 1945. "Lenin and Trotsky's companions believed in this, they never stopped believing it even while committing their most dreadful mistakes." This relates to an essential point Rosa Luxemburg made in her 1918 critique *The Russian Revolution*: "What is in order is to distinguish the essential from the non-essential, the kernel from the accidental excrescencies in the politics of the Bolsheviks."[2]

The fact remains that by 1919 the "dictatorship of the proletariat" came to mean a dictatorship exercised by the Russian Communist Party, the name adopted by the Bolsheviks in 1918. This has often been seen as the defining attribute of "Leninism." Yet Lev Kamenev scoffed at the notion that "the Russian Communists came into power with a prepared plan for a standing army, Extraordinary Commissions [the Cheka, secret police], and limitations of political liberty, to which the Russian proletariat was obliged to recur for self-defense after bitter experience."[3]

Immediately after power was transferred to the soviets, he recalled, the opponents of working-class rule were unable to maintain an effective resistance. The revolution had "its period of 'rosy illusions,'" Kamenev continued. "All the political parties—up to Miliukov's [pro-capitalist Kadet] party—continued to exist openly. All the bourgeois newspapers continued to circulate. Capital punishment was abolished. The army was demobilized." Even fierce opponents of the revolution arrested during the insurrection were generously set free (including pro-tsarist generals and reactionary officers who would soon put their expertise to use in the violent service of their own beliefs).

Kamenev went on to describe increasingly severe civil war conditions that finally changed this situation, ending a period of "over six months (November 1917 to April–May 1918) [that] passed from the moment of the formation of the soviet power to the practical application by the proletariat of any harsh dictatorial measures." This is corroborated in findings of anti-Leninist scholar Alfred G. Meyer that "the unceremonious dissolution of the Constituent Assembly" in January 1918 hardly constituted the inauguration of Bolshevik dictatorship:

for some months afterwards there was no violent terror. The nonsocialist press was not closed until the summer of the same year. The Cheka began its reign of terror only after the beginning of the Civil War and the attempted assassination of Lenin, and this terror is in marked contrast with the lenient treatment that White [counter-revolutionary] generals received immediately after the revolution.[4]

Regarding the crescendo of ruthless measures, culminating in the "Red Terror," Lenin expressed an outward intransigence and a fierce determination for carrying out all "necessary expedients" to ensure the Revolution's survival. At the same time, he more than once expressed anguish over what was happening. Indeed, the "evil" qualities attributed both to Lenin and to Leninism are largely associated with what unfolded in this period.*

Lenin and other Bolsheviks also sought to restrain some of the negative policies they had helped unleash, strengthening trade unions to defend workers, initiating a New Economic Policy to ease the lives of the peasants, and advancing the quality of life and cultural level of many sectors of the population in the surviving Soviet Republic. Such Leninist policies will be examined in Chapters 9 and 10 of this book. But the country's continuing isolation in a hostile capitalist world meant the radical democracy and freedom, for which the Revolution was made, were destined to give way to more authoritarian outcomes.

"In the middle of the First World War, at that time of the most massive human blood-letting ever, refinements of morality seemed

---

* *Mass murderer* is a tag that has more than once been applied to Lenin because of the Red Terror policies, and the related fact that he was a leader of the Soviet Republic during a devastating civil war in which terrible slaughter and multiple human rights abuses took place. The term has very different definitions. For example, it is commonly used to describe one or more persons directly murdering at least several others in a single "incident" (which no one claims was true of Lenin). It has also been used more broadly to refer to political leaders who order the deaths of others, or who are responsible for policies from which many deaths result; sometimes battle deaths are included in the calculations. While Lenin can be fit into such broader definitions, the same is true of other figures: Winston Churchill and other defenders of the British Empire; such wartime U.S. Presidents as Harry Truman, Franklin D. Roosevelt, and Abraham Lincoln (plus the latter's pro-slavery counterpart Jefferson Davis); and many more.

not only constricting but obscene," Christopher Read has reflected. "A few sacrifices, a moment of ruthlessness, was not only justified but demanded if millions could be saved from death at the front and from the worldwide tentacles of imperialist exploitation." He concludes brutally: "To lay the foundations of a new world, a more perfect, classless and human world, it was the revolutionary's duty to have dirty hands."[5]

The Russian civil war of 1918–21 – generating 350,000 combat deaths, with an additional 450,000 combatants dying of disease—was horrific and brutalizing.[6] The Red Army was organized by Leon Trotsky, the secret police or Cheka by Felix Dzerzhinsky (Rosa Luxemburg's close comrade in the Polish revolutionary movement). Both were highly principled as well as highly efficient, Trotsky in leading the Red Army in ferocious battles, Dzerzhinsky in leading the Cheka in ferocious repressions. Some argue the counter-revolutionary White Terror was significantly more violent and murderous than the resulting Red Terror, others estimate roughly 100,000 were killed by each side. But both were murderous, devastating, and often out of control. In 1921, the observant sympathizer Albert Rhys Williams wrote:

> "Repressions, tyranny, violence," cry the enemies. "They have abolished free speech, free press, free assembly. They have imposed drastic military conscription and compulsory labor. They have been incompetent in government, inefficient in industry. They have subordinated the soviets to the Communist Party. They have lowered their Communist ideals, changed and shifted their program and compromised with the capitalists."
>
> Some of these charges are exaggerated. Many can be explained. But they cannot all be explained away. Friends of the Soviet grieve over them. Their enemies have summoned the world to shudder and protest against them. ...[7]

The memoirs of a veteran revolutionary, the anarchist-turned-Bolshevik Victor Serge, describe the process:

> "Totalitarianism" did not yet exist as a word; as an actuality it began to press hard on us, even without our being aware of it.

> ... What with the political monopoly, the Cheka, and the Red Army, all that now existed of the "Commune-State" of our dreams was a theoretical myth. The war, the internal measures against counter-revolution, and the famine (which had created a bureaucratic rationing-apparatus) had killed off Soviet democracy. How could it revive and when? The Party lived in the certain knowledge that the slightest relaxation of its authority could give the day to reaction.[8]

"We were forced to use terror in response to the terror employed by the Entente, when the mighty powers of the world flung their hordes against us, stopping at nothing," Lenin explained in February 1920. "We could not have lasted two days had we not replied to these attempts of officers and whiteguards in a merciless fashion. This meant the use of terror, but this was forced on us by the terrorist methods of the Entente." Just as the state of siege imposed by the civil war and foreign interventions made the Red Terror necessary, according to Lenin, the victory of revolutionary forces would soon end it. "We say that the use of violence arises from the need to crush the exploiters, the landowners and capitalists. When this is accomplished, we shall renounce all extraordinary measures." He looked forward to the time when "it will be impossible to apply the death penalty in Russia."[9]

Yet as Victor Serge's later reflections indicate, the authoritarian expedients, once implemented, were not so easily set aside. Even when the Red Terror was finally concluded, the death penalty remained on the books. Nor was the vibrantly multi-party democracy flourishing in the soviets up to 1918 brought back to life. And Serge pinpointed a related problem:

> The state of siege had now entered the Party itself, which was increasingly run from the top, by the Secretaries. We were at a loss to find a remedy for this bureaucratization: we knew that the party had been invaded by careerist, adventurist and mercenary elements who came over in swarms to the side that had the power. Within the Party the sole remedy of this evil had to be, and in fact was, the discreet dictatorship of the old, honest, and incorruptible members, in other words the Old Guard.[10]

CRITICISM AND SELF-CRITICISM

The most perceptive critics of Lenin in this period were those who knew him, who appreciated aspects of his achievement, and who shared major aspects of his revolutionary commitments.

Maria Spiridonova's Left SRs had joined with the Bolsheviks in the new Soviet regime, but they refused to accept the decision to make far-reaching concessions to German imperialism in order to withdraw Russia from the First World War. No less anti-war than the Bolsheviks, the Left SRs argued that rather than compromise, the Soviet regime should fight a revolutionary war to defeat the German reactionaries. In early 1918, they broke from the Bolsheviks, walked out of the Soviet government, assassinated the German Ambassador, and attempted to foment a rebellion. "Our party must take upon itself the burden of leadership of the insurrection," Spiridonova told her comrades. "We shall call upon the masses to rise, we shall incite, ignite, and organize. Only by means of the insurrection shall we be able to overcome that which is moving upon us." She concluded: "We are entering a new stage of political development, a stage when we probably shall be the ruling party."[11]

All of this proved illusory and suicidal, and it was a terrible blow to the young Soviet Republic. A shocked Lenin mobilized effectively to repress the uprising and jail the Left SR leaders. Such developments closed off what might have been an opportunity to maintain an essential modicum of soviet democracy, and it undoubtedly facilitated the desperate choice to unleash the Red Terror. These developments also made it easier for the regime to embark on misguided policies in regard to the peasantry, the constituency with which the SRs were especially attuned.

As she watched the unfolding of the Red Terror from her prison cell, and particularly sensitive to violence being done to broad swaths of the peasant majority, Spiridonova issued an eloquent open letter to Lenin. "Your party had great tasks and began them finely," she recalled. "The October Revolution, in which we marched side by side, was bound to conquer, because its foundations and watchwords were rooted in historical reality and were solidly supported by all the working masses." But by November of 1918 this had all changed:

> In the name of the proletariat you have wiped out all the moral achievements of our revolution. Things that cry aloud to Heaven have been done by the provincial Chekas, by the all-Russian Cheka. A blood-thirsty mockery of the souls and bodies of men, torture and treachery, and then—murder, murder without end, done without inquiry, on denunciation only, without waiting for any proof of guilt.[12]

Such things had been foretold by Lenin's old comrade and Menshevik opponent Julius Martov. Acknowledging Lenin's Bolsheviks had won the support of the revolutionary working class, Martov saw this as an indication of the workers' political immaturity. The Mensheviks continued to insist socialist revolution in backward Russia was hopelessly utopian, and the proletariat—still a small minority of the population—could not possibly sustain its political rule.

"Under the guise of 'proletarian power' ... the most reprehensible vulgarity is let loose," Martov wrote, "with all its specifically Russian vices of lack of culture, base careerism, bribery, parasitism, dissoluteness, irresponsibility, and so on." He warned: "we are moving, through anarchy, ... toward some kind of Caesarism, based on the whole people's loss of faith in the possibility of self-government." Since its inception, the Bolshevik state "had become overgrown with a thick layer of careerists, speculators, new bureaucrats, and plain scoundrels," Martov argued, "and had in fact ceased to be the state power of the toilers, workers, and peasants." The Mensheviks following Martov sought to establish "the unity of the proletarian movement on the basis of independent class politics and its liberation from anarchistic and utopian adulterations," at the same time fostering the capitalist economic development that would eventually create the material basis for genuine socialism.[13]

Yet, especially as the civil war intensified, the Bolsheviks came to feel that all efforts to dislodge them (whether violent or peaceful) were intolerable, that "if the Russian workers' dictatorship with its Terror collapsed, its place would be taken, not by democracy, but by the White Terror of Kolchak and Denikin," in the words of Karl Radek.[14] It was precisely such fear that caused Lenin to make some of his most authoritarian statements. This was particularly evident when the Soviet regime—seeing its popular support dangerously eroding—retreated from some of its more militant orientations at the close of the civil war:

> Indeed, the sermons which ... the Mensheviks and Socialist-Revolutionaries preach express their true nature: "The revolution has gone too far. What you are saying now we have been saying all the time, permit us to say it again." But we say in reply: "Permit us to put you before a firing squad for saying that. Either you refrain from expressing your views, or, if you insist on expressing your political views publicly in the present circumstances, when our position is far more difficult than it was when the white guards were directly attacking us, then you will have only yourselves to blame if we treat you as the worst and most pernicious white guard elements."[15]

Lenin sought the emigration from Soviet Russia of left-wing opponents such as Martov, in part to protect them from firing squads and repression. Here too, however, we can see what the tough-minded yet also liberal-minded philosopher Bertrand Russell meant in his 1920 critique: "It is, of course, evident that in these measures the Bolsheviks have been compelled to travel a long way from the ideals which originally inspired the revolution."[16]

Russell added: "I recognize to the full the reasons for the bad state of affairs, in the past history of Russia and the recent policy of the Entente," the wartime coalition of Britain, France, and the United States seeking to overturn the revolutionary regime, through economic blockade and militarily intervention, plus financing and supplying the counter-revolutionary White armies in the brutal civil war. Despite scathing criticisms, he believed, "the Bolsheviks have only a very limited share of responsibility for the evils from which Russia is suffering."[17]

Russell's critique and rejection of Bolshevism in 1920 was unrelenting. He concluded that "the price mankind has to pay to achieve Communism by Bolshevik methods is too terrible," but also "even after paying the price, I do not believe the result would be what the Bolsheviks profess to desire."[18]

Still, Russell believed the Bolshevik regime "represents what is most efficient in Russia, and does more to prevent chaos than any possible alternative government would do," noting that Maxim Gorky (one of the sharpest left-wing critics of the Bolsheviks at this time) "supports the Government—as I should do, if I were a Russian—not because he thinks it faultless, but because the possible alternatives are worse." He also commented:

> It seems evident, from the attitude of the capitalist world to Soviet Russia, of the Entente to the Central Empires, and of England to Ireland and India, that there is no depth of cruelty, perfidy or brutality from which the present [capitalist] holders of power will shrink when they feel themselves threatened.[19]

The original ideals of the 1917 Revolution were explicit in one of the most articulate critiques, which was advanced by a faction inside the Russian Communist Party, the Workers' Opposition. Its most prominent personalities were Alexander Shlyapnikov and Alexandra Kollontai. Both had been closely associated with Lenin as he had pushed forward to the Revolution of October 1917—and now they crossed swords with him around the meaning of proletarian rule.

In a widely distributed document entitled *The Workers' Opposition*, it was argued that a "bureaucratic state system" had replaced the "self-activity of the working masses" with "a hierarchy of 'permissions' and 'decrees.'" The document added: "We give no freedom to class activity, we are afraid of criticism, we have ceased to rely on the masses: hence we have bureaucracy with us."[20] Many non-revolutionary elements had been drawn into the state apparatus, it was argued. In addition, any party standing at the head of the Soviet state is compelled to consider the needs of non-proletarian layers in society (the vast peasantry, urban petty bourgeoisie, and so on) and the pressures of world capitalism. All of this created a gap between leaders of the party and state, on the one hand, and the working class, on the other.

The document observed that "during these three years of the revolution, the economic situation of the working class, of those who work in factories and mills, has not only not been improved, but has become more unbearable." The outlook of "the working masses" was described in this way: "The leaders are one thing, and we are something altogether different. Maybe it is true that the leaders know better how to rule over the country, but they fail to understand our needs, our life in the shops, its requirements and immediate needs; they do not understand and do not know." In fact, the leaders, "having severed all ties with the masses, carry out their own policy and build up industry without any regard to our opinions and creative abilities," and "distrust of the workers by the leaders is steadily growing."[21]

The solution seemed simple enough: "The Workers' Opposition has said what has long ago been printed in The *Communist Manifesto* by Marx and Engels: the building of communism can and must be the work of the toiling masses themselves. The building of communism belongs to the workers."[22] Such notions resonated powerfully among working-class Communists and others.

Lenin led the way in anxiously, angrily, aggressively denouncing the Workers' Opposition (and other oppositions such as Left Communists, Democratic Centralists, etc.). He voiced concern over the "fever" of factionalism becoming "chronic and dangerous." Particularly anxious about what he perceived as (under the circumstances) romantically utopian demands for working-class control of decision-making being advanced by the Workers' Opposition, he initiated measures to limit this faction's influence, and to discredit and marginalize its partisans.* The Workers' Opposition was smeared as representing an "anarcho-syndicalist" deviation, although Shlyapnikov denied the charge, noting that he and his co-thinkers did not "repudiate political struggle, the dictatorship of the proletariat, the party's leading role, nor the significance of the soviets as bodies of power." As historian Barbara Allen notes,

* Biographer Barbara Allen notes, in *Alexander Shlyapnikov 1885–1937*, that Shlyapnikov's judgment a decade later, partially vindicating Lenin's critique: "Without repudiating its ideals, he conceded that its programme could not be fulfilled in Russia in the early 1920s."

"their approach was neither syndicalist nor anarchist, but was rooted in the Bolshevik Party's multi-faceted tradition." Shlyapnikov warned: "Here, perhaps, you will suppress and smash us; but from this you will only lose."[23]

Lenin and his comrades faced an extremely difficult situation in the country as a whole, with moods within the exhausted peasantry and in much of the battered and decimated working class turning against policies of the Soviet regime and the Russian Communist Party which controlled it. If the Communists were dislodged, it was felt, the only forces sufficiently organized and determined to take control were those of the anti-democratic counter-revolutionaries. At the Tenth Party Congress in 1921, Lenin introduced another emergency measure—a resolution banning factions within the party, which was overwhelmingly adopted.

Yet Lenin continued to support the right of party members to form inner-party groups: "To form ourselves into different groups (especially before a congress), is of course permissible (and so is to canvass for votes). But it must be done within the limits of communism (and not syndicalism) and in such a way as not to provoke laughter." (The "syndicalism" and "laughter" references are aimed at the Workers' Opposition.) Expressing the hope that "the Party is learning not to blow up its disagreements," he approvingly quoted Trotsky's suggestion that "ideological struggle within the Party does not mean mutual ostracism but mutual influence."[24]

But moods outside of the Communist Party were not easily placated. Peasant rebellions continued, often led by both Right SRs and Left SRs, and there was an armed uprising in 1921 of disgruntled sailors and workers at the Kronstadt naval base (once a bastion of Bolshevik support) just outside of Petrograd, with some demanding Soviets without Communists.* When it was bloodily repressed, there were many—such as one-time anarchist supporters Emma Goldman and Alexander Berkman—who added to the chorus of critiques under such titles as *My Disillusionment in Russia* and *The Bolshevik Myth*.

* Paul Avrich's *Kronstadt 1921* provides essential information on the uprising, its context, and its brutal repression.

Upon his arrival with Goldman in the Soviet Republic of early 1920, Berkman had "sensed a new spirit in the bearing and looks of the people, a new will and huge energy tumultuously seeking an outlet." In these years of the Red Terror, he also "saw much that was wrong and evil, the dangerous tendency toward bureaucracy," and continuing "inequality and injustice." Yet he believed revolutionary Russia "would outgrow these evils with the return of a more ordered life, if the [anti-Bolshevik Western] Allies would cease their interference and lift the blockade." He was greeted warmly when he visited Lenin. "He is below medium height and bald; his narrow blue eyes have a steady look, a sly twinkle in the corners." Berkman "liked his face—it is open and honest and not the least pose about him." Goldman was amazed by Lenin's "glee over anything he considered funny in himself or his visitors." Berkman sized him up: "His manner is free and confident; he gave me the impression of a man so convinced of the justice of his cause that doubt can find no place in his reactions."[25]

Yet their anarchist principles prevented Goldman and Berkman from fully embracing Lenin's cause, and an accumulation of negative experiences and insights during these years of Red Terror further distanced them from the regime. With the repression of the Kronstadt rebellion, Berkman concluded: "Terror and despotism have crushed the life born in October." Goldman concurred: "Whatever their pretenses in the past, the Bolsheviks now proved themselves the most pernicious enemies of the Revolution. I could have nothing further to do with them."[26]

While a fierce partisan of the Bolshevik Revolution, Rosa Luxemburg had analyzed early contradictions that would undermine the goals of Lenin and the Bolsheviks. In her draft critique written as the process was beginning in 1918, she had hit upon some of the key problems.

"The socialist system of society should only be, and can only be, an historical product," she wrote,

> born out of the school of its own experiences, born in the course of its realization, as a result of the developments of living history, which—just like organic nature of which, in the last analysis, it forms a part—has the fine habit of always producing along with

> any real social need the means to its satisfaction, along with the task simultaneously the solution.

She emphasized that "only experience is capable of correcting and opening new ways. Only unobstructed, effervescing life falls into a thousand new forms and improvisations, brings to light creative new force, itself corrects all mistaken attempts. … The whole mass of the people must take part in it."[27] She described the impending danger to the Bolshevik Revolution in this way:

> Without general elections, without unrestricted freedom of press and assembly, without a free struggle of opinion, life dies out in every public institution, becomes a mere semblance of life, in which only the bureaucracy remains as the active element. Public life gradually falls asleep, a few dozen party leaders of inexhaustible energy and boundless experience direct and rule. Among them, in reality only a dozen outstanding heads do the leading and an elite of the working class is invited from time to time to meetings where they are to applaud the speeches of the leaders, and to approve proposed resolutions unanimously—at bottom, then, a clique affair—a dictatorship, to be sure, not the dictatorship of the proletariat but only the dictatorship of a handful of politicians …[28]

Luxemburg was also of the opinion, however, that such problems could not be resolved within the confines of what had been the Russian Empire. Revolutions elsewhere were essential if the Russian Revolution was to be saved. "The fate of the revolution in Russia depended fully upon international events," she emphasized. "That the Bolsheviks have based their policy entirely upon the world proletarian revolution is the clearest proof of their political far-sightedness and firmness of principle and of the bold scope of their policies." Writing to a Polish comrade living in Soviet Russia, she commented: "It is clear that, under such conditions, i.e., being caught in the pincers of the imperialist powers from all sides, neither socialism nor the dictatorship of the proletariat can become a reality, but at the most a caricature of both."[29]

"Socialist democracy is not something that only begins in the Promised Land, once the substructure—the socialist economy—has been established; it does not come as a ready-made Christmas present for the obedient populace who, in the interim, have loyally supported the handful of socialist dictators," Luxemburg emphasized in her 1918 critique. "Socialist democracy commences simultaneously with the dismantling of class domination and the construction of socialism."[30]

Such notions were by no means alien to Lenin himself, and as late as 1922 he asserted: "The idea of building communist society exclusively with the hands of the Communists is childish, absolutely childish. We Communists are but a drop in the ocean, a drop in the ocean of the people." Yet a return to the vibrant, multi-party norms of the revolutionary soviets of 1917 now hardly seemed possible. The process of helping tens of millions to learn how to create socialism seemed to require dedicated Communist Party members acting as tutors and guides, including within the Party itself. As Serge had noted, there reigned the "discreet dictatorship of the old, honest, and incorruptible members, in other words the Old Guard."[31] Such efforts to square the circle proved neither adequate nor durable.

LOSSES

As Soviet Russia was engulfed by civil war, foreign invasion, economic collapse, famine, and terrible epidemics of typhus, cholera, and influenza, the loss of life was massive and pervasive. On top of three million First World War casualties, hundreds of thousands perished during the Russian civil war (including the interlocked Red and White Terror), and millions more died from famine and disease.[32] The proliferation of deaths reached deep into Bolshevik ranks, including circles close to Lenin.

In 1918, Socialist-Revolutionaries began initiating assassination attempts against who they perceived as the new Bolshevik tyrants. Lenin himself was shot, and his wound was dangerous, but he survived. On the same day, an assassin's bullet killed Petrograd Cheka chief Moishei Uritsky (a former Menshevik and, in fact, a moderate when it came to repressive measures)—and this double shooting had helped launch the Red Terror.

Another loss contributing to the process of brutalization was the 1918 execution of the 26 commissars in Baku (Bolsheviks allied with Left SRs), and notable among these was Stepan Shahumian, a longtime revolutionary Marxist leader in Georgia of Armenian extraction, with strengths as an intellectual and practical organizer. He had a reputation as the "Caucasian Lenin" due to his role as "indisputable leader" of Bolshevism and the Russian Revolution in the Caucasus (although Stalin had a competing claim for "Caucasian Lenin" status). Shahumian's close relationship with Lenin was in part due to their collaboration in discussions of "the national question." A comrade remembered "his deep truthfulness, which came out in all his actions, words, gestures, movements," and historian Ronald Suny—characterizing Shahumian as "moderate, democratic"—tells us that "during his administration in Baku in 1917–1918 the Bolsheviks did not use state terror to hold on to power. When his government lost a crucial vote in the local soviet, Shahumian and his comrades stepped down."[33] Local anti-Communists, supported by British advisors, quickly moved to capture Shahumian and his comrades, and to have them shot.

But disease, typically, tended to be the bigger killer. In 1919 Jacob Sverdlov died of influenza at the age of 33. He had earned a reputation as an efficient, balanced, absolutely trusted practical worker, which gave him key internal organizational responsibilities among the Bolsheviks, and Lenin valued him highly. (Sverdlov had more than once found himself in exile, in tsarist times, with a different practical worker, Joseph Stalin. Another exile recalled: "In contrast to Sverdlov, who cared for people and whom everyone loved, Stalin was closed up and morose.") Sverdlov's death left a gap filled by a secretariat of three trusted comrades: Nikolai Krestinski, Leonid Serebriakov, and Eugen Preobrazhensky. In 1922 they were replaced by Stalin, through the newly created position of the Communist Party's General Secretary.[34] Stalin brought his own distinctive qualities to the various tasks Sverdlov had carried out.

One of the most devastating losses for Lenin personally was the death of Inessa Armand, who died of cholera in 1920. There would be controversy over the nature of his relationship with her. She had for years been a stalwart Bolshevik, playing important organizational roles, and particularly active in the Bolsheviks' engagement with the women's rights and anti-war movements. An intimate of both Krupskaya and Lenin, the quality of his engagement with her brings to mind his extremely close relationship with his sister Olga, who had also died of typhoid long before, when he and she were becoming revolutionaries. There is evidence that the relationship between Lenin and Armand may have involved physical intimacy—not all historians agree. Angelica Balabanoff attended Armand's 1920 funeral, as did Lenin, and her recollection is vivid:

> He was utterly broken by her death. … I cast sidelong glances at Lenin. He was plunged in despair, his cap down over his eyes; small as he was, he seemed to shrink and grow smaller. … I never saw him look like that before. It was something more than the loss of a "good Bolshevik" or a good friend. He had lost someone very dear and very close to him and made no effort to conceal it.[35]

The author of the journalistic masterpiece *Ten Days That Shook the World*, John Reed, died from cholera one month after Armand. He had thrown himself body and soul into the revolutionary cause, deeply inspired by what he had seen of soviet democracy in the making and what had seemed the tangible promise of a socialist future, perhaps in his lifetime. That was not to be, and some who were close to him have indicated how disturbed he was by the grim developments unfolding in the years following 1917—a feeling shared by many, Lenin included.

LENIN'S GREATEST DEFEAT

Luxemburg noted what Lenin and the Bolsheviks had stressed more than once: "The whole calculation behind the Russian fight for freedom is based on the tacit presumption that the revolution in Russia ought to become the signal for the revolutionary rising of the proletariat in the West: in France, England and Italy, but above all in Germany." Without such an international revolutionary development, she commented, "even the greatest energy and the greatest sacrifices of the proletariat in a single country must inevitably become tangled in a maze of contradiction and blunders." Luxemburg's critique was written from "the inside," by someone who passionately supported the Bolshevik Revolution, who argued that "the future belongs to Bolshevism,"[36] and who was helping to organize the German Communist Party, hoping to help make a German revolution to open the way to the forward movement of Russian and German and global socialism.

The failure of the international revolution to triumph in a variety of countries outside of Russia created the "maze of contradictions and blunders" in which the Bolsheviks found themselves. Lenin himself wrestled with the disturbing realities for which he bore some responsibility. Victor Serge and Natalia Sedova, both of whom were in a position to observe Lenin at fairly close range, later summarized aspects of his response to the growing crisis of Bolshevism:

> Lenin's speeches and writings of 1921–2, while still self-assured and authoritative, did not conceal his uneasiness and occasional bitterness. Reminiscences by his contemporaries show that Vladimir Ilyich was, like so many people he attacked, highly critical of the conduct and outlook of those Party leaders who favored a bureaucratic dictatorship. At times, Lenin was brutally frank in his defense of the people—a brutality that no doubt reflected his anguish. "What mistakes we have made!" he said repeatedly. "It would be criminal to deny that we have exceeded all bounds ..." Or again: "Our attempt to implement socialism here and now has failed. ... The dictatorship shows that never before has the proletariat been in such a desperate situation ..." We must "abandon the construction of socialism and fall back on state capitalism in many economic spheres." We are "uncouth"; we live in "administrative chaos", in "waves of illegality". He coined words like *Kom-chvantso* and *Kom-vranio* (com-conceit and com-deceit, where "com" was an abbreviation for communist); he compared some Party leaders to those brutal satraps of the old regime who had been dubbed *derzhimordas*, after the repulsive bully in Gogol's satire.[37]

Lenin's thinking in this period became scathingly self-critical. As Tamás Krausz has noted, democracy was "one of the cornerstones of his political concept," within which "bourgeois democracy becomes plebian democracy and then a workers' democracy (semi-state), presupposing a transformation within the power structure of the social-economic change of regimes as a whole." He never renounced this orientation, but it is, to put it mildly, difficult to reconcile with the deepening catastrophes welling up in the "besieged fortress" of the early Soviet Republic. "There is no doubt," Hannah Arendt commented in *The Origins of Totalitarianism*, "that Lenin suffered his greatest defeat when, with the outbreak of the civil war [in 1918], the supreme power that he planned to concentrate in the soviets passed into the hands of the party bureaucracy."[38]

Arno J. Mayer has expressed the tragedy of the Bolshevik Revolution more poignantly than most. He comments that of all the parties on the scene in 1917, "the Bolshevik party was by far the best organized and disciplined, as well as the most adaptable." This is balanced by his observation that "the Bolshevik project was an inconstant amalgam of ideology and circumstance, of intention and improvisation, of necessity and choice, of fate and chance." He emphasizes that "the way the Bolsheviks took power was consistent with their credo of direct and defiant action, and their authoritarian rule following Red October [1917] was bound to provoke resistances which they were, of course, determined to counter and repress." Their initial intention was to help lead the way to socialist revolution, anticipating partnership with other political forces on the working class and peasant left prepared to follow this course. Yet Lenin's Bolsheviks were not prepared (perhaps no party could have been prepared) for the tidal waves that would hit them. As Mayer puts it, "just as they were unprepared for the enormity of the crisis, so they were caught unawares by its Furies, which they were not alone to quicken."[39]

Lenin was unable to solve the problems he confronted, but there is something to be learned from what we will touch on in the final chapter—his final struggles and "testaments."

9
Unexplored Mountain (1921–23)

Lenin saw *catastrophe* as central to the evolving realities of his time. He not only recognized this fact but embraced it as an essential element in the Bolshevik strategic orientation. Catastrophe is also central to the evolving realities of our own time, suggesting that Lenin's orientation may have relevance for activism of today and tomorrow.

Yet the wave of catastrophe sweeping over Russia, Europe, and the world was not resolved by what Lenin and his comrades did. Things turned out badly, and catastrophe expanded. In the previous chapter we see the initial catastrophe assuming multiple dimensions, overwhelming what had been an impressive revolutionary coherence, disrupting the principled harmony of ends and means. The first seven chapters of this book present a coherent arc of development in Lenin's revolutionary perspectives. The eighth chapter indicates how that coherence was shattered.

A common way of telling the Lenin story has been to force a coherence that wasn't there: insisting authoritarianism was embedded in the methods, goals, and outcomes of what Lenin thought and did. In fact, the methods and goals of Lenin's revolutionary project were basically (*not perfectly*, but *basically*) anti-authoritarian, consistent with a commitment to profoundly radical conceptions of democracy and freedom.

Most of Lenin's life was focused on crafting the perspective, the analysis, the organization, the movement, the strategy, and the struggle that could culminate in the 1917 Revolution. There is a coherence, consistency, and continuity in all of that, a basic harmony of desired ends and practical means. Democratic-minded activists may be able to learn much from a serious consideration of that part of the story.

But what is one to do with what happened next? "In 1917 Lenin stood tall among the leaders of other Russian parties," Lars Lih has argued, "because they had enough sense to be frightened out of their wits by the oncoming disaster—the social and economic breakdown that was just around the corner—whereas he saw it as an opportunity." The revolutionary voyage which Lenin charted "involved more suffering than anyone had bargained for" because, in Lih's opinion, it was begun with "unsound assumptions." Lenin's revolutionary ark consequently "ended up far from where its builder planned."[1]

This chapter has three purposes. First is to identify possible "unsound assumptions" of Lenin and his co-thinkers. One could argue that these were "reasonable hopes" or "revolutionary gambles" that didn't turn out well—but they certainly culminated in a crisis of Bolshevik perspectives. Second is to challenge the notion that there was an essential continuity between what Lenin thought, said, and did with what unfolded under the Stalin regime that followed. Third is to identify aspects of Lenin's practical approach in the face of Bolshevism's crisis of perspectives—what he, characteristically, tried to *do* about it.

CRISIS OF PERSPECTIVES

There were three interrelated beliefs whose breakdown resulted in a crisis of Lenin's revolutionary perspectives of 1917: a belief in the possibility of a mixed economy, a belief in the capacities of soviet democracy for dealing with the problems that would face revolutionary Russia, and a belief in the imminence of a triumphant world revolution. As the first two assumptions gave way to brutal realities, recourse was made to emergency solutions in the form of what came to be known as "war communism." This was designed to allow for the survival of the Soviet Republic until revolutions finally triumphed in other lands.

Lenin did not believe socialism was possible in the Russia of 1917–23. He believed that socialism would need to be based on a highly integrated and technologically advanced economy, providing a level of economic abundance that would not be achieved in Russia for many years and could not—given the realities and interdependence of the global economy—be achieved in a single country. The best that revolutionary Russia could do in the period immediately following 1917 would be establishing a state-regulated capitalism, combined with social policies beneficial to the laboring masses, and with the development of some economic sectors operating according to socialist principles—or what is commonly known as a "mixed economy." It would in this way be possible to *begin a process* of transition to socialism, but the creation of socialism could only be consummated through future developments.

Before the Bolsheviks took power, Lenin himself made this point time and again. In his April Theses, he stressed that "it is not our immediate task to 'introduce' socialism, but only to bring social production and the distribution of products at once under the control of the soviets of Workers' Deputies." The eyewitness sociologist E.A. Ross observed in 1918 that "while there are plenty of syndicalists urging the workmen of each factory to organize, cast out the owner and his agents, and run it as their own, the Bolsheviks are guilty of no such folly."[2]

Against what he termed "left-wing childishness," Lenin argued that the workers "have no experience of independent work in organizing giant enterprises which serve the needs of scores of millions of people." It was necessary, he insisted, "to learn from the capitalist organizers" and to proceed "cautiously" and "gradually." He stressed: "The difference between socialization and simple confiscation is that confiscation can be carried out by 'determination' alone, without the ability to calculate and distribute properly, whereas socialization cannot be brought about without this ability." Against romantic and impatient conceptions, he insisted that "the bricks of which socialism will be composed have not yet been made."[3]

Journalist-historian William Henry Chamberlin aptly describes Lenin's orientation:

> When workers' delegations came to him asking for the nationalization of their factories, Lenin at this time was in the habit of putting embarrassing questions to them. Did they know accurately what their factories produced, or what markets could be

found for their products? Were they prepared to operate the factory efficiently if the state placed it in their hands?

Under such questioning, some workers' delegations had second thoughts. "If they could not answer these questions satisfactorily Lenin would recommend that they make haste slowly and consent to an arrangement under which the capitalist would have a share in the management of the factory and would provide technical knowledge and experience for its operation."[4]

The early orientation of Lenin—a mixed economy under the general control of a workers' state—collapsed within eight months. There were three primary factors that brought this about: the mass radicalization among the workers combined with confusion over the meaning of workers' control; the onset of civil war and foreign invasion; and the growing tendency among Russian capitalists to sabotage, de-capitalize, or simply abandon their enterprises. The result was the replacement of capitalism by the rapid takeover of the economy by the Soviet government. This shift came to be called "war communism."

All the reasons for resisting a rapid state takeover of the economy, unfortunately, were sound. The shift brought about economic chaos and, in a twist of irony, gravely undermined the power of the workers. "This expropriation of industry, verging ever closer to total nationalization," wrote Victor Serge, "placed an increasingly numerous population of workers within the responsibility of the socialist state, and compelled it hastily to establish a body of functionaries, managers and administrators who could not be recruited straight away from among the working class. The bureaucracy was born, and was rapidly becoming a threat."[5]

From 1918 to 1919, the government apparatus had grown from 114,539 to 529,841. In roughly the same period the Bolshevik organization, renamed the Communist Party, grew from 115,000 to 251,000. "The functionaries were thus far more numerous than the party membership," Serge noted, "and they infiltrated into the ranks of the party."[6] This was accompanied by the collapse of the economy, the spread of famine, the brutalizing civil war, which all combined to make war communism a devastating and authoritarian experience, suffused with a desperate commitment to revolutionary ideals, but no less tragic for all that.

Before coming to power, the Bolsheviks had called for dealing with the collapse of both political authority and food supply with the most thoroughgoing revolutionary democracy. "Democratic soviets could overcome the food-supply crisis by crushing the sabotage that was its main cause" is Lih's summation of the initial strategy. "But events quickly revealed that the soviets and other local organizations would not make real sacrifices to support the new authority unless direct local benefit was obvious." This relates to Eric Blanc's observation: "Running a state machine in the context of war and economic free fall proved to be significantly more difficult than anticipated." A frustrated Bolshevik functionary complained: "They say that the voice of the people is the voice of God. We hearkened to the voice of the people, ... but what came of it? The most pathetic results possible."[7] For many, "all power to the soviets" had meant all power to the localities—which was disastrous for the effort to ensure that people throughout the new Soviet Republic would have enough to eat. In the swirl of events, and fairly rapidly, decisive decision-making power shifted from the soviets to the functionaries.

The Menshevik Simon Liberman, serving the Soviet regime as a sympathetic specialist, later recalled that Lenin saw all state authority as "something transitory, a mere temporary phase of the all-important journey toward social justice."[8] But (as his comrade Martov had foretold) the crescendo of catastrophes brought on by civil war and economic collapse obliterated the vibrant soviet democracy of 1917, and the "emergency measure" of eliminating opposition parties turned what was left of the soviets into relatively lifeless bodies, controlled by the Communist Party and rubber-stamping decisions already made from above. The authoritarianism of the Soviet state became more extensive and deeply rooted, despite the humane and libertarian assumptions.

Many believed a democratic balance could be restored as working-class revolutions swept to victory beyond Russia. These would ensure that the Soviet Republic would not be restricted to its own impoverished circumstances and isolated in a ferociously hostile capitalist world. One might argue that this was, in fact, *not* an unsound assumption. After all, there was extensive and deepening radicalization and considerable revolutionary ferment throughout much of Europe. Rather, this turned out to be a gamble that Lenin and his comrades lost. As a result, it was no longer possible for the Bolshevik regime to remain true to the inspiring revolutionary-democratic scenario of 1917 and, at the same time, to survive.

We have seen that much of Lenin's attention and energy, between 1919 and 1922, were focused on efforts to extend the world revolution through the Communist International. As some of those who had worked most closely with him (Krupskaya, Zinoviev, Kamenev, Radek, Trotsky and others) would assert not long after his death, the construction of socialism in the Soviet Republic required the spread of revolution beyond the Soviet Republic—"socialism will be victorious in our country," they would declare in the platform of the united opposition, "in inseparable connection with the revolutions of the European and world proletariat and with the struggle of the East against the imperialist yoke."[9] This was the perspective formally shared by all Bolshevik comrades until 1924.

At the same time, we find Lenin pushing to advance social and cultural development among the masses of workers and peasants, also seeking to push back bureaucratic functioning of the revolutionary regime. His final struggle with death was interwoven with his struggle against repressive, brutal policies and practices of comrades in the central leadership of the Russian Communist Party. We will turn much of our attention to this in the present chapter and in the next. But attention must first be given to the question of whether what is termed *Stalinism* was the "legitimate" and necessary outcome of what Lenin was reaching for. (A succinct definition of Stalinism might be: authoritarian modernization in the name of socialism.[10])

SEEDS OF STALINISM—BUT NOT STALINISM

Cascading catastrophes took a severe toll on what Lenin wrote and said and did in the five years after 1917. At the conclusion of that five years, he was felled by a series of strokes, dying (as his father, also a stroke victim, had done) at age 54. Lih suggests that by 1919, "he becomes defensive and halting as he searches for a way to match his ideological scenario with events."[11] At the same time, up until his incapacitation and death, we can see Lenin struggling to help preserve and push forward the revolution he had helped to make, and—once he realized his death was imminent—seeking to help orient those who would continue that struggle.

Seeds of Stalinism can be found in what the Bolsheviks did in the first five years after the 1917 Revolution. But Bolshevism or Leninism were qualitatively different from Stalinism. A comparison sometimes made between the French and Russian Revolutions is relevant. Specifically, comparisons have often been made between Lenin's Bolsheviks and the Jacobins of the French Revolution. Among the most radical of the revolutionaries in France in 1789–94, the Jacobins were absolutely committed to "the rights of man" and to the creation of a truly democratic republic—but in the brutalizing struggle against multiple enemies to achieve these goals, they unleashed the "reign of terror" which swept up not only active counter-revolutionaries but also many innocents among the common people, even dedicated partisans of the revolution.

Reflecting in his personal notebooks of 1945 on the cause to which he had dedicated so much of his life, Victor Serge was insistent that "neither the doctrine nor the intentions of the Bolshevik party aimed at establishing a totalitarian police state with the vastest concentration camps in the world." Recalling the Red Terror and the hard times of "war communism," he added: "The Bolshevik party saw in the perils it confronted the excuse for its Jacobin methods." His conclusion was repeated more than once: "I think it is undeniable that its Jacobinism contained the seed of Stalinist totalitarianism, but Bolshevism also contained other seeds, other possibilities of evolution. The proof is in the struggles, the initiative, and the final sacrifice of its various oppositions."[12]

One example will suffice. Martemyan N. Ryutin was a leader in one of the last oppositions, the Union of Marxists-Leninists in 1932. It was quickly repressed, but what it reveals merits consideration. Ryutin had been a party stalwart from 1914 to 1930, and under Stalin's leadership had orchestrated strong-arm efforts to repress oppositionists in the mid-to-late 1920s. Then he was horrified as Stalin's murderous "revolution from above" initiated the forced collectivization of the peasants' land. The dissident current that he represented in the Russian Communist Party had quite different origins from the Left Opposition with which Serge had identified, but its analysis was similar. The analytical platform of Ryutin's group, *Stalin and the Crisis of Proletarian Dictatorship*, argued that the apparatus of the Communist Party had been transformed into "an organ standing above the masses and hostile to them, into an organ that chastises and terrorizes them." Acknowledging that "the Stalinist clique ... does not see the real character of its degeneration," Ryutin and his co-thinkers insisted, nevertheless, that "Stalin is killing Leninism under the banner of Leninism, the proletarian revolution under the banner of the proletarian revolution, and socialist construction under the banner of socialist construction." Providing a searching, scathing analysis, the Ryutin platform concludes the task of "every honest Bolshevik" involves "putting an end to Stalin the dictator and his clique," returning to "the path of correct Leninist theory and policy and by that ensur[ing] the victory of communism."[13]

All of which throws into question Stalin's contention that what he did was consistent with Lenin's goals and methods. The belief that "socialism cannot be implemented by a minority, by the Party," was articulated in 1918 by Lenin himself, who explained: "It can be implemented only by tens of millions when they have learned to do it by themselves."[14]

George F. Kennan approached the matter from a different vantage-point. He was a U.S. State Department official with a deep knowledge of Soviet history and considerable experience in the Soviet Union as he helped craft U.S. policy in the early Cold War. Kennan gave attention to the interplay of personalities and leadership styles. In his examination of *Russia and the West under Lenin and Stalin*, Kennan suggested Lenin "was spared that whole great burden of personal insecurity which rested so heavily on Stalin. He never had to doubt his hold on the respect and admiration of his colleagues." The result was that Lenin "could rule them through the love they bore him, whereas Stalin was obliged to rule them through their fears."[15]

Kennan's perception of Lenin's personality comes through in descriptions from those who worked with him. One of these was the Menshevik economic advisor to the Soviets in 1918–26, Simon Liberman. "He could indeed be all attention, all charm, apparently putting all his cards on the table." At their first meeting, Liberman felt sufficiently comfortable to express sharp criticisms of certain Bolshevik economic decrees. "Of course, we make mistakes," Lenin responded. "There cannot be a revolution without errors. But we are learning from our errors and are glad when we can correct them." Liberman was drawn in by this approach, later commenting that "one remarkable gift you noticed in Lenin at once: he could quickly draw people to himself, even when they were outsiders." He added: "There is an ancient saying that the closer you move to a mountain, the bigger it seems; the closer you move to a man, the smaller he is. Lenin was one of the very rare exceptions to this rule." Noting that "Lenin had a deep faith in the 'goodness' of the revolution," Liberman elaborated:

> He was inflexible in his principles, yet flexible and full of compromises in practice—in handling people. That is why, when he did not consider a person his political opponent, Lenin was governed by his own humaneness and even gentleness.[16]

A person such as Liberman could not have described Stalin in this way. Whittaker Chambers, a knowledgeable ex-Communist with impeccably anti-Communist credentials, starkly emphasized the distinction. "To become the embodiment of the revolutionary idea in history," he wrote, "Stalin had to corrupt Communism absolutely," adding: "He sustained this corruption by a blend of cunning and brute force. History knows nothing similar on such a scale." From the opposite side of the political spectrum, the Marxist theorist Georg Lukács—with a long and rich history in the Communist movement—offered the judgment that "Leninism, in which the spirit of Marx lived, was converted into its diametrical opposite." This murderous corruption of Communism, "systematically built by Stalin and his apparatus," must "be torn to pieces."[17]

Such revolutionary critics as Lukács, Serge, and Ryutin believed that, despite the Russian Revolution's ultimate degeneration, mistakes and even crimes related to the civil war and the subsequent period, and then the horrific crimes of Stalinism, this revolution nevertheless opened a new era in human history, one that had an overall positive and lasting impact on society. They didn't deny that Stalinism arose from within the Bolshevik tradition. But for them, Stalinism was not just different from Lenin's Bolshevism—it was its negation.[18]

Lenin's final years involve systematic efforts—insufficiently strong, to be sure—to tear to pieces an incipient "Stalinism" that was beginning to crystallize within his party. His primary purpose, as he did this, was to help create a new balance consistent with the revolutionary goals to which he had committed his life, the advance toward a society of the free and the equal.

REVOLUTIONARY REFLECTIONS

One of Lenin's central priorities was to convey to workers and revolutionaries of all countries an understanding of the Russian Revolution that would serve to advance revolutionary consciousness around the world. One senses that he was also seeking to clarify the Revolution's meaning in his own mind.

An important element in this effort was his embrace of the remarkable eyewitness account by John Reed, a left-wing journalist from the United States—*Ten Days That Shook the World.* Reed's classic portrayed the revolution as profoundly democratic, animated precisely by aspirations among a majority of Russia's workers and peasants for a government and an economic order that would be of the people, by the people, and for the people.

"Here is a book which I should like to see published in millions of copies and translated into all languages," Lenin wrote. "It gives a truthful and most vivid exposition of the events so significant to the comprehension of what really is the Proletarian Revolution and the Dictatorship of the Proletariat." Nadezhda Krupskaya, intimately in tune with Lenin's thinking, elaborated that it was

> a wonderfully vivid and forceful description of the first days of the October Revolution. It is not a mere enumeration of facts, nor a collection of documents, but a succession of scenes from life, so typical that any participant in the revolution cannot but remember similar scenes he had witnessed himself. And these

> shots from life reflected with astonishing veracity the sentiments of the masses, the sentiments that determined every act of the Revolution.[19]

A very different classic account was written by a left-wing Menshevik, Nikolai N. Sukhanov, who, like Simon Lieberman and others, had stayed on to offer his expertise to the Soviet Republic as an economic advisor. His seven volumes of reminiscences were packed with valuable information, impressions, and critical analyses. It is also noteworthy that Sukhanov's account was legally published in 1922 by a state-run enterprise in the Soviet Republic. It "created a great stir," according to its English-language translator and editor—"required reading for party circles and considered an indispensable source-book for the study of the revolution."[20] Lenin's critique, "Our Revolution," was written in January 1923, two months before he was incapacitated by his third stroke.

Lenin was sharply critical of the "heroes of the Second International," adding (perhaps with Sukhanov in mind) "even the best of them." He saw them as "fainthearted" when it came to deviating from the model of German Social Democracy. "What strikes one is their slavish imitation of the past," he complained. Their conception of Marxism was "impossibly pedantic," completely failing to understand "revolutionary dialectics" and Marx's own example that "in times of revolution the utmost flexibility is demanded." Marx's dynamic approach to revolution was something they "walk around and about ... like a cat around a bowl of hot porridge."[21]

Sukhanov, Lenin complained, sees "capitalism and bourgeois democracy in Western Europe following a definite path of development" and projects this as a universal model. "Certain amendments" were required, Lenin insisted, highlighting a key methodological point: "While the development of world history as a whole follows general laws it is by no means precluded, but, on the contrary, presumed, that certain periods of development may display peculiarities in either the form or the sequence of this development."[22]

For example, "because Russia stands on the borderline" between European and non-European countries, she was "bound to reveal certain distinguishing features; although these, of course, are in keeping with the general line of world development, they distinguish her revolution from those which took place in the West European countries and introduce certain partial innovations as the revolution moves on to the countries of the East."[23]

Related to this was the controversy of Bolsheviks and Mensheviks around whether Russia's revolution would be advanced by a worker-peasant alliance or a worker-capitalist alliance. Here Lenin drew on Marx's writings that had envisioned "a combination of a 'peasant war' with the working-class movement" to bring revolutionary victory.[24]

Acknowledging that "the objective economic premises for socialism do not exist in our country," he asked:

> What about the people that found itself in a revolutionary situation such as that created during the first imperialist war? Might it not, influenced by the hopelessness of its situation, fling itself into a struggle that would offer it at least some chance of securing conditions for the further development of civilization that were somewhat unusual?"[25]

Similar points were made a year earlier in his "Notes of a Publicist." Lenin began with a dramatic analogy:

> Let us picture to ourselves a man ascending a very high, steep and hitherto unexplored mountain. Let us assume that he has overcome unprecedented difficulties and dangers and has succeeded in reaching a much higher point than any of his predecessors, but still has not reached the summit. He finds himself in a position where it is not only difficult and dangerous to proceed in the direction and along the path he has chosen, but positively impossible. He is forced to turn back, descend, seek another path, longer, perhaps, but one that will enable him to reach the summit. The descent from the height that no one before him has reached proves, perhaps, to be more dangerous and difficult for our imaginary traveler than the ascent—it is easier to slip; it is not so easy to choose a foothold; there is not that exhilaration

> that one feels in going upwards, straight to the goal, etc. One has to tie a rope round oneself, spend hours with all alpenstock to cut footholds or a projection to which the rope could be tied firmly; one has to move at a snail's pace, and move downwards, descend, away from the goal; and one does not know where this extremely dangerous and painful descent will end, or whether there is a fairly safe detour by which one can ascend more boldly, more quickly and more directly to the summit ....
>
> The voices from below ring with malicious joy. They do not conceal it; they chuckle gleefully and shout: "He'll fall in a minute! Serve him right, the lunatic!" Others ... moan and raise their eyes to heaven in sorrow, as if to say: "It grieves us sorely to see our fears justified! But did not we, who have spent all our lives working out a judicious plan for scaling this mountain, demand that the ascent be postponed until our plan was complete? And if we so vehemently protested against taking this path, which this lunatic is now abandoning (look, look, he has turned back! He is descending! A single step is taking him hours of preparation! And yet we were roundly abused when time and again we demanded moderation and caution!), if we so fervently censured this lunatic and warned everybody against imitating and helping him, we did so entirely because of our devotion to the great plan to scale this mountain, and in order to prevent this great plan from being generally discredited![26]

Lenin emphasized what he viewed as the positive achievements. "We have created a Soviet type of state and by that we have ushered in a new era in world history, the era of the political rule of the proletariat, which is to supersede the era of bourgeois rule," he wrote. He integrated the internationalist element: "Nobody can deprive us of this, either, although the Soviet type of state will have the finishing touches put to it only with the aid of the practical experience of the working class of several countries." Focusing attention on "the ruin, poverty, backwardness and starvation prevailing in our country," he insisted that "in the *economics* that prepare the way for socialism we have *begun to make progress*," related to new policies he was helping to advance.[27]

NURTURING THE NEW SOCIETY

It will not be possible here to evaluate the viability or effectiveness of all that Lenin sought to do in overcoming the catastrophic breakdown of the revolutionary-democratic orientation that had guided him up through 1917. That would involve another and different book.* What follows, then, is little more than a quick and suggestive survey.

Pushing past "war communism" at the conclusion of the civil war was seen as essential to the economic recovery of Soviet Russia. "Early in 1921 Lenin realized that with the peasants' uprising in Tambov and the sailors' rebellion in Kronstadt the masses of the Russian people had just about reached the end of their rope," noted Simon Liberman. "Lenin firmly resolved that Russia should follow his New Economic Policy, ... a partial re-establishment of free trade in small industry, and a whole series of concessions to the peasantry."[28]

With the retreat from "war communism" and partial return to capitalist economic functioning represented by the New Economic Policy (NEP), it was now "admitted on all sides ... there is no communism in Russia." So wrote sympathetic journalist Anna Louise Strong in the early 1920s. "But the Communists go further. They say there never was any communism." Strong elaborated that "the equal sharing and sacrifice that marked the dark days of the famine was not communism at all, but merely the necessary war tactics of a besieged city." She emphasized that *war communism*

> was not the kind of communism that anyone wants again. They seized the peasants' grain to feed the cities and the army; they divided it equally at first, to keep everyone alive. Industry had been broken in the long collapse before the Revolution; they created a centralized apparatus to see that at least the war needs of supplies and munitions were met. It was an insufficient amount, but enough so that they won.[29]

---

* Some efforts in this direction can be found in my study *October Song*, from which some elements have been drawn in the writing of this chapter.

NEP was not simply Lenin's policy—it was embraced by his comrades. "The very people who fought on all the fronts of the civil war … are working for the economic restoration of the country, in the name of the same aims, with the same energy, the same readiness to give of themselves completely." So explained Trotsky, who added: "The difficulties here are truly incredible, our economic and cultural backwardness is immeasurable, but a knowledge of our own backwardness, when it takes hold of the wide masses of the people, becomes in itself the greatest force towards culture." Trotsky concluded: "This force has been awakened by the Revolution. We have it, and on it we are building."[30]

Historian E.H. Carr later recounted that "not only had the peasant for the first time since the revolution a surplus to sell and legal authority and encouragement to sell it, but the terms of trade were exceptionally favorable to him." Carr notes NEP's initial outcome: "If the countryside was profiting at the expense of the town, the town was deriving visible benefits, however unequal the distribution and however high the eventual cost, from the greater abundance of supplies."[31]

As Carr's comments suggest, NEP brought the short-term economic gains so desperately needed by the beleaguered Soviet Republic, but future "costs" were looming ahead. Lenin searched for ways to enhance the power of Soviet Russia's worker and peasant majority, enabling it to meet the new challenges.

Hand-in-hand with the NEP was the end of the Red Terror. While insisting on the essential role of the Cheka since its consolidation in 1918 (led by incorruptible but severe Felix Dzerzhinsky), Lenin was also responsive to much of the criticism voiced by such prominent sympathizers as Maxim Gorky and leading Communist comrades. By November 1921 he was writing to Lev Kamenev (an early advocate for dismantling the power of the Cheka): "Comrade Kamenev! My position is closer to yours than to Dzerzhinsky's. I advise you not to give way, and to raise [the issue] in the Politburo. Then we shall make a stand for the very maximum."[32]

Lenin was also concerned to draw on the insights and expertise of non-Communists to help nurture the new society. He favored working with technical specialists and economic experts who were far from being Bolsheviks, identifying with Mensheviks, Socialist-

Revolutionaries, Kadets, etc. This included such figures as Simon Liberman, Nikolai N. Sukhanov, Nikolai Volsky-Valentinov, Nikolai Kondratiev, and Alexander V. Chayanov. He pressed for them to be hired and supported by the Soviet regime. In the NEP period, they formed a sort of "brain trust," engaged in essential research and policy design. In 1921, pushing back comrades who judged Chayanov to be politically dubious, Lenin insisted "we need wise heads, we are left with too few of them." At the Eleventh Party Congress, in the spring of 1922, historian James Heinzen notes that "under pressure from Lenin," it was resolved that such specialists "must be protected from the antagonism of unfriendly party officials," and instead should be consulted more frequently.[33]

In *The Origins of Totalitarianism*, Hannah Arendt indicated that Lenin was far from reaching for the extreme authoritarianism often attributed to him. "Lenin seized at once on all possible differentiations" within Soviet life, she wrote—not to eliminate them but to strengthen them, in order to "bring some structure into the population, and he became convinced that in such stratification lay the salvation of the revolution." Arendt perceived efforts on his part to secure the development of an independent peasant class, strengthening the working class by encouraging independent trade unions, facilitate the reappearance of businessmen, and help to generate a significant degree of cultural freedom and artistic diversity. "He introduced further distinguishing features by organizing, and sometimes inventing, as many nationalities as possible, furthering national consciousness and awareness of historical and cultural differences even among the most primitive of tribes in the Soviet Union."[34]

In Chapter 4 of this book, we touched on Lenin's keen appreciation of creative literature and the arts, which he believed should be free from rigid notions of "correctness." In the 1930s authoritarian norms of "socialist realism" would be imposed on artists and writers by the Stalin regime. This approach was alien to the dominant trend in the Bolshevik regime's Commissariat of Enlightenment, headed by Anatoly Lunacharsky, whose taste for avant-garde innovations went well beyond what Lenin was comfortable with. But for this very reason, Lenin saw Lunacharsky as the person who should oversee the development of Soviet culture.

Lenin's own cultural tastes were relatively conservative. As he explained to German Communist leader Clara Zetkin (who tended to agree with him): "It is beyond me to consider the products of expressionism, futurism, cubism and other 'isms' the highest manifestation of artistic genius. I do not understand them. I experience no joy from them." But far from seeking to repress them, he said in the next breath: "Yes dear Clara, it can't be helped. We're both old fogies. For us it is enough that we remain young and are among the foremost at least in matters concerning the revolution. But we won't be able to keep pace with the new art; we'll just have to come trailing behind." Adding that "our opinion on art is not the important thing," he emphasized: "Art belongs to the people." His primary concern was that to help "art to get closer to the people and the people to art we must start by raising general educational and cultural standards."[35]

Sharp and exuberant challenges were posed to classical and traditional creations by innovators of the Russian and Soviet avant-garde, such as the poet Vladimir Mayakovsky, the theater director Vselovod Meyerhold, artists Alexander Rodchenko, Varvara Stepanova, and many others who saw what they offered as the true cultural expression of the revolutionary Russia. While appreciative of the avant-garde innovators, Lunacharsky resisted their pressure to grant them a privileged position as the "official" artistic representatives of the Soviet Republic. "He encouraged Communist artists and scholars," as historian Sheila Fitzpatrick has documented, "but not in persecution of their colleagues or bids for monopoly."[36]

Openness, experimentation, and diversity were encouraged, as was the broadening participation of young workers and peasants in fields of cultural creativity. But Lenin and Lunacharsky were of one mind on the priority of raising educational and cultural standards for the bulk of the laboring population. Lenin insisted "proletarian culture … is not clutched out of thin air" or "the invention of those who call themselves experts in proletarian culture." Rather, more and more laboring people must engage with "the culture created by the entire development" of humanity. "Proletarian culture must be the logical development of the store of knowledge mankind has accumulated under the yoke of capitalist, landowner and bureaucratic society." Lunacharsky elaborated: "The laboring masses thirst after education," and the regime's responsibility was to offer "schools, books, theatres, and so on" to facilitate "the people themselves, consciously or unconsciously" so that they evolve "their own culture" under their own democratic control. "But the proletariat must draw on the art of the past in order to produce its own."[37]

Lenin also was compelled to wrestle with his greatest defeat—the failure of soviet democracy to withstand the calamities engulfing Russia in 1918, with power now in the hands of the burgeoning bureaucratic apparatus of the Communist Party and state. Far from overcoming this bureaucracy, NEP had fed into it. The improved economic conditions enabled it to grow, providing greater material privileges to layers of full-time state employees, and giving them an enhanced material interest in preserving their own authority.

Even before NEP, in the 1920–21 debates on the role of trade unions, Lenin had noted "what we actually have ... is a workers' state with bureaucratic distortions," which he argued necessitated the existence of independent trade unions to help defend the workers against bureaucratic excesses. He criticized a strong tendency among comrades to defend rather than rectify the bureaucratic excesses. The excesses grew, and Lenin more than once expressed concern that the revolutionary party was not in control of the bureaucratic machine. Rather, the party seemed to be coming under the control of the bureaucracy, with even its basic revolutionary vocabulary being defined in ways consistent with bureaucratic requirements. "There is nothing more mistaken," Lenin complained as early as 1918, "than confusing democratic centralism with bureaucracy and routinism."[38]

To push back in the revolutionary-democratic direction, Lenin fought for two major innovations: the development of a Central Control Commission and an entity called the Workers' and Peasants' Inspection. The Control Commission was to be made up of respected and independent-minded comrades, not in the central leadership, who would be empowered to supervise the party apparatus, at the same time helping defend the rights of individual comrades. The Workers' and Peasants' Inspection was to consist of three or four hundred respected and independent-minded representatives of the working class and peasantry who would play a similar role in regard to the state.

Lenin was successful in having these entities established. But they would soon be overwhelmed by and absorbed into the bureaucracy. A key role in facilitating this was the dedicated and practical-minded comrade who was serving as the General Secretary of the Russian Communist Party.

Nadezhda Krupskaya had for years overseen much of this work, but as the tasks dramatically expanded in 1917, the magnified position was held by Jacob Sverdlov (who died in 1919). The position was designed to keep track of party membership composition, to oversee assignments within the party, to oversee the recording of party events, and to keep party leaders and members informed of party activities. In 1922, the position received the name "General Secretary," and Joseph Stalin was chosen to fill it.

Stalin transformed the position into one of considerable influence and power. It placed him at the intersection of the increasingly interlocked apparatuses of party and state. Of modest demeanor and a practical organizer of proven capabilities, he initially generated little concern that anything problematical was happening. Lenin became increasingly aware that his proposed solutions were not moving forward in the way that he had hoped. This was not the end of Lenin's efforts—but his time soon ran out.

10
Testament and Aftermath

From 1922 to 1924, Lenin was hit by four strokes—the kind that had killed his father. The first disrupted and impeded his normal functioning, the second ended his ability to participate in leadership bodies of party and state, the third almost totally incapacitated him, and the fourth killed him.

Alfred Rosmer, an early activist working for the new Communist International, describes Lenin at its Fourth World Congress in 1922, which took place as Lenin was still recovering from his first stroke in May of that year. Rosmer later recalled:

> Those who were seeing him for the first time said: "It's the same Lenin." But the others could not allow themselves such illusions. Instead of the alert Lenin they had known, the man they had before them was deeply marked by paralysis. His features remained fixed and he walked like a robot. His usual simple, rapid, self-confident speech had given way to a halting, hesitant delivery. Sometimes he couldn't find the words he wanted. The comrade who had been sent to assist him was doing the job badly, so Radek sent him away and took his place.[1]

Max Eastman, who had never seen Lenin before, was frankly charmed "when Karl Radek stepped up beside him and like a cupbearer passed him from time to time the word he was groping for." Lenin struck him not as someone laboring through physical difficulties, but rather as an unpretentious "selfless intellectual" who, using a language not his own (German), and "with expert help ... was taking us inside his mind and showing us how the truth looks."[2]

A few months later, while still convalescing, Lenin was becoming increasingly engaged with the problems confronting the Soviet

Republic. Lev Kamenev, after an hour-long conversation with his ailing comrade, addressed the question "what does Lenin condemn?" The answer: "Very much and first of all, with special emphasis, our bureaucratic apparatus."[3]

The second stroke in December 1922 put an end to this level of functionality. Lenin was restricted to a restful country home in Gorki, with a staff of assistants and medical personnel, as well as Krupskaya and one or another sister. With increasing difficulty, he engaged in the elaboration of a multi-layered "testament." He sought to take the initiative in what would be the final conflict of his life, reaching to save what he could of the revolution to which he had devoted the whole of his life. No more speeches could be made, and his writing had to be painstakingly dictated to secretaries who would take down his formulations, revise them after he was able to review them—all with a two-hour per day work limit. His doctors also did not want him to have discussions with visiting comrades that might be "upsetting," although being cut off from the political engagement that had been the fire and glow of his life, especially as the bureaucratic machine was overwhelming the Soviet Republic, may have been more upsetting than anything else.

Her biographer Robert McNeal suggests Krupskaya "seems to have thought that in these months Lenin was more sympathetic to some of the pre-revolutionary comrades with whom he had quarreled than his current Bolshevik comrades." She later recalled that he asked her about prominent Mensheviks Pavel Axelrod and Julius Martov, the Bolshevik-turned-Menshevik Nikolai Volsky-Valentinov, and erstwhile Bolshevik co-worker Alexander Bogdanov. McNeal speculates that "in Lenin's last months his thoughts were with the men whose humanitarian qualities had helped make them losers, rather than with the new 'bureaucrats' whom he wished to attack."[4]

The third stroke on March 10, 1923 took away his ability to speak, forcing him to communicate with grunts, grimaces, and gestures. He could understand others when they spoke to him, and he valued Krupskaya patiently reading to him—some non-fiction blended in with novels and short stories, but hardly enough to be in touch with the political battles that continued in his absence. "About a month before his death," she later confided to Trotsky, "as he was looking through your book, Vladimir Ilyich stopped at the place where you sum up Marx and Lenin,* and asked me to read it over again to him; he listened very attentively, and then looked it over again himself."[5]

There were strolls in nature, often with a wheelchair. With a stick and orthopedic shoes, he could sometimes walk. Krupskaya helped him learn how to say words again—an important one being "so," which could signify *yes*.[6] His visitors slowed to a trickle. Bolshevik economist Eugen Preobrazhensky, who had co-authored with Nikolai Bukharin the 1919 classic *The ABC of Communism*, described his final visit to Lenin:

> I decided to keep a happy and cheerful face at all times. I approached him. He pressed my hand firmly, I instinctively embraced him. But his face! It cost me a great effort to keep my mask and not cry like a baby. In this face there was so much suffering, not only the sufferings of the present moment. It was as if on his face there were photographed and frozen all the sufferings he had undergone in this whole period.[7]

In October, pushing aside the "rules" established by the doctors, Lenin obstinately insisted he be driven to Moscow to visit his study and flat in the Kremlin. Krupskaya and his sister Maria accompanied him. His chauffeur remembered he was in high spirits. Lenin paced in his study, gathered some notebooks and volumes

* There is such comparison in Trotsky's April 23, 1920 *Pravda* article entitled "Lenin's National Characteristics" (available in Leon Trotsky, *On Lenin: Notes towards a Biography*), which says in part: "The very style of Marx, rich and brilliant, combining vigor and flexibility, anger and irony, austerity and sophistication, is marked by all the literary and aesthetic heritage of German political and social writings that go back to the Reformation and beyond. Lenin's literary and oratorical style is extremely simple, utilitarian, spare, as is his whole nature. ... It is simply the outward expression of an inner concentration of forces, a concentration for action." Also: "The whole of Marx can be found in *The Communist Manifesto*, in the preface to his *Critique*, in *Das Kapital*. Even if he were not the founder of the First International, he would forever remain what he had been till now. Not so Lenin, whose whole personality is centered in revolutionary action. His scientific works were only preliminary to action. If he had never published a single book, he would forever have entered history just as he had entered it now: as a leader of the proletarian revolution, a founder of the Third International."

of Hegel. He saw a little of Moscow on the following morning, and then returned to the estate in Gorki. "Lenin was noticeably in low spirits," according to the chauffeur. "This was his last visit to Moscow and the Kremlin."[8]

Three months later, on January 21, 1924, the fourth and lethal stroke hit.

LENIN'S MULTI-LAYERED TESTAMENT

Moshe Lewin's *Lenin's Last Struggle* documents Lenin's efforts, in the final phase of his life, to push back against the growth of bureaucratic despotism, and to defend as best he could the revolution's original goals.

Two major policy questions came into play as part of this struggle: the question of the Communist Party maintaining control of foreign trade (essential for preventing the Soviet economy under the New Economic Policy [NEP] from becoming subordinated to foreign capital); and the question of nationalities in the Soviet-controlled territories of what had been the tsarist empire. Lenin discovered, to his horror, examples of a bullying "great Russian chauvinism" among leading comrades, bureaucratic insensitivity and mismanagement (including repression and violence)—all of which reinforced his concerns over "bureaucratic deformations."

On these issues Lenin formed a bloc with Trotsky and intended to initiate a fight at the upcoming party congress. Lenin also discovered Stalin was trying to control his access to information, and to supervise Lenin's convalescence in a manner that would isolate him, also attempting to ride roughshod over Nadezhda Krupskaya. This provided the framework within which he composed what has often been tagged "Lenin's Last Testament."

The word *testament* has different meanings. It can mean a tribute or an expression of one's convictions. It can involve the distribution of a person's possessions after death. An archaic meaning is a covenant between God and the human race. These last two meanings can be excluded. Lenin didn't believe himself to be God, nor did he believe in God at all. And he was not seeking to distribute his possessions. What is referred to could be seen as a tribute to what he believes in, an expression of his convictions, and his sharing of beliefs on the question he had been dealing with for most of his life—*What Is to Be Done?*

The document commonly known as "Lenin's Testament" focuses on thoughts about the leadership of the Russian Communist Party after his death. But that is too narrow—his actual testament had multiple layers. Aspects of this can be found in the previous chapter: reflections on the Russian Revolution; thoughts on ways to nurture the new society initiated by the revolution; ways to advance fundamental revolutionary-democratic goals, particularly in the face of a threatening bureaucracy.

Combined with this effort to transition away from a bureaucratic state, Lenin pressed, in his article "On Cooperation," for a transition toward a cooperative economy. He projected "a whole historical epoch" involving one or two decades of NEP interconnected with organizing the population into an expanding network of cooperatives (supported by generous state loans). Perhaps reflecting discussions with the anarchist Kropotkin, he envisioned this as a process inseparable from a far-reaching "cultural revolution."[9] By cultural revolution, Lenin meant the creation of universal literacy and educating people into norms of efficiency that would enable them to create an economic, material base for socialism.

He first repeated the Marxist estimate of cooperatives associated with Robert Owen and other utopian socialists. They envisioned the collective organization of laborers who work together in an organized fashion to provide a good, culturally enriched, healthy life for all, with increasingly improved working conditions. Owen and the others had not taken into account "such fundamental questions as the class struggle, the capture of political power by the working class, the overthrow of the rule of the exploiting class."[10] But since such fundamental questions had been boldly addressed by the 1917 Revolution, the growth of cooperatives could become identical with the growth of socialism. Lenin gave special emphasis to the importance of such cooperative economic policies in improving the lives of increasing numbers of Russia's vast peasantry, and winning more and more peasants to socialism.

The orientation in "On Cooperation" is consistent with other policy perspectives he had been advancing—the New Economic Policy, cultural approaches associated with the Commissariat of Enlightenment, and the proposed Workers' and Peasants' Inspection.

Although the Workers' and Peasants' Inspection proposal had been adopted, it was overseen by Stalin, whose sensibilities were not consistent with what Lenin intended. This led to the semi-polemical article "Better Fewer, But Better." The article begins by complaining about the inefficiency of the Soviet state apparatus and about considerable Communist hyperbole around the flippant catchphrase "proletarian culture." Experiences since 1917 provided considerable ground for "mistrust and skepticism." Rather than imposing superficial policies in the name of revolution, "we should be satisfied with real bourgeois culture," Lenin wryly commented, to "dispense with the cruder types of pre-bourgeois culture, i.e., bureaucratic culture or serf culture."[11]

Lenin repeatedly emphasizes that "our state apparatus is so deplorable, not to say wretched." He elaborates: "The most harmful thing would be to rely on the assumption that we know at least something, or that we have any considerable number of elements necessary for the building of a really new state apparatus, one really worthy to be called socialist, Soviet, etc." Then, again, comes the sledgehammer: "No, we are ridiculously deficient of such an apparatus, and even of the elements of it, and we must remember that we should not stint time on building it, and that it will take many, many years." His immediate prescription:

> In order to renovate our state apparatus we must at all costs set out, first, to learn, secondly, to learn, and thirdly, to learn, and then see to it that learning shall not remain a dead letter, or a fashionable catch-phrase (and we should admit in all frankness that this happens very often with us), that learning shall really become part of our very being, that it shall actually and fully become a constituent element of our social life.[12]

Lenin's impatience with pseudo-revolutionary pretentiousness is a central feature in this document. "We have been bustling for five years trying to improve our state apparatus, but it has been mere bustle," he complains, "which has proved useless in these five years, or even futile, or even harmful." This makes it harder to think clearly or do anything serious: "This bustle created the impression that we were doing something, but in effect it was only clogging up our institutions and our brains."[13]

Lenin's assessment of the Workers' and Peasants' Inspection was brutal:

> Let us say frankly that the People's Commissariat of the Workers' and Peasants' Inspection does not at present enjoy the slightest authority. Everybody knows that no other institutions are worse organized than those of our Workers' and Peasants' Inspection, and that under present conditions nothing can be expected from this People's Commissariat.

Rather than ballooning its size with more comrades having a superficial understanding, or seeking quick fixes to boast about, it was necessary to move more slowly, more carefully, recruiting to the People's Commissariat of the Workers' and Peasants' Inspection more knowledgeable, more serious, more thoughtful workers who would actually be capable of accomplishing something. The quality of those engaging in this work was far more important than the quantity of appointees to this new People's Commissariat.[14]

Lenin placed all this in the revolutionary-internationalist framework that had guided him all along. "It is not easy for us," he acknowledged, "to keep going until the socialist revolution is victorious in more developed countries." The fact remained that "we are confronted with the question—shall we be able to hold on with our small and very small peasant production, and in our present state of ruin, until the West-European capitalist countries consummate their development towards socialism?"[15]

Various points in "Better Fewer, But Better"—but also all the other layers of Lenin's testament—dovetailed with the key question of party leadership. This brings us to the letter to the upcoming Twelfth Congress of the Communist Party, commonly referred to as "Lenin's Testament." The letter was made up of several parts, dictated with considerable effort to secretaries over an extended period. Lenin took it very seriously.

It reflected a determination on Lenin's part to undercut the authority Stalin was acquiring in both the Communist Party and the young Soviet state. There are indications that the creation of the very position giving Stalin such power—General Secretary—and the fact that he occupied that position had come about through his own manipulations. "Lenin later deeply regretted that he had trusted Stalin" (according to prominent party veteran Vladimir Nevsky). Complaining to Krupskaya that Stalin "is lacking elementary honesty, the simplest human honesty," Lenin—according to his younger sister Maria Ulyanova—while valuing him as a practical worker, "genuinely disliked Stalin during his last days."[16]

In early sections of his letter to the Twelfth Congress, Lenin seems intent on providing a balanced assessment of those whom he envisions being the central leadership team on the Political Committee: Trotsky, Stalin, Zinoviev, Kamenev, Bukharin, Piatakov. In warning against a Trotsky/Stalin split, he terms Trotsky a man of "outstanding ability" who is "perhaps the most capable man" on the Central Committee—but displaying "excessive self-assurance" and "excessive preoccupation with the purely administrative side of the work." He comments that Stalin, "having become general secretary, has concentrated unlimited authority in his hands," adding: "I am not sure whether he will always be capable of using that authority with sufficient caution."[17] In all this, he appears to envision the team, despite his criticisms and warnings, functioning as a collective leadership, and the "testament" goes on to touch on other matters—issues of Soviet policy. But he then adds this jarring addendum:

> Stalin is too rude and this defect, although quite tolerable in our midst and in dealings among us Communists, becomes intolerable in a General Secretary. That is why I suggest that the comrades think about a way of removing Stalin from that post and appointing another man in his stead who in all other respects differs from Comrade Stalin in having only one advantage, namely, that of being more tolerant, more loyal, more polite and more considerate to the comrades, less capricious, etc.[18]

Another layer of Lenin's "testament" can be seen in Krupskaya's unsuccessful effort to head off his deification. This was consistent with Lenin's efforts, after 1917, to push back against well-meaning assaults on his common humanity and democratic sensibilities. There were deep-rooted traditions in Russia (similar to those elsewhere) to worship the Adored Leader whose authority was unquestioned and upon whom special privileges and multiple luxuries were lavished.

While Lenin rejected such tendencies with extreme distaste, however, others in the leadership favored making use of such deep-rooted popular impulses, which some felt could be used to bolster the authority of the regime. This culminated in the decision (opposed by Kamenev, Bukharin, and Trotsky) to mummify and preserve Lenin's body in a special mausoleum in Moscow's Red Square. His closest relatives, as well as Krupskaya, had opposed this, and Lenin himself would have been horrified. In an open letter shortly after his death, Krupskaya wrote:

> Comrades, workers and peasants! I have a great request to make of you: do not allow your grief for Ilych to express itself in external veneration of his person. Do not create memorials to him, palaces named after him, magnificent celebrations in his memory, etc. All of this meant so little to him in his lifetime: he found it all so trying. Remember how much poverty and disorder we have in our country. If you want to honor the name of Vladimir Ilyich, build day care centers, kindergartens, homes, schools … etc., and most importantly try in all things to fulfill his legacy.[19]

WHAT CAME NEXT

In the aftermath of Lenin's death, there was a struggle resembling the conflict Lenin had warned against in his letter to the Twelfth Party Congress, although it took a more complex form than he had envisioned. By the late 1920s, Stalin triumphed. In achieving the top position in the Soviet hierarchy, Stalin made ample use of precedents and norms that had become common in the period of "war communism," and these became integral to the manner in which he interpreted and carried out his version of Lenin's legacy.

Some saw this proclaimed continuity with Lenin as what could be termed a *changed* continuity. *New York Times* correspondent

Walter Duranty noted a growing number of old Bolsheviks "were showing signs of restiveness, partly because they saw that Stalinism was progressing from Leninism (as Leninism had progressed from Marxism) towards a form and development of its own, partly because they were jealous and alarmed by Stalin's growing predominance."[20]

A shrewd and somewhat cynical observer, Duranty was sympathetic to Stalin, though with a decidedly non-revolutionary detachment. In his opinion, "Stalin deserved his victory because he was the strongest, and because his policies were most fitted to the Russian character and folkways in that they established Asiatic absolutism and put the interests of Russian Socialism before those of international Socialism." Years later, eminent historian Moshe Lewin described the same development in different terms. "One group of old Bolsheviks after another was to engage in rearguard actions in an attempt to rectify the course of events in one fashion or another," he noted. "But their political tradition and organization, rooted in the history of Russian and European Social-Democracy, were rapidly swept away by the mass of new members and new organizational structures which pressed that formation into an entirely different mold."[21]

The Russian Communist Party ballooned from tens of thousands to hundreds of thousands and ultimately to millions as it became the Communist Party of the Soviet Union. Many of the new members were drawn to what they perceived as an idealistic and triumphant organization rebuilding society in the interests of laboring people such as themselves, but many also sought privileges to be garnered by being on the winning side. Most were quite new to Marxist ideas and socialist commitments. "The original cadres found themselves flooded by a mass of newcomers who shared neither their ideology nor their ethos," observed Lewin. Stalin's position as General Secretary of the Communist Party placed him in the key position to oversee the process. "The process of the party's conversion into an apparatus—careers, discipline, ranks, abolition of all political rights—was an absolute scandal for the oppositions of 1924–8. But their old party was dead." Lewin concludes "people should not be misled by old names and ideologies: in a fluid political context, names last longer than substances."[22]

It is interesting to consider how Stalin was perceived by a seasoned oppositionist who was not satisfied with mere demonization of his one-time comrade. Looking back in 1943, Victor Serge concluded Stalin "believes in his mission: he sees himself as the savior of a revolution threatened by ideologues, the idealistic and the unrealistic." Serge added that Stalin "fought them as he could, with his inferiority complex and his jealousies, his terror of men superior to him and whom he couldn't understand." Stalin viewed himself as Lenin's rightful heir, but his method for dealing with troublesome comrades was very much his own: "He cast them from his savior's path by the only methods he had at his disposal: terror and lies, the methods of a limited intelligence governed by suspicion and placed at the service of a great vitality."[23] This "great vitality" refers not simply to Stalin's own life-force and will-to-power, but to the revolutionary cause to which he remained committed, in his own fashion.

Stalin himself—in acknowledging his own mistakes of 1917, during a 1924 controversy around Trotsky's polemic *Lessons of October*—had described the pre-October Bolshevik party as a democratic collective: "our Party would be a caste and not a revolutionary party if it did not permit different shades of opinion in its ranks." He emphasized that serious "disagreements among us" need not undermine the Bolsheviks' revolutionary unity. He would soon adopt and propagate a very different point of view, and as his most perceptive biographer comments, "had Stalin heeded his own words ... a different Communist Party would have emerged than the one forged under Stalin."[24]

The Stalin regime evolved into a "demented bureaucracy" (as observant Austrian Communist Ernst Fischer reflected). Only persecuted and reviled fragments of the Leninist core could remain true to the goal in which "future generations," according to Trotsky's testament, would cleanse life "of all evil, oppression, and violence, and enjoy it to the full." John McIlroy and Alan Campbell (drawing on Moshe Lewin's phrase) have suggested: "Stalinism was as different from socialism as the hippopotamus from the giraffe."[25]

Regarding Lenin's dictum "there can be no revolutionary movement without revolutionary theory," ex-Communist Angelo Tasca explained in 1949:

> Lenin would no doubt have understood this to call for the conscious development, within the revolutionary movement, of a corpus of theory; but ... present-day Communist theory is something that you find all ready for you, cut and dried, in Party "manuals" and "courses of study." ... Study groups ... will be required to read aloud and comment on such materials (newspapers, reports, bulletins) as have been forwarded by the Central Committee. ... The truths revealed to Marx and Engels and their prophets Lenin and Stalin are not open to discussion: one merely keeps on verifying them by observing the facts of the objective situation.[26]

Stalin played a central role in editing and helping to compose the *History of the Communist Party of the Soviet Union (Bolsheviks), Short Course*, utilized to educate Soviet citizens from all walks of life and Communists around the world between 1938 and 1956 about the meaning and history of this "party of a new type" (a term Lenin never used). In the Soviet Union over 40 million copies were published in more than a dozen languages, and hundreds of thousands more were published in Beijing, Budapest, London, New York, Paris, Prague, Warsaw and elsewhere—shaping the understanding of many millions (friends and foes) on how socialism and Communism should be understood; on the history of Russia, the Soviet Union, and the revolutionary movement; and on the very meaning of "Leninism":

> The Communist Party of the Soviet Union (Bolsheviks) has traversed a long and glorious road, leading from the first tiny Marxist circles and groups ... to the great Party of the Bolsheviks, which now directs the first Socialist State of the Workers and Peasants in the world. ...
>
> The C.P.S.U.(B) grew and gained strength in a fight over fundamental principles waged against the petty-bourgeois parties within the working-class movement—the Socialist-Revolutionaries (and earlier still, against their predecessors, the Narodniks), the Mensheviks, Anarchists and bourgeois nationalists of all shades—and within the Party itself, against the

> Menshevik, opportunist trends—the Trotskyites, Bukharinites, nationalist deviators and other anti-Leninist groups. …
>
> The study of the history of the C.P.S.U.(B) strengthens our certainty of the ultimate victory of the great cause of the Party of Lenin-Stalin, the victory of Communism throughout the world. …[27]

The book, according to latter-day critics, taught readers "to assume a passive, submissive relationship toward political authority," the Communist Party of which Stalin was the highest representative. It "was always correct and … any shortcomings or problems interfering with the realization of the official line were the result of sabotage and wrecking on the part of the U.S.S.R.'s foes."[28]

One example of the book's pervasive and enduring influence can be found in the novelist Stefan Heym, a young refugee from Hitler's Germany, drawn to the German Communist movement as the *Short Course* was profoundly influencing the education of cadres and idealists in Communist ranks. His left-wing novels of the 1940s and 1950s had global impact. By the 1960s, however, Heym was a dissident whose writings were banned in his own East Germany. After the Communist collapse and German reunification of 1989, he was elected to the Bundestag as a representative of the newly formed Party of Democratic Socialism, projecting an anti-Stalinist and humane socialist vision. Heym's novel of the 1990s, *Radek*, reflects these sensibilities. Yet one still finds the understanding of "Leninism" propagated in Stalin's *Short Course*: "Lenin had his party, a party of a new type, as he called it, small but professional, and sworn to him, and subordinate to his instructions."[29]

The Stalin era saw immense gains: the industrialization and modernization of what had been the backward Russian Empire; universal literacy, education, health care and other social benefits for all; the immense sacrifices that defeated the brutal onslaught of Nazi Germany during the Second World War, which in turn helped catapult the Soviet Union into orbit as a great world power. Yet dissident Soviet historian Roy Medvedev argued:

> It was not Stalin who taught the Soviet people to read and write ... It was the October revolution that opened the road to education and culture for the Soviet people. Our country would have traveled the road far more quickly if Stalin had not destroyed the hundreds of thousands of the intelligentsia, both old and new. Prisoners in Stalin's concentration camps accomplished a great deal, building almost all the canals and hydroelectric stations in the U.S.S.R., many railways, factories, pipelines, even tall buildings in Moscow. But industry would have developed faster if these millions of innocent people had been employed as free workers. Likewise, Stalin's use of force against the peasantry slowed down the growth rate of agriculture with painful effects for the whole Soviet economy to the present day. He did not speed up but rather slowed down the overall rate of development that our country might have enjoyed. The "price" our people paid, its sacrifices, underline not the difficulty of the task but Stalin's cruel recklessness.[30]

Regardless of accomplishments attributed to the Stalinist order, with its distorted versions of Leninism and Communism, it ultimately proved unsustainable. Before the collapse of this order, when it seemed to represent a compelling global power in the wake of the Second World War, the eloquent survivor and witness Victor Serge touched on what was becoming a central dilemma of the mid-twentieth century:

> Until 1917, throughout history, the poor and the exploited had been eternally beaten. For the first time, through Bolshevism, the harsh "natural" law appeared annulled. The masses' feeling of inferiority gave way to confidence, pride, a new optimism. Some roots of Stalinism are still embedded in the soil of these feelings. In a good many minds there is a frank conflict between truth, facts, and newly acquired faith. If the balance sheet of the Revolution ends in an appalling deficit, they ask, how can there be hope? Many ... flinch from this brutally superficial conclusion and prefer blindness, deception and totalitarian discipline. Others are poisoned with bitterness. In both cases rational understanding yields to irrational rationalization.[31]

Communism's collapse and the end of the Cold War heralded the worldwide triumph of a dynamic capitalism, powered by multinational corporations, in multiple ways shaping the lives of the billions of laborers and consumers all across our planet. Some envisioned a bright new era of what was tagged "globalization"—presumably ensuring abundance and democracy, with liberty and justice for all.

Instead, there has been a proliferation of problems and crises, and these—dovetailing with Communism's collapse and the disorientation and disintegration of an organized left-wing working-class movement—has generated a conservative and right-wing onslaught throughout much of the world. Serge put his finger on aspects of its early beginnings: "The reactionaries have a clear interest in confusing Stalinist totalitarianism—the exterminator of Bolshevism—with Bolshevism itself and thus eventually with socialism, Marxism, and even liberalism."[32]

This has had a powerful impact on the writing of history, but also in the realm of social policy and contemporary politics—including the phenomenon of right-wing "populist" authoritarianism entering the political mainstream, contesting for power and in a growing number of cases coming to power in countries around the world.

Inside the former Soviet Union, with Communism's collapse, attitudes toward Lenin have been complex and contradictory. Boris Yeltsin's regime launched an anti-Lenin campaign, sharply challenged by less powerful historians (among whom were Soviet-era dissidents). Subsequently, the regime of "anti-revolutionary conservative" Vladimir Putin went on to sharply denounce Lenin for undermining Russian power, while arguing that "Stalin got it right."[33]

ENGAGING WITH CATASTROPHE

An objective assessment of world history over the past two centuries seems to reveal rising tides of catastrophe. One way of dealing with this has been tagged "cognitive dissonance."[34] It is a dynamic that can be found across the political spectrum and can be found among a variety of thoughtful and caring people.

Each of us has a worldview with which we make sense of reality. If confronted with evidence conflicting with that worldview, our minds experience an uncomfortable dissonance (or conflict). Instead of changing our worldview, which may have guided us through most of our lives, we are inclined to dismiss the evidence. Along with that, we dismiss (through ridicule, slander, and other forms of disrespect) those who provide such unpleasant evidence. A current example involves many people who deny the documented reality of climate change. We have seen Victor Serge explaining how this operated among people not wanting to acknowledge the horrific realities associated with the Stalin regime.

This can also be found in conflicting analyses of Lenin. Some have a worldview inclining them to look positively on Lenin, causing them to reject, avoid, or downplay the negative realities presented in Chapter 8 of this book. The worldview of others inclines them to look negatively on Lenin, causing them to reject, avoid, or downplay material presented in the bulk of this book. Yet it doesn't make historiographical or political sense to focus on Lenin's first 48 years without seeking to comprehend his last five years. And it hardly makes sense to dismiss the first 48 years and simply focus on the last five. For a serious historian, and for a serious political activist, it is obvious that Lenin's life can best be understood by taking it as a whole—finding challenges, insights, and understandings unavailable with an exclusive focus on only one portion of his life.

For those inclined to see Lenin in negative terms, there is a tendency to focus on what is perceived to be problematical (either potentially or actually)—especially around issues involving elitism and violence. There are at least two ways in which this may prevent a serious understanding: (1) the adoption of a moralistic stance, and (2) the refusal to consider all of reality.

Challenging a "moralistic stance" does not mean being dismissive of moral considerations. It refers to a stance in which one's *primary concern* is not to achieve genuine understanding or social improvement, *but to define oneself as a "good" or superior person.* Adopting this stance might also involve identifying with some historical figure presumed to be closer to the ideal of perfection—

perhaps Rosa Luxemburg, perhaps Mohandas Gandhi, perhaps Mikhail Bakunin, perhaps all three of these very different and not necessarily compatible figures.*

The "refusal to consider all of reality" can involve three different problems. One would be to rip words of Lenin's out of context, so that the ripped-out words have a connotation different from or even the opposite of what Lenin is actually saying. Another is not to consider the actual historical context which Lenin's words are addressing—again, not understanding the point he is actually making, and assuming the quoted words represent for him a generalized principle to which, in fact, he does not adhere. A third problem involves forgetting that Lenin is functioning in a world dominated by elites who systematically use violence—casting him as a monster among presumed angels.

The third problem is most common. On the matter of his condoning violence, one might fixate on Lenin with no reference to those who led the dominant social order—as if Lenin is the only practitioner of violence, but not Tsar Nicholas II or Alexander Kerensky, not Generals Kornilov or Denikin, and certainly not Winston Churchill or Woodrow Wilson. Similarly, Lenin aside, each of the six people mentioned in the preceding sentence can be legitimately accused of elitism, at least five of them (unlike Lenin) were conscious racists, and it can be documented that four of them (unlike Lenin) were conscious opponents of *rule by the people*—so again, a question-mark hovers over the meaning of the anti-Lenin criticism.

For those believing in democracy, it is a truism that a majority of the people rarely favor one or another idea—unless a minority, which presumes to have better ideas, actively persuades the majority. Yet if the minority is led or inspired by Lenin, this is often tagged as *elitism*. Without such so-called "elitism," however, there can be no politics at all—aside from being part of a passive herd going along with the status quo.

---

* Too often, the presumed morally superior figure is understood in a shallow or romanticized way. Relevant to this point are: Paul Le Blanc, *The Living Flame: The Revolutionary Passion of Rosa Luxemburg* (also see Scott and Le Blanc, "Introduction," in *The Complete Works of Rosa Luxemburg*, Vol. 5); Talat Ahmed, *Mohandas Gandhi: Experiments in Civil Disobedience*; E.H. Carr, *Michael Bakunin*.

SUMMING UP

Facts are stubborn things. As catastrophic realities accumulate, growing numbers of people find such catastrophes unacceptable and ask: *what is to be done*?

A reasonable guide to action, in Lenin's view, could be found in the body of thought and methodology known as Marxism. He embraced its class analysis, its commitment to the oppressed and laboring majority of humanity, and the revolutionary-democratic goal of bringing society under the control of its vast laboring majority. With a keen understanding of undemocratic power in society and politics, he committed to building alternative structures, genuinely democratic in the revolutionary struggle and in the ethos permeating the revolutionary goal.

Lenin's Marxism comprehended reality as complex, ever-changing, and contradictory. He believed "any truth, if 'overdone' ..., if exaggerated, or if carried beyond the limits of its actual applicability, can be reduced to an absurdity."[35] Rooted in national and cultural realities of his homeland, he was also profoundly internationalist in his revolutionary understanding and commitment. The depth of Lenin's commitment was reflected in an ongoing dissatisfaction with amateurishness, and a quest for political, strategic, tactical, and organizational seriousness. We can see an ongoing effort (not always successful) to achieve uncompromising clarity on realities, principles, goals—but this was complemented with an inclination toward considerable tactical flexibility. And he believed his contributions could only be developed within and applied through a coherent, democratic, revolutionary collective of vibrant and strong-minded individuals sharing the revolutionary commitment. This has a compelling quality that seems indelible. "Of course," writes post-Soviet dissident Ilya Budraitsksis, "you can demolish every Lenin monument on earth, but that does not mean that communism has vanished once and for all."[36]

There is certainly *more* to be said. Some of the "more" can found in the preceding pages. But for those of an activist bent who want this "more" to move into the future, there are limits on what can be said here. Layers of new generations will be facing catastrophes. So did Lenin and his comrades—but they were part of a global phenomenon of the late nineteenth century, which had largely vanished by the late twentieth century: a mass movement of organized labor committed to the economic democracy of socialism. Mike Davis points out: "There is no historical precedent or vantage point for understanding what will happen in the 2050s, when a peak species population of 9 to 11 billion struggles to adapt to climate chaos and depleted fossil energy." He goes on to imagine "a global revolution that reintegrates the labor of the informal working classes, as well as the rural poor, in the sustainable reconstruction of their built environments and livelihoods." He also confesses this seems "an utterly unrealistic scenario."[37]

Yet Lenin says: "We should dream!" He adds:

> The rift between dreams and reality causes no harm if only the person dreaming believes seriously in his dream, if he attentively observes life, compares his observations with his castles in the air, and if, generally speaking, he works conscientiously for the achievement of his fantasies. If there is some connection between dreams and life then all is well.[38]

Philip Rahv's comment of 1971 still holds true: "Historically we are living on volcanic ground."[39] Those of my generation inspired by Lenin and his comrades have been likened to children enamored of the reptile giants roaming the world in a long-gone epoch. And yet, the catastrophes which brought Lenin and his comrades into being, and then overwhelmed them, have not stopped happening. In *Jurassic Park*, the film about the return of the dinosaurs, the character Ian Malcolm emphasizes: "Life finds a way."

An interesting notion, Lenin might have responded, but what is to be done?

Epilogue: Commit Yourself and Then See …

Read Lenin. Be careful.

—C. Wright Mills
"Letter to the New Left"

The very nature of Lenin's orientation compels an engagement with the "what is to be done?" question in our own, specific here-and-now. What is the relevance of Lenin's orientation for activists of today and tomorrow? There are layers of such activists coming together not only in Britain and the United States, but throughout Europe and the Americas, as well as in Asia, Africa, Australia, and even among islands independent of the great continents. This is due to the deepening economic, social, political, and environmental crises with which capitalism is afflicting us.

My thoughts naturally turn to the double-barreled admonition of radical sociologist C. Wright Mills. The need for more of us to "read Lenin" inspired the creation of the Pluto Press anthology of his writings*—but a keen sense that I must "be careful" now comes into play.

Much of what I have to say is grounded in experiences from my own country. Experiences from the histories and cultures of other lands would surely enrich this discussion.

When I was a young "New Left" activist, I came to know two audacious, thoughtful, charismatic people who moved to a working-class neighborhood in Pittsburgh for the purpose of organizing a socialist revolution. Roughly my age, they had been in Paris during the heady days of the momentous student-worker upsurge of May–June 1968. Their experiences imbued them with the conviction that a working-class revolution was necessary and

* Lenin, *Revolution, Democracy, Socialism: Selected Writings*, ed. Paul Le Blanc (Pluto Press, 2008).

possible, but they were also persuaded of the need for a revolutionary organization with a Leninist orientation. They committed themselves to making it so, more than doubling their numbers in a short period of time (making a group of five).

The group took to heart Lenin's stricture that without revolutionary theory, there can be no revolutionary movement. One of them therefore acquired and began to study the *Collected Works* of Lenin. This intimate theoretical connection meant that he would assume the function of "central committee," handing down decisions for the others to implement as disciplined comrades. Given Lenin's stress on the importance of a newspaper, they published a four-page revolutionary newspaper. They soon discovered, of course, that all of this was not producing the desired results. When the group and its newspaper went out of existence, its members were able to move on to a more effective use of their creative energies.

There have been somewhat larger groups whose would-be Leninism also proved incapable of producing the desired results. All too often—animated by a stilted understanding of what Lenin actually said, actually meant, actually did—the result has been the creation of one or another sect, disconnected from the experience, consciousness, and struggles of the working class, creating a universe of its own, whose primary function has been the preservation of that rarified universe. Sometimes the sect endures, stultifying or exhausting the creative energies of its participants. We have to do better than that.

A key to Lenin is the fundamental commitment to being rooted in the *actual struggles* of the *working class*—not conceptually and rhetorically, but in fact.

THE WONDROUS, MUNDANE, MULTIFACETED, ACTUAL WORKING CLASS—ALL OF US*

It is possible (and among certain socialist, Communist, anarcho-syndicalist currents, it is the norm) to idealize and deify

* This section and the next are drawn from the essay "Reflections on Coherence and Comradeship," in Le Blanc, *Revolutionary Collective*.

the working class. This can become a huge barrier to revolutionaries who wish to overcome multiple forms of exploitation—thinking of people as glorified abstractions instead of actual people.

Actual people have a variety of ages and cultural preferences, different genders and sexual orientations, different sets of biases and prejudices, different levels of knowledge and insight, various neuroses and other mental-emotional problems, divergent attitudes on multiple questions, and more. All of this is true of the working class, given that it is composed of actual people.

The classical definition of the working class is: those who make a living (get enough money to buy basic necessities and perhaps some luxuries) by selling their *ability to work* (their *labor-power*) to an employer. Out of the labor-power, the employer squeezes actual labor in order to create the wealth that is partly given to the workers (usually as little as possible), with the rest of this labor-created wealth going to the employer. In the early decades of the Industrial Revolution in patriarchal and capitalist Europe, men were often considered the "real" workers (even though many women worked), and factory workers were often considered the "real" working class. But men and women, and many, many children too, were part of the working class the way we have defined it, and that was the case whether they produced goods or services, regardless of specific and proliferating occupations, skill sets, levels of income, levels of occupational pride, etc.

Capitalism is the most dynamic form of economy in human history—continually generating what Kim Moody has termed "new terrain" in the global economy, continually transforming the occupational structure and experience of the working class, thereby "reshaping the battleground of class war."[1] As an alert, critical-minded, creative Marxist, Lenin engaged with such realities and integrated them into his revolutionary orientation.

As a class, the immense collectivity of people just described have been oppressed and exploited in order to enrich the tiny and powerful minority that owns and controls our economy. But there are powerful and terrible forms of oppression that bear down—in multiple ways—on people through their non-class identities, including race, ethnicity, gender, sexuality, religion, age, distinctive physical specifics, and more. Not only must fighting against such oppression be central to all that activists do in the struggle for human liberation, but the interrelationship of such forms of oppression, and of the struggles against them, must be understood.

In particular, the *class struggle* must be seen as involving determined, creative, uncompromising struggle against all forms of oppression. "Working-class consciousness cannot be genuine political consciousness unless the workers are trained to respond to all cases of tyranny, oppression, violence, and abuse, no matter what class is affected," Lenin once emphasized. He specified that this includes oppression around freedom of speech and expression, cultural freedom, the rights of religious minorities, the rights of racial and ethnic groups, the rights of women, of soldiers, of students, of peasants. He argued that such oppression must be seen by the worker (here Lenin was presumably speaking of male workers) as coming from "those same dark forces that are oppressing and crushing him at every step of his life." A revolutionary must be a "tribune of the people, who is able to react to every manifestation of tyranny and oppression, no matter where it appears, no matter what stratum or class of people it affects."[2]

Also worth considering, in this regard, are comments of George Breitman, a seasoned working-class intellectual, who put the matter this way half a century ago in the United States:

> The radicalization of the worker can begin off the job as well as on. It can begin from the fact that the worker is a woman as well as a man; that the worker is Black or Chicano or a member of some other oppressed minority as well as white; that the worker is a father or mother whose son can be drafted; that the worker is young as well as middle-aged or about to retire. If we grasp the fact that the working class is stratified and divided in many ways—the capitalists prefer it that way—then we will be better able to understand how the radicalization will develop among workers and how to intervene more effectively. Those who haven't already learned important lessons from the radicalization of oppressed minorities, youth and women had better hurry up and learn them, because most of the people involved in these radicalizations are workers or come from working-class families.[3]

COLLECTIVES AND CADRES

Many adages from past movements and struggles continue to resonate: an injury to one is an injury to all, in unity there is strength, if we fail to hang together we may be hanged separately, etc. There will be no inevitable triumph of human rights, freedom, creativity, community, and a better future. Such things must be fought for, and they must be fought for against oppressive and exploitative elites that are powerful and well organized, with immense resources. They can only be overcome by the force of the majority, but only if that majority has the necessary consciousness and a high degree of organization.

Obviously, not every human being who is part of "the majority" has the same thoughts and values. Some are drawn to multiple forms of bigotry and/or fear and/or passivity and/or submissiveness, etc. Only a portion—a layer—of the working-class majority is at this moment inclined toward a revolutionary class-consciousness, commitment against all forms of oppression, and inclination to fight for a better world. Within this layer, there are some who have developed some skills in actually fighting back, in analyzing what's what, and in waging effective struggles. Anarcho-syndicalists have referred to this as "the militant minority," and such a minority has sometimes been able to provide leadership in sustained struggles that result in victories. Many among those inclined to read a book such as this might be part of the *broad vanguard layer* of the working class.

Based on what has been said so far, it seems clear that this vanguard layer or militant minority must not substitute itself for the majority (let alone arrogantly claim that it *is* the majority). Rather, it must seek to win more and more individuals, more and more of the majority, to forms of consciousness and activity through which they too will either become part of the vanguard layer or increasingly conscious and active supporters of what that layer is reaching for—against all forms of oppression, and for a world in which the free development of each will become the condition for the free development of all.

Just as the entire working class or the majority of the population is not telepathically connected, thinking the same thoughts and automatically inclined to carry out the same actions, so those who are part of the vanguard layer do not all have the same thoughts and understanding, including about pathways that make sense and what to do next. To be effective, individuals who are part of this layer must join together to pool their energies, their ideas, their resources, their insights, their commitments. Without the development of such a collaboration of thinking and activism, without a political collective (in fact, a network of collectives), there can be no effective plans of action that can be carried out to change the world.

Such collectives cannot be sustained, cannot grow, cannot carry out the broad array of educational, consciousness-raising, and practical political activities, without people who have developed the skills to make this so. The word *cadre* has been used as a tag for such people.

Such a person has developed the interactive blend of knowledge, understanding, experience, and skills to do the things that must be done.

- How does one organize a meeting that is coherent and democratic and effective and has good practical results? How are those good practical results achieved, and how can various comrades be helped to make sure that they are achieved? How can one's specific collective be sustained in order to ensure the development and effectiveness of its various comrades and the collective as a whole?
- How does one size up an actual situation in the community or the workplace, figure out the kinds of things that need to be done, and figure out how they can be done in order to realize a specific goal? How does one organize an educational forum, a picket line, a strike, a rally, a mass demonstration, an election campaign, a struggle for a specific reform, etc.?
- What can we learn from other struggles, at other times, from other places, that can help us be strong and effective in our own struggles? How can these be applied to our specific situations?

Not everyone can answer such questions—but a cadre is someone who can answer some of them, helping create collaboration in which further answers can be developed and tested in practical action. A cadre is someone who can help ensure that the collective can be what it must be, who can help others see the need to become part of the collective, and who can help members of the collective (and even people who are not members of the collective) to become cadres in the sense that is suggested here.

With the proliferation of cadres, with more and more and more activists developing as cadres, there could be the growth of a mass movement capable of being effective in the fight against all forms of oppression, forging pathways in the struggle for a better world of the free and the equal.

PRACTICAL ACTIVISM, PRINCIPLED POLITICS, REVOLUTIONARY PATIENCE

It is not possible to declare a revolutionary organization into existence. Without the accumulation of experience, cadres, relationships, and authority within the working class, a would-be revolutionary organization cannot actually become a revolutionary organization. This can only be achieved through practical activism.

For some would-be revolutionary organizations, its members seem to feel it is sufficient to develop and express revolutionary thoughts, revolutionary "positions." These can be developed through discussions and study groups. But defining and expressing "politically correct" positions becomes primary for many would-be revolutionary groups. This may take the form of arguing against the capitalist ruling class, or against non-revolutionary groups, or against other would-be revolutionary groups. It is certainly the case, as we have seen, that Lenin was fully prepared to engage in polemics and arguments. But what was primary for him was helping to mobilize *practical struggles* capable of materially defending and advancing the urgent needs of workers and the oppressed—struggles that can make sense to people in the here-and-now but also tilt toward mass revolutionary consciousness and, if fought effectively, insurgency and power-shift—ultimately, revolution.

For Lenin, theory, education, and the articulation of "principled positions" was inseparable from such practical work. The Bolsheviks engaged in practical campaigns that helped define them, that created a practical framework of struggle in which they might form *united fronts* and, in some cases, converge with other groups prepared to fight the good fight and push toward victory. Only in that way could an organization of would-be revolutionaries become a revolutionary organization. This approach was simply expressed in the explanation of V.R. Dunne, leader of the militant and victorious Minneapolis teamster strike of 1934: "Our policy was to organize and build strong unions so workers could have something to say about their own lives and assist in changing the present order into a socialist society."[4]

One key revolutionary principle involves the political independence of the working class—the refusal to subordinate the struggles of the working class to the leadership of pro-capitalist parties. "No democracy in the world puts aside the class struggle and the ubiquitous power of money," Lenin noted, adding that while in a country such as the United States capitalists and workers had equal political rights, in fact "they are not equal in class status: one class, capitalists, own the means of production and live on the unearned product of the labor of the workers; the other, the class of wage-workers, ... own no means of production and live by selling their labor-power in the market." He warned that the "so-called bipartisan system" of the pro-capitalist parties, Democrats and Republicans, "has been one of the most powerful means of preventing the rise of an independent working class, i.e., genuinely socialist party."[5]

Another principle involves opposition to all forms of racism, ethnic bigotry, or oppression based on gender or sexuality. A third involves opposition to imperialism and war. A fourth, becoming increasingly urgent in our time, is uncompromising opposition to the destruction of a livable environment. A fifth principle is a commitment to genuine democracy (rule by the people) as essential both to our future world and within the movement to create that better future. A sixth principle involves an internationalist orientation—solidarity across borders, a commitment to global collaboration among the workers and oppressed of all countries.

How can one apply such principles in a manner that can advance the struggle for power, democracy, and well-being of the working class? Different approaches, analyses, campaigns, and programs might be followed to achieve this. The process of testing different perspectives and learning from actual struggles—accompanied by debates and splits, but also united efforts and fusions—will be necessary on the way to creating a revolutionary party worthy of the name.

Lenin insisted "we must at all costs set out, first, to learn, secondly, to learn, and thirdly, to learn, and then see to it that ... learning shall really become part of our very being, that it shall actually and fully become a constituent element of our social life."[6] But he also insisted we must learn through doing—learning through actual struggles against oppression and exploitation, collectively evaluating that experience, and thinking through what to do next.

It is crucial to learn from practical experience, but also from historical experience. This involves not simply learning from the Russian Bolsheviks, but also from one's own radical traditions. The outstanding Marxist writer Harry Braverman emphasized this point in describing a founder of the U.S. Communist Party (later expelled for opposing Stalinism), James P. Cannon. Although breaking from his mentor in the 1950s, the earlier impact was vibrantly recalled:

> He spoke to us in the accents of the Russian revolution and of the Leninism which had gone forth from the Soviet Union in the twenties and the thirties. But there was in his voice something more that attracted us. And that was the echoes of the radicalism of the pre-World War I years, the popular radicalism of Debs, Haywood, and John Reed. And he spoke with great force and passion.[7]

Cannon made a similar point in a late-in-life interview: "A revolutionist's spirit and attitude is not determined by the popular mood of the moment. We have a historical view and we don't allow the movement to fade away when it runs into changed times, which can happen as we know from experience." Cannon emphasized a key element in Leninism: "People must learn how to work together and think together so that the work and thought of each individual becomes a contribution to the whole." He added that it was essential "to create an atmosphere in the party where everyone is valued and everyone has a full opportunity to show what they can do for the party." Those who stood out, in this natural political process, would assume a certain "moral authority" that, in a healthy situation, would cause them to become part of the organization's leadership. What was needed, he concluded was not "one person who becomes a one-man leader but a group of people who combined their talents as well as their faults and make a collective leadership. That's what we need everywhere."[8]

Chronology of Lenin's Life

1870: Vladimir Ilyich Ulyanov born in Simbirsk: his father (Ilya), a teacher and school inspector, son of a tailor and former serf; his mother (Maria), from a cultured middle-class background; fourth child, with an older sister (Anna), an older brother (Alexander), two younger sisters (Olga, Maria), a younger brother (Dmitri), and two other siblings who died in infancy. All surviving children will become active in the revolutionary movement.

1874: Father becomes director of schools in Simbirsk and active state councilor.

1886: Father dies of brain hemorrhage (or stroke), age 54; Vladimir rejects religion.

1887: Brother Alexander arrested and executed for plotting to kill the tsar. Vladimir wins gold medal in final grammar school examinations; enters Kazan University as law student; takes part in student protests and is briefly arrested; expelled from Kazan University.

1891: Permitted to take examinations in law at St. Petersburg University, receiving high marks. Involved with revolutionary literature and groups. Sister Olga dies of typhoid.

1892: Awarded a first-class law degree from St. Petersburg University; begins practice of law.

1893: Emerges as a prominent Marxist in circles of revolutionary-minded students and youth.

1894: Writes *What the "Friends of the People" Are and How They Fight the Social Democrats*, defending Marxism and criticizing Populism. Becomes close to Nadezhda Krupskaya, a Marxist school teacher focusing on adult education.

1895: Develops agitational and educational materials for Russian workers. Travels to Switzerland, France, Germany, connecting with George Plekhanov and other Russian Marxists (Pavel Axelrod, Vera Zasulich) of the Emancipation of Labor Group. Meets prominent socialists, including Paul Lafargue and Laura (Marx) Lafargue, Wilhelm Liebknecht. Deepens his studies of Marxism. Continues revolutionary work in Russia through the League of Struggle for the Emancipation of the Working Class. Arrested.

1896: From prison, continues study and writing, maintains contacts with League of Struggle.

1897: Exiled to Siberia, while continuing studies, writing, and contacts with revolutionaries.

1898: Declares adherence to the new Russian Social Democratic Labor Party (RSDLP). Joined in exile by Nadezhda Krupskaya, and they are married.

1899: Publishes *The Development of Capitalism in Russia.*

1900: Siberian exile ends. Works closely with Julius Martov, A.N. Potresov, and others—including the Emancipation of Labor Group—to develop an underground paper *Iskra*. First issue of *Iskra* appears, featuring his article "Urgent Tasks of Our Movement."

1901: Adopts pseudonym "Lenin." Functioning in Germany (where he is joined by Krupskaya), develops relations with Karl Kautsky, Rosa Luxemburg, and others. Oversees production of *Iskra.*

1902: Publication of *What Is to Be Done?*, representing standpoint of *Iskra* supporters (although some will denounce it and Lenin after 1903 split in the RSDLP). Lenin and Krupskaya move to London. Continues to work closely with Martov, Plekhanov, and other *Iskra*-ites in preparation for the Second Congress of the RSDLP. Initially develops close relations with Trotsky.

1903: Lenin prioritizes worker-peasant alliance in *To the Rural Poor.* Second Congress of RSDLP in Brussels and London initially results in triumph of *Iskra* supporters—but then a deep split over seemingly secondary organizational matters. A majority (Bolsheviks) align with Lenin and Plekhanov, a minority (Mensheviks) includes Martov, Potresov, Axelrod, Zasulich, and others. Plekhanov goes over to the Mensheviks, who take control of *Iskra*. Fierce campaign of denunciation is launched against Lenin.

1904: Lenin discusses Bolshevik/Menshevik split in *One Step Forward, Two Steps Back*, seeking reunification of factions until more substantial political differences emerge.

1905: Lenin amid revolutionary upheaval—1

Non-violent mass march of workers, led by Father Georgi Gapon, is brutally fired upon by the tsar's troops. This—combining with long-standing grievances among peasants, workers, and intellectuals, plus the Russo-Japanese War—generates a nationwide insurgency. Movements for democratic reforms push forward, poor peasants aggressively reach out for land, mass strikes and trade union organizing flourish, democratic councils (*soviets*) spring up in working-class districts. Thousands of workers flood into RSDLP (regardless of faction).

Returning to Russia, Lenin calls for facilitating broader working-class participation in the Bolshevik faction of the RSDLP and for embracing the new soviets. He advocates armed uprising, which he helps organize in Moscow. His *Two Tactics of Social Democracy in the Democratic Revolution* advocates a worker-peasant alliance to overthrow tsarism, in contrast to Menshevik perspectives of a more moderate worker-capitalist alliance. Responding to a militant appeal from Father Gapon, he formulates what will become the *united front* tactic.

1906: Since 1905 events brought a political convergence of Bolsheviks and Mensheviks, Lenin favors unity efforts, also embracing the Menshevik call for "democratic centralism." Moves to Finland to help direct, with Alexander Bogdanov, Bolshevik activity within Russia. Anticipating imminent revolutionary resurgence, Lenin supports forms of urban guerrilla warfare (including bank robberies), overseen by Bogdanov and Leonid Krasin.

1907: Failure of revolutionary resurgence to materialize. Tsarist regime strengthens authoritarian policies, backing away from reformist promises made under earlier revolutionary pressures. Demoralization and division among revolutionaries—some abandon political activity altogether, while many (tagged "Liquidators") among Mensheviks adapt by ending underground activity in favor of functioning legally within the limited space allowed by the regime. Lenin insists on a separation of the RSDLP from the Liquidators. Lenin also breaks from those Bolsheviks (headed by Bogdanov) who reject electoral, trade union, and social reform efforts, because they anticipate imminent renewal of revolutionary armed struggle. Rosa Luxemburg, Lenin, and Martov collaborate closely to craft a revolutionary anti-war resolution adopted by the Socialist International.

1908: Lenin and Krupskaya move to Geneva. Sharp struggle opens in Bolshevik faction regarding the appropriate tactical orientation; Lenin is accused of veering toward Menshevism and abandoning essential principles of Bolshevism. Perceiving a link between Bogdanov's "Ultra-Left" tactics and his philosophical innovations, Lenin develops a detailed and polemical philosophical critique.

1909: Lenin and Krupskaya move to Paris. Publication of Lenin's philosophical polemic *Materialism and Empiriocriticism*. Lenin intensifies struggle against the Liquidators in the RSDLP (who are shielded by Mensheviks around Martov), also sharpening his struggle within the Bolshevik faction against Bogdanov's perspectives. Majority in the Bolshevik faction embrace Lenin's orientation, with a formal split from "Ultra Lefts" around Bogdanov.

1910: Amid fierce factional struggle on two fronts against Liquidators and "Ultra Lefts," Lenin actively pursues Bolshevik merger with "party Mensheviks" associated with Plekhanov, to form a cohesive and effective "party core" of the RSDLP.

1911: Leninist-Bolsheviks initiate a school for working-class activists in Longjumeau near Paris. Efforts intensify for an RSDLP congress around the "core" of Plekhanov's "party Mensheviks" and Leninist-Bolsheviks. Such efforts are sharply denounced by Martov, Trotsky, Luxemburg, and a diverse collection of others.

1912–14: Lenin and his comrades organize what they project as an authoritative RSDLP congress in Prague, passing resolutions and establishing structures designed to make the party an effective force. With refusal of non-Bolsheviks (except for a couple of "party Mensheviks" *without* Plekhanov's support) to participate, this amounts to creation of an independent Bolshevik party. Renewed working-class radicalization and upsurge begins in Russia, sparked by massacre of striking workers by government forces in the Lena goldfields. Lenin and Krupskaya move to Poland to be closer to Russian events. The Bolshevik version of RSDLP—despite competition from the Mensheviks and others—proves most effective in connecting with radical upsurge.

1914: Outbreak of First World War compels Lenin and Krupskaya to move to neutralist Switzerland. Lenin calls for *turning the imperialist war into a civil war* (social revolution). He begins deeper study of philosophy—especially Hegel on dialectics—in his *Philosophical Notebooks.*

1915: Lenin participates in Zimmerwald conference of anti-war socialists. He collaborates with Zinoviev to write *Socialism and War.* Lenin produces a series of articles and polemics emphasizing the relationship of democratic demands and "the national question" to socialist revolution—for example, *The Revolutionary Proletariat and the Right of Nations to Self-Determination.*

1916: Lenin participates in Kienthal conference of anti-war socialists. Writes *Imperialism, the Highest Stage of Capitalism: A Popular Outline.* Learns of his mother's death (age 81).

1917: **Lenin amid revolutionary upheaval—2**

Protests of women workers on International Women's Day (March 8, or February 23 according to Russia's old calendar) escalate into mass working-class insurgency. This is joined by much of the army (largely peasants in uniform). Tsar's abdication results in two power centers claiming to favor democracy: (1) pro-capitalist Provisional Government of traditional politicians; (2) pro-socialist workers' and soldiers' councils (soviets) of those who actually overthrew the tsar. Soviets favor an end to the war, land to the peasants, bread for the laboring masses, but under moderate socialist leadership are initially supportive of the Provisional Government. Provisional Government seeks to continue Russian involvement in the First World War and hesitates to initiate land reform.

Lenin calls for a revolutionary reorientation—through *Letters from Afar*, *Letters on Tactics*, *April Theses* and other writings. Upon his return to Russia, this finds expression in what became key Bolshevik slogans: Peace, bread, land! Down with the Provisional Government! All power to the soviets! Amid ups and downs of revolutionary ferment in 1917, Lenin pens *The State and Revolution*. Many revolutionaries flock to the Bolshevik banner (the most famous being Leon Trotsky), and a broad-based insurgency establishes the democratic power of the soviets, placing Lenin and the Bolsheviks in the leadership of Soviet Russia.

1918: Treaty of Brest-Litovsk

Involved a controversial compromise with German military as price for ending Russian participation in First World War, resulting in Left Socialist Revolutionary Party violently breaking off its alliance with the Bolsheviks.

1918–21: Lenin amid civil war

Renamed "Russian Communist Party," Bolsheviks face mounting calamities: foreign invasions, a complex and brutalizing civil war, multiple assassinations and assassination attempts (Lenin himself is badly wounded), and efforts from opponents from both Right and Left to destabilize the new regime. Increasingly authoritarian measures, dictatorship by the Communist Party, and initiation of a "Red Terror" are employed to ensure survival.

Crises generated by First World War combine with hostility and flight of Russia's capitalist class, plus foreign economic boycott and blockade. Revolutionary Russia's economy collapses. Highly centralized and repressive economic policies—dubbed "war communism"—are implemented, contributing to an already swelling governmental bureaucratic apparatus.

1919: Lenin and Russian comrades, combined with supporters and revolutionaries of other lands, create a Communist International (also known as the Comintern or Third International), designed to help organize Communist parties and revolutionary struggles in all countries, holding four congresses during Lenin's lifetime (1919, 1920, 1921, 1922), absorbing much of his energy and attention.

1920: Concerned with pushing back "Ultra-Left" tendencies within the Communist International, Lenin writes *Left-Wing Communism, an Infantile Disorder*, pressing for greater tactical flexibility. He also increasingly seeks to control and push back bureaucracy.

1921: Kronstadt rebellion, in larger context of peasant uprisings and workers' strikes against policies of "war communism." The New

Economic Policy implemented (1921–28), ending "war communism" and inaugurating greater openness and market mechanisms, bringing economic relief and revitalization. In wake of fierce controversies, factions banned (presumably temporarily) in Communist Party. One-party dictatorship consolidates.

1922–23: Between incapacitating strokes, Lenin composes a multi-layered final testament: "Our Revolution" (responding to socialist criticisms); a letter to upcoming Congress of the Russian Communist Party on issues of party leadership; "On Cooperation"; "How We Should Reorganize the Peasants' and Workers' Inspection"; and "Better Fewer, But Better."

1924: Final stroke in January. Lenin dies (age 54).

Biographical Notes

Abramovitch, Raphael (1880–1963): a Menshevik leader in the Russian Social Democratic Labor Party

Alexander II (1818–1881): as tsar, promoted liberal reforms, ended serfdom; assassinated by revolutionaries

Alexander III (1845–1894): as tsar, promoted conservative reaction, undoing many reforms of his father

Alexinsky, Gregor (1879–1967): prominent Bolshevik, aligned with Bogdanov against Lenin; broke with revolutionary movement during the First World War; attacked opponents of the war as being paid German agents

Armand, Inessa (1874–1920): French-Russian revolutionary activist, prominent among Bolsheviks, close to Lenin

Axelrod, Pavel (1850–1928): pioneering Russian Marxist, close to George Plekhanov, prominent in Menshevik faction of Russian Social Democratic Labor Party

Bakaiev, Ivan (1887–1936): active in 1905 Revolution, 1917 Revolutions and Russian civil war; Bolshevik since 1906, associated with Zinoviev in opposition to Stalin

Bakunin, Mikhail (1814–1876): Russian revolutionary anarchist, socialist and founder of collectivist anarchism, influenced by Pierre-Joseph Proudhon and Karl Marx; became a rival and opponent of Marx in later years

Balabanoff, Angelica (1875–1965): Russian-Italian revolutionary activist, secretary of the Communist International from 1919 to 1920; broke with Communism, becoming a socialist leader in Italy

Beatty, Bessie (1886–1947): U.S. journalist, part of a reporting team covering the Russian Revolution, including John Reed, Louise Bryant, and Albert Rhys Williams

Berkman, Alexander (1870–1936): prominent Russian-American anarchist and author

Bogdanov, Alexander (1873–1928): physician, economist, philosopher, science fiction writer, cultural activist; with Lenin leader of the Bolshevik faction from 1904 to 1907; represented an orientation from which Lenin broke; led and lost sharp conflict (1907–10) in Bolshevik faction

Bonch-Bruevich, Vladimir D. (1873–1955): one of the earliest Bolsheviks, cultural scholar, organizer and administrator, worked closely with Lenin; in later years served as a museum director

Brusnev, M.I. (1864–1937): Russian revolutionary and explorer; helped form one of the first Marxist groups inside Russia in the early 1890s; arrested and exiled in Siberia; became politically inactive after 1907

Bryant, Louise (1885–1936): U.S. journalist, part of a reporting team covering the Russian Revolution, including John Reed, Albert Rhys Williams, and Bessie Beatty

Bukharin, Nikolai (1888–1938): Marxist philosopher, economist, theorist, and revolutionary activist, Bolshevik since 1907; opponent of some of Lenin's policies, he shifted to become a supporter during the period of the New Economic Policy; aligned with, then broke from Stalin; eventually purged and executed

Butler, Octavia (1947–2006): African-American author, multiple recipient of the Hugo and Nebula awards; in 1995, became first science fiction writer to receive a MacArthur Fellowship

Cannon, James P. (1890–1974): in his youth associated with the Socialist Party of America and the Industrial Workers of the World (IWW), he became a founder of the U.S. Communist movement and later of U.S. Trotskyism

Chambers, Whittaker (1901–1961): U.S. writer, editor, translator, in the Communist movement from 1925 to 1938; spied for Soviet Union; broke from Communism; conservative anti-Communist from 1940s until his death

Chayanov, Alexander V. (1888–1937): economist, sociologist, advocate of peasant-friendly policies and cooperatives, highly valued by Lenin for his expertise; repressed by Stalin regime in the late 1920s and early 1930s

Chekov, Anton (1860–1904): Russian playwright and short-story writer, considered to be among the great writers

Chernov, Victor (1873–1952): a leader of Socialist-Revolutionary Party, in the 1917 Provisional Government under Alexander Kerensky, later supported civil war against Soviet regime

Chernyshevsky, Nikolai (1828–1889): Russian revolutionary social critic, journalist, novelist, democrat, and socialist philosopher, author of radical novel *What Is to Be Done?*, imprisoned by the tsarist regime

Churchill, Winston (1874–1965): helped lead two world wars and coordination of foreign invasions of Soviet Russia, defending interests of the British Empire; Prime Minister 1940–45, 1951–55

Clemenceau, Georges (1841–1929): served as Prime Minister of France from 1906 to 1909 and again from 1917 until 1920, helped orchestrate hostile efforts against Soviet Russia

Dallin, David (1889–1962): prominent Menshevik in the Russian Social Democratic Labor Party

Dan, Theodore (1871–1947): a Menshevik leader in the Russian Social Democratic Labor Party

Davis, Jefferson (1808–1889): led breakaway from the United States and a Civil War in defense of slavery

Debs, Eugene V. (1855–1926): radical trade unionist, leader of the 1894 Pullman Strike, and immensely popular representative of the Socialist Party of America

Denikin, Anton (1872–1947): Lieutenant General in the Imperial Russian Army, later served as a commander of counter-revolutionary military forces during the Russian civil war

Drobnis, Y.N. (1890–1937): working-class activist in revolutionary movement since 1905, participated in 1917 Revolution and civil war; involved with a succession of Left opposition groups; arrested, broken, and shot

Duranty, Walter (1884–1957): U.S. journalist, correspondent to U.S.S.R. for *New York Times*, sympathetic to Stalin

Durnovo, Pyotr (1845–1915): Russian noble, frequently in government. Known in the era of the Russian Revolution of 1905 as "the counter-revolution's butcher." Warned against dangers of entering the First World War

Dzerzhinsky, Felix (1877–1926): a leading Polish revolutionary socialist close to Rosa Luxemburg, spent many years in tsarist prisons, joined Bolsheviks in 1917, became head of Cheka

Eastman, Max (1883–1969): U.S. socialist writer, editor, translator; sympathetic to Bolshevik Revolution, spent time in early Soviet Republic; disillusioned in the late 1930s, became conservative anti-Communist from 1940s to 1960s

Engels, Frederick (1820–1895): with Karl Marx, founder of "scientific socialism" or Marxism

Francis, David (1850–1927): Missouri businessman and politician, served as U.S. Ambassador to Russia in 1916–17, hostile to revolutionaries

Gandhi, Mohandas (1869–1948): Indian revolutionary, pioneered techniques of non-violent resistance

Gapon, Father Georgi (1870–1906): Russian Orthodox Priest, popular working-class leader leading up to 1905 upsurge; killed by members of

Socialist-Revolutionary Party in 1906 when it was discovered he had ties with the tsarist secret police

Gogol, Nikolai (1809–1852): Russian novelist, short-story writer and playwright of Ukrainian origin, one of the great writers

Goldman, Emma (1869–1940): prominent Russian-American anarchist and author

Gorky, Maxim (1868–1936): novelist, short-story writer, playwright, essayist, close to Bolsheviks up to 1917

Gusev, S.I. (1874–1933): early Bolshevik activist and organizer

Haywood, William D. (1869–1928): popularly known as "Big Bill" Haywood, a central leader of the Industrial Workers of the World (IWW)

Hegel, Georg Wilhelm Friedrich (1870–1831): influential German philosopher, elaborated dialectical perspectives

Heym, Stefan (1913–2001): left-wing German novelist

Hilferding, Rudolf (1877–1941): Austrian-born Marxist economist, socialist theorist, politician and theoretician in Social Democratic Party of Germany; his study *Finance Capital* traced realities of imperialism

Ho Chi Minh (1890–1969): Vietnamese revolutionary, participated in founding of Communist International; became leader of Vietnamese liberation struggle; served as Prime Minister and then President of North Vietnam

Hobson, John A. (1858–1940): liberal English economist, best known for his writing on imperialism

Hughes, Langston (1901–1967): African-American poet, associated with Harlem Renaissance

James, C.L.R. (1901–1989): Marxist activist in Trinidad, Britain, and the United States; tireless political activist; especially known for 1937 work *World Revolution* and 1938 study on the Haitian Revolution, *The Black Jacobins*

Joffe, Adolph (1883–1927): active Russian revolutionary since 1900, joined Russian Social Democratic Labor Party in 1903, close to Leon Trotsky, became prominent Bolshevik in 1917, served as diplomat in early Soviet regime

Jogiches, Leo (1867–1919): a leading Polish revolutionary socialist close to Rosa Luxemburg

Kaganovitch, Lazar (1893–1991): working-class activist, joined Bolsheviks in 1911, involved in 1917 Revolution and civil war, aligned with Stalin beginning in 1920s

Kamenev, Lev (1883–1936): early Bolshevik, close associate of Lenin, initially aligned with Stalin against Trotsky, then in United Opposition against Stalin; perished in purges

Kautsky, Karl (1854–1938): revolutionary interpreter of Marxism, prominent theorist in German Social Democratic Party and Socialist International, shifted away from revolutionary orientation beginning in 1910

Kerensky, Alexander (1881–1970): lawyer, moderate socialist, became head of Provisional Government in 1917

Kolchak, Alexander (1874–1920): admiral in Imperial Russian Navy, later served as a commander of counter-revolutionary military forces during the Russian civil war

Kollontai, Alexandra (1872–1952): Marxist theorist focused on women's rights; Menshevik, became a Bolshevik in 1915; Commissar of Welfare in Soviet regime; supported Workers' Opposition; became a Soviet diplomat

Kondratiev, Nikolai (1892–1938): Socialist-Revolutionary; economic theorist, served as non-Bolshevik expert in early Soviet regime; repressed as the Stalin regime consolidated its policies in the late 1920s

Kornilov, Lavr (1870–1918): reactionary general, appointed head of the army by Provisional Government President Kerensky, sought to crush Soviets

Krasin, Leonid (1870–1926): engineer, early Bolshevik leader, aligned with Bogdanov; rejoined Bolsheviks in 1918, became an important diplomat for the Soviet regime

Kremer, Arkadi (1865–1935): active in Russian Marxist movement since late 1880s; a foundational figure in Jewish Labor Bund

Krestinski, Nikolai (1883–1938): early Bolshevik; was party secretary between 1919 and 1921, economic administrator, and diplomat; eventually targeted for purge, arrest, execution

Kropotkin, Peter (1842–1921): an aristocrat who became a revolutionary advocate of anarcho-communism, as well as an historian, scientist, and philosopher

Krupskaya, Nadezhda K. (1869–1939): teacher and Marxist activist beginning in the 1890s, a founding member and first general secretary of Bolshevism, author of *Reminiscences of Lenin*

Kuibyshev, Valarian (1888–1935): joined Bolsheviks in 1904; cycles of organizing, arrests, escapes culminated in the Soviet Revolution of 1917, Red Army service in the civil war, and various government assignments

Levine, Isaac Don (1892–1981): U.S. journalist, specialist on the Soviet Union, prominent anti-Communist

Liberman, Simon (1882–1946): Menshevik; economic expert to Soviet regime, close to Lenin; left U.S.S.R. in 1926

Lincoln, Abraham (1809–1865): 16th President of the United States, during American Civil War

Lloyd George, David (1863–1945): Liberal British politician, Prime Minister 1916–22

Lukács, Georg (1885–1971): Marxist theorist who developed important studies of Marx, Hegel, Lenin, literature and culture; a leader of the Hungarian Communist Party in 1919 but politically marginalized in the late 1920s

Lunacharsky, Anatoly (1875–1933): Marxist scholar, critic, journalist; joined Bolsheviks in 1904; aligned with Bogdanov against Lenin; supported Bolsheviks in 1917; director of Commissariat of Enlightenment (Education)

Lutovinov, Yury (1887–1924): joined Bolsheviks in 1904, prominent working-class activist in the metalworkers' union; held important positions in early Soviet government; associated with the Workers' Opposition

Luxemburg, Rosa (1871–1919): Polish revolutionary Marxist active in the left wing of the German Social Democratic Party; outstanding theorist on mass strike, imperialism, and more; supported Russian Revolution with criticisms; a founder of German Communist Party shortly before her death in an abortive uprising

Malinovsky, Roman (1876–1918): became a leading worker-Bolshevik in 1912, but was in the pay of the tsarist secret police; caught and executed after the Russian Revolution

Marchlewski, Julian (1866–1925): a leading Polish revolutionary socialist close to Rosa Luxemburg, active in 1905 upsurge, joined Bolsheviks in 1906

Martov, Julius (1873–1923): a Menshevik leader in the Russian Social Democratic Labor Party

Marx, Karl (1818–1883): with Frederick Engels, founder of "scientific socialism" or Marxism

Mayakovsky, Vladimir (1893–1930): futurist poet, leading figure in Soviet artistic avant-garde

Meyerhold, Vselovod (1874–1940): theater producer, director, prominent in Soviet artistic avant-garde of 1920s; repressed by Stalin regime

Miliukov, Pavel (1859–1943): Russian historian, a leader of the liberal Constitutional Democratic Party, prominent figure in Provisional Government of 1917

Mussolini, Benito (1883–1945): ex-socialist founder and leader of Italian fascism, ruled Italy from 1922 to 1943

Nevsky, Vladimir (1876–1937): revolutionary activist since 1897, joined the Russian Social Democratic Labor Party in 1898 and Bolsheviks in 1904, active in 1917 Revolution; became prominent Soviet scholar and historian; repressed by Stalin regime

Nicholas II (1868–1918): as tsar preserved his father's policies of conservative reaction; the last tsar

Nicolaevsky, Boris I. (1887–1966): Bolshevik-turned-Menshevik, active in revolutionary movement since 1901; became prominent archivist and researcher

Owen, Robert (1777–1858): British manufacturer, reformer, utopian socialist

Paine, Tom (1737–1809): British-born radical democrat, active in the American and French Revolutions, author of numerous revolutionary pamphlets

Piatakov, Georgy (1890–1937): joined the Russian Social Democratic Labor Party in 1910 and Bolsheviks in 1912; prominent figure in the early Soviet regime; oppositional views made him a target for repression and execution by Stalin regime

Piatnitsky, Osip (1882–1938): joined the Russian Social Democratic Labor Party in 1899, *Iskra* group in 1901, Bolshevik faction in 1903; activist through 1917; key figure in Communist International in the 1920s and early 1930s; repressed, executed by Stalin regime

Pisarev, Dmitry (1840–1868): radical democratic Russian literary critic and philosopher

Plekhanov, George (1856–1918): philosopher and social critic known as the "father of Russian Marxism," initiator of the Emancipation of Labor Group, associated with the Menshevik faction of the Russian Social Democratic Labor Party

Pokrovsky, Mikhail (1868–1932): prominent Marxist historian, became a Bolshevik in 1905, with Bogdanov, rejoined the Bolsheviks in 1917, worked with Lunacharsky in Commissariat of Enlightenment

Potresov, Alexander (1869–1934): early member of the Russian Social Democratic Labor Party, aligned with Lenin and Martov; became Menshevik

Preobrazhensky, Eugen (1886–1937): active Bolshevik in the early 1900s, prominent in the organization in years leading to 1917 Revolutions; important economist and theorist; opposed policies of Stalin regime; repressed, shot

Pushkin, Alexander (1799–1837): Russian poet, playwright, novelist, considered to be among the great writers

Radek, Karl (1885–1939): active in Polish and German socialist movements, with the Russian Revolution became a prominent figure in the Communist International; opposed, capitulated to, purged by Stalin

Reed, John (1887–1920): U.S. journalist, part of a reporting team covering the Russian Revolution, including Louise Bryant, Albert Rhys Williams, and Bessie Beatty

Rodchenko, Alexander (1891–1956): artist, photographer, prominent in Soviet artistic avant-garde of 1920s

Rodney, Walter (1942–1980): Guyanese historian, academic, martyred Pan-African and Marxist activist

Roosevelt, Franklin D. (1882–1945): 32nd President of the United States, during the Second World War

Rosmer, Alfred (1877–1964): French revolutionary syndicalist, joined the Communist movement in 1917, helped build the French Communist Party and the Communist International; expelled around the Stalin-Trotsky conflict

Ross, E.A. (1866–1951): U.S. sociologist whose visits to Soviet Russia resulted in three very substantial and informative studies of the revolution from 1918 to 1923

Roy, M.N. (1887–1954): a founder and leader of the Indian Communist Party and prominent member of the early Communist International, pushed out with the consolidation of Stalin's regime

Russell, Bertrand (1872–1970): British philosopher, socialist, and pacifist; early critic of the Soviet regime

Rykov, Alexei (1881–1938): activist and organizer among the original Bolsheviks; influential figure in early Soviet regime; with Bukharin he was aligned with Stalin in mid-1920s, then in opposition; finally purged and shot

Ryutin, Martemyan N. (1890–1937): joined Bolsheviks in 1914, participated in 1917 Revolutions and Russian civil war; at first supported Stalin against oppositionists, then sharply denounced the policies of Stalin regime; repressed

Saint-Simon, Claude-Henri (1760–1825): influential French social, economic, and political theorist; utopian socialist

Savinkov, Boris (1879–1925): Socialist-Revolutionary involved in terrorist activities; in Provisional Government associated with Kerensky and Kornilov, engaged in conspiracies and in armed struggle against early Bolshevik regime

Schwarz, Solomon (1883–1973): socialist and trade union activist, Bolshevik-turned-Menshevik

Sedova, Natalia (1882–1962): revolutionary activist beginning in the early 1900s, and Trotsky's life partner from 1903 to 1940

Serebriakov, Leonid (1890–1937): joined Bolsheviks in 1905; active in 1917 Revolution; on Secretariat of Central Committee of the Communist Party; various other assignments; opposed policies of Stalin regime; repressed, shot

Serge, Victor (1890–1947): former anarchist, joined Bolsheviks in 1917; centrally involved in early Communist International; oppositionist to rise of Stalin regime; writer, poet, essayist, survivor, witness

Shahumian, Stepan (1878–1918): Bolshevik since 1903; leader of revolutionary struggles in Baku, martyred amid civil war and foreign intervention

Shlyapnikov, Alexander (1885–1937): leading Bolshevik trade union militant; aligned with Lenin in 1917 Revolution; Commissar of Labor until he organized Workers' Opposition; later repressed by Stalin regime, shot

Smilga, Ivar (1892–1938): joined the Russian Social Democratic Labor Party at age 14, in wake of 1905 upsurge; a leading Petrograd Bolshevik by 1914; active in 1917 Revolution and civil war; governmental responsibilities; opposed Stalin; repressed, shot

Smirnov, I. N. (1881–1936): engaged in patient labor and socialist organizing year after year; in the wake of 1917, played heroic role in the civil war; in 1920s helped manage the economy; opposed Stalin's policies; repressed, shot

Sokolnikov, Grigory (1888–1939): Bolshevik since 1905, active in Bolshevik Revolution of 1917, and in Red Army during civil war; Commissar of Finance before victimization by Stalin regime

Souvarine, Boris (1895–1984): a founder of the French Communist Party and prominent activist in the early Communist International, pushed out of the Communist movement in 1924 for resistance to Stalin's influence

Spiridonova, Maria (1884–1941): prominent in Left Socialist-Revolutionary Party; favored coalition regime with Communists, but soon broke with and went into opposition against the Soviet regime

Stalin, Joseph (1878–1953): Bolshevik activist in the early 1900s, rising into the leadership by 1912; became General Secretary of Russian Communist Party in 1922, consolidated his control of the Soviet government in the late 1920s

Steinberg, Isaac (1883–1957): prominent in Left Socialist-Revolutionary Party; Minister of Justice in coalition regime of Communists and Left Socialist-Revolutionaries, but soon broke with and went into opposition against the Soviet regime

Stepanova, Varvara (1894–1958): artist, designer, prominent in Soviet artistic avant-garde of 1920s

Strong, Anna Louise (1885–1970): U.S. journalist and radical activist who lived and worked in Soviet Russia from the early 1920s to 1949

Sukhanov, N.N. (1882–1940): Menshevik author of influential work on the Russian Revolution; served as an economic expert to Soviet regime in 1920s; repressed as the Stalin regime consolidated its policies in the late 1920s

Sverdlov, Jacob (1885–1919): active in the Bolshevik organization from the beginning, by 1917 he was playing a central role as part of a four-person bureau of the Central Committee: Lenin, Trotsky, Sverdlov, and Stalin

Tasca, Angelo (1892–1960): a founder of the Italian Communist Party; returned to Socialist Party in 1929; lived in exile in France, in 1940s collaborated with the Vichy regime, secretly assisting a Belgian anti-fascist network; Cold War anti-Communist

Terracini, Umberto (1895–1983): a leader of the Italian Communist Party

Tolstoy, Leo (1828–1910): Russian novelist, essayist, short-story writer, considered to be among the great writers

Tomsky, Mikhail (1880–1936): joined the Russian Social Democratic Labor Party in 1904, became a Bolshevik trade union activist; became head of Soviet trade unions in 1922; committed suicide in face of arrest by Stalin regime

Tristan, Flora (1803–1844): French-Peruvian socialist and feminist writer, radical activist

Trotsky, Leon (1879–1940): revolutionary leader, Marxist theorist, joined Bolsheviks in 1917, helped plan October insurrection, organized and led Red Army, helped lead opposition to Stalin regime

Truman, Harry (1884–1972): 33rd President of the United States at end of the Second World War and during Korean War

Turgenev, Ivan (1818–1883): Russian novelist, short-story writer, poet; considered to be among the great writers

Ulyanov, Alexander (1866–1887): Lenin's older brother; executed for participating in a revolutionary group that conspired to assassinate the tsar

Ulyanov, Anna (1864–1935): Lenin's older sister

Ulyanov, Dmitri (1874–1843): Lenin's youngest brother

Ulyanov, Ilya Nikolaevich (1831–1886): Lenin's father

Ulyanov, Maria Alexandrovna Blank (1835–1916): Lenin's mother

Ulyanov, Maria (1878–1937): Lenin's youngest sister

Ulyanov, Olga (1871–1891): Lenin's younger sister

Ulyanov, Vladimir Ilyich (1870–1924): Lenin

Uritsky, Moishei (1873–1918): Menshevik in 1903, joined Bolsheviks in 1917, active in 1917 Revolution, then became head of the Petrograd Cheka. His assassination helped unleash the Red Terror

Vanzetti, Bartolomeo (1888–1927): iconic Italian-American anarchist; executed, along with his comrade Nicolo Sacco, after years of imprisonment, based on what many believed a phony murder charge and an unfair trial

Volsky-Valentinov, Nikolai (1880–1964): Bolshevik, then Menshevik; economic expert to Soviet regime; left U.S.S.R. in 1928

Voronsky, Alexander (1884–1937): Bolshevik activist since 1904; literary critic, editor; in consultation with Lenin and Gorky, launched influential journal *Red Virgin Soil*; close to Lunacharsky and Trotsky; repressed by Stalin

Washington, George (1732–1799): commander of Continental Army during American Revolution, 1st President of the United States

Weinstone, William (1897–1985): U.S. Marxist scholar, editor, labor activist, prominent Communist Party member from 1919 until his death

Williams, Albert Rhys (1883–1962): U.S. journalist, part of a reporting team covering the Russian Revolution, including John Reed, Louise Bryant, and Bessie Beatty

Wilson, Woodrow (1856–1924): 28th President of the United States, during the First World War

Zasulich, Vera (1849–1919): pioneering Russian Marxist, close to George Plekhanov, prominent in Menshevik faction of the Russian Social Democratic Labor Party

Zetkin, Clara (1857–1933): active leader of women's movement in German Social Democratic Party, close to Rosa Luxemburg, became a leader of the German Communist Party

Zinoviev, Gregory (1883–1936): close associate of Lenin, first leader of the Communist International, initially aligned with Stalin against Trotsky, then in United Opposition against Stalin; perished in purges

Notes

See Bibliography for full reference details.

PROLOGUE: WHAT'S THE POINT

1. Le Blanc, "Conclusions on Coherence and Comradeship," in *Revolutionary Collective*, 188–204; Le Blanc, *Left Americana*, 161–76.
2. See Halstead, *Out Now!*
3. Le Blanc, *Left Americana*, 213–15, 230–2. This involved the formerly Trotskyist Socialist Workers' Party in the United States. Similar afflictions could be found among U.S. Maoists who, according to Max Elbaum, succumbed to "a miniaturized Leninism" in which "sixty-year-old polemics written as guidelines for a party of thousands to interact with a movement of millions were interpreted through the prism of how organizations of hundreds (or even dozens) should interact with movements of thousands (or less)." The result—"mechanical formulas and organizational narrow-mindedness" (*Left Americana*, 193).
4. Rahv, *Essays on Literature and Politics, 1932–1972*, 353.
5. Possony, *Lenin, The Compulsive Revolutionary*, 392.
6. Luxemburg, *Letters*, 290; Abramovitch quoted in Levine, *The Man Lenin*, 34.
7. Balabanoff, *Impressions of Lenin*, 149.
8. Churchill on Lenin quoted in Ali, *The Dilemmas of Lenin*, 70; Churchill on Mussolini quoted in Seymour, "The Real Winston Churchill"; Eastman, *Marx, Lenin and the Science of Revolution*, 150, 151.
9. Levine, *The Man Lenin*, 192. The careful scholar Georges Haupt notes: "His rigor was not rigidity but the evaluation of every possible variation on the possible in order to be prepared for any eventuality" (Haupt, "War and Revolution in Lenin," in *Aspects of International Socialism 1871–1914*, 151).
10. Frankfurter and Jackson, eds, *The Letters of Sacco and Vanzetti*, 116–17.
11. Ho Chi Minh, *Ho Chi Minh on Revolution*, 40.
12. Hughes, "Lenin," in Faith Berry, ed., *Good Morning Revolution*, 94.
13. Medhurst, *No Less Than Mystic*, 35.

14. Read, *Lenin*, 261; Radek in Richardson, *In Defence of the Russian Revolution*, 76.
15. Molotov, *Molotov Remembers*, 133; Stalin, *The Essential Stalin*, 155.
16. Kamenev, "The Literary Legacy and Collected Works of Illyitch"; Lenin, "Letters on Tactics," *Collected Works*, Vol. 24, 43.
17. Suny, *Stalin*, 659–60.
18. Souvarine, *Stalin*, 121–2; Rodney, *Decolonial Marxism*, 40.
19. Lenin, "Our Revolution," *Collected Works*, Vol. 33, 477.
20. Fischer, *The Life of Lenin*, 479.
21. John Riddell, note to author, 7 March 2022.
22. Blanc, *Revolutionary Social Democracy*, 42, 43.
23. Gorky, *Mother*, 136, 345; Lenin and Gorky, *Lenin and Gorky*, 332, 329.
24. Kropotkin, *The Conquest of Bread*, 25, 26, 23, 28.
25. Lenin, "The State and Revolution," *Collected Works*, Vol. 25, 465, 467.
26. Bonch-Bruevich, "Meeting with Kropotkin," in Tamara Deutscher, ed., *Not By Politics Alone*, 76, 77; Avrich, *The Russian Anarchists*, 227. Post-Soviet dissident Ilya Budraitskis observes "Lenin's 'dictatorship of the proletariat' is a dictatorship to end all dictatorships," grounded in the notion that "the masses," needing no condescending saviors, can shape their own destiny (Budraitskis, *Dissidents among Dissidents*, 98).
27. Malm, *Corona, Climate, Chronic Emergency*, 148; Camfield, *Future on Fire*, 59–60; Angus, *Facing the Anthropocene*, 214; Heron and Dean, "Climate Leninism and Revolutionary Transition"; Butler, *Parable of the Sower*, 357.
28. Butler, *Parable of the Sower*, 47, 137; Butler, *Parable of the Talents*, 68.

1. WHO WAS LENIN?

1. Deutscher, *Lenin's Childhood*, 24.
2. Turton, *Forgotten Lives*, 10, 17.
3. Pomper, *Lenin's Brother*, 207.
4. Turton, *Forgotten Lives*, 15, 14; Valentinov, *The Early Years of Lenin*, 121.
5. Deutscher, *Lenin's Childhood*, 44; Suny, *Stalin*, 414.
6. Zinoviev, *History of the Bolshevik Party*, 17.
7. Pomper, *Lenin's Brother*, 44; Deutscher, *Lenin's Childhood*, 58.
8. Turton, *Forgotten Lives*, 27.
9. Ibid., 26.
10. Ibid., 28.
11. Harding, ed. *Marxism in Russia*, 69, 70, 71.

12. Bukharin, *Lenin as a Marxist*, 17–18, 23 reproduced in Richardson, ed., *In Defence of the Russian Revolution*, 255, 258.
13. Lenin, "Letters on Tactics," *Collected Works*, Vol. 24, 43.
14. Lukács, *Lenin*, 11–12.
15. Ulyanova-Yelizarova et al., *Reminiscences of Lenin by His Relatives*, 44.
16. Lenin, "The Urgent Tasks of Our Movement," *Collected Works*, Vol. 4, 371–2.
17. Marik, *Revolutionary Democracy*, 289.
18. Krupskaya, *Reminiscences of Lenin*, 12, 13, 15.
19. Ibid., 18–20.
20. Valentinov, *Encounters with Lenin*, 142.
21. Heym, *Radek, a Novel*, 68, 126.
22. McNeal, *Bride of the Revolution*, 67–8.
23. Valentinov, *Encounters with Lenin*, 60, 141.
24. Trotsky, *My Life*, 152.
25. Levine, *The Man Lenin*, 160, 162; Elwood, *The Non-Geometric Lenin*, 166.
26. McDermid and Hillyer,"In Lenin's Shadow," 155.
27. Lunacharsky, *Revolutionary Silhouettes*, 41, 44; Trotsky, *On Lenin*, 166–7.
28. Rabinowitch, Rabinowitch with Kristof, eds, *Revolution and Politics in Russia*, 29.
29. Pokrovsky, *Revolutionary Silhouettes*, 195, 197.
30. Williams, *Lenin—the Man and His Work*, 45–6; Williams, *Journey into Revolution*, 51, 62.
31. Tucker, *Stalin as Revolutionary 1879–1929*, 51, 53–4.

2. THEORY, ORGANIZATION, ACTION (1901–05)

1. Lenin, *What Is to Be Done? Collected Works*, Vol. 5, 369.
2. Ibid., 369.
3. Ibid., 369–70.
4. Bogdanoff [Bogdanov], *A Short Course of Economic Science*, 336.
5. Scott, *Seeing Like a State*, 151.
6. Suny, *Stalin*, 137.
7. Bogdanoff [Bogdanov], *A Short Course of Economic Science*, 341–2.
8. Molyneux, *Marxism and the Party*, 164–5.
9. Zinoviev, *History of the Bolshevik Party*, 34.
10. Suny, *Stalin*, 102.
11. Alliluev quoted in Suny, *Stalin*, 103.
12. Harding, ed., *Marxism in Russia*, 192, 202.

13. Ibid., 194, 200.
14. Ibid., 205.
15. Lenin, *What Is to Be Done? Collected Works*, Vol. 5, 472.
16. Ibid., 472.
17. Ibid., 473.
18. Ibid., 423.
19. Ibid., 402, 423.
20. Dan, *The Origins of Bolshevism*, 236, 237–8.
21. Pearce, ed., *1903*, 10; Le Blanc, *Lenin and the Revolutionary Party*, 63.
22. Martov in Pearce, ed., *1903*, 311–12, 320–1.
23. Lenin in Pearce, ed., *1903*, 326–9; Lenin, *One Step Forward, Two Steps Back, Collected Works*, Vol. 7, 258.
24. Lenin, *One Step Forward, Two Steps Back, Collected Works*, Vol. 7, 344–5.
25. Piatnitsky, *Memoirs of a Bolshevik*, 59–60.
26. Krupskaya, *Reminiscences of Lenin*, 96; White, *Red Hamlet*, 103, 108.
27. Axelrod quoted in Dan, *The Origins of Bolshevism*, 297; also see Ascher, *Pavel Axelrod and the Development of Menshevism*, 218–23.
28. Lenin, "The Zemstvo Campaign and *Iskra*'s Plan," *Collected Works*, Vol. 7, 503.
29. Ibid., 514, 515.
30. Lenin, *To the Rural Poor, Collected Works*, Vol. 6, 428.
31. Schwarz, *The Russian Revolution of 1905*, 66, 69.
32. Lenin, "The St. Petersburg Strike," *Collected Works*, Vol. 8, 90, 91.
33. Schwarz, *The Russian Revolution of 1905*, 66, 69, 70.
34. Lenin, "Letter to S.I. Gusev, October 13, 1905," *Collected Works*, Vol. 34, 358–9.
35. Schwarz, *The Russian Revolution of 1905*, 181, 183; on all of this, also see Le Blanc, *Lenin and the Revolutionary Party*, 98–106.
36. Lenin, "Our Tasks and the Soviet of Workers' Deputies," *Collected Works*, Vol. 10, 19, 20, 21.

3. THE REVOLUTIONARY EXPLOSION OF 1905

1. Lenin, *What Is to be Done? Collected Works*, Vol. 5, 479.
2. Harcave, *First Blood*, 285, 286, 287.
3. Lenin, "Speech on the Question of the Relations between Workers and Intellectuals within the Social-Democratic Organizations," *Collected Works*, Vol. 8, 408.
4. Krupskaya, *Reminiscences of Lenin*, 117.
5. Lenin, *Collected Works*, Vol. 10, 45.

6. Read, *Lenin*, 82; Lenin in Tucker, ed., *The Lenin Anthology*, editor's note, 148.
7. Lenin, *Collected Works*, Vol. 10, 47.
8. Voronsky, *Art as the Cognition of Life*, 144, 100, 129.
9. Krupskaya, *Reminiscences of Lenin*, 111–12.
10. Ibid., 118.
11. Lenin, "A Militant Agreement for the Uprising," *Collected Works*, Vol. 8, 163.
12. Ibid., 163.
13. Ibid., 163–4.
14. Ibid., 164.
15. Ibid., 164, 165.
16. Ibid., 165.
17. Hunt, *The Political Ideas of Marx and Engels*, Vol. 1, 295.
18. Ibid., 314.
19. Lenin, *Two Tactics of Social-Democracy in the Democratic Revolution*, *Collected Works*, Vol. 9, 52, 56, 60; Mayer, *The Persistence of the Old Order*; also see discussion in Heller, *The Birth of Capitalism*, 139–45.
20. Lenin, *Two Tactics of Social-Democracy in the Democratic Revolution*, *Collected Works*, Vol. 9, 60, 56–7.
21. Abramovitch, *The Soviet Revolution 1917–1939*, 214; Lenin, *Two Tactics of Social-Democracy in the Democratic Revolution*, *Collected Works*, Vol. 9, 48.
22. Lenin, "The Reorganization of the Party," *Collected Works*, Vol. 10, 32.
23. Lenin, *Two Tactics of Social-Democracy in the Democratic Revolution*, *Collected Works*, Vol. 9, 132.
24. Lenin, "Lessons of the Moscow Uprising," *Collected Works*, Vol. 11, 173.
25. Krupskaya, *Reminiscences of Lenin*, 113–14, translation slightly modified.
26. Lenin, "Tasks of Army Contingents," *Collected Works*, Vol. 9, 420.
27. Krupskaya, *Reminiscences of Lenin*, 142.
28. Lenin, "The Present Situation and the Tasks of the Workers' Party," *Collected Works*, Vol. 10, 114.
29. Lenin, "Lessons of the Moscow Uprising," *Collected Works*, Vol. 11, 178.
30. Lenin quoted in Suny, *Stalin*, 409–10.
31. Ibid., 651.

4. COMRADES AND COHERENCE (1905–14)

1. Suny, *Stalin*, 236, 238, 241.

2. Blanc, "Did the Bolsheviks Advocate Socialist Revolution in 1917?"; ibid., 247.
3. Peters, *The Communist Party*, 23.
4. Meyer, *Leninism*, 92, 93, 100.
5. Menshevik and Bolshevik resolutions quoted in Le Blanc, *Lenin and the Revolutionary Party*, 116.
6. Bogdanov quoted in White, *Red Hamlet*, 129; Lenin, "Report on the Unity Congress of the R.S.D.L.P.," *Collected Works*, Vol. 10, 380–1.
7. Krupskaya, *Reminiscences of Lenin*, 89.
8. Read, *Lenin*, 67.
9. Lenin, "A Tactical Platform for the Unity Congress of the R.S.D.L.P.," *Collected Works*, Vol. 10, 152.
10. Krupskaya, *Reminiscences of Lenin*, 167.
11. Pokrovsky, *Russia in World History*, 190.
12. Bogdanov quoted in Le Blanc, *Revolutionary Collective*, 63.
13. Krupskaya, *Reminiscences of Lenin*, 193.
14. Zinoviev, *History of the Bolshevik Party*, 153–4.
15. Lenin, "Notes of a Publicist (1910)," *Collected Works*, Vol. 16, 212.
16. Ibid., 214.
17. Bogdanov quoted in White, *Red Hamlet*, 300, 302, 337.
18. Piatnitsky, *Memoirs of a Bolshevik*, 165.
19. Krupskaya, *Reminiscences of Lenin*, 229–30, 231.
20. Elwood, *The Non-Geometric Lenin*, 35.
21. Broué, *Memoirs of a Bolshevik*, 61 quoted in Le Blanc, *Lenin and the Revolutionary Party*, 183.
22. Lenin, "Report of the C.C. of the R.S.D.L.P. to the Brussels Conference and Instructions to the C.C. Delegation," *Collected Works*, Vol. 20, 500.
23. Ibid., 500–1.
24. Ibid., 501.
25. Dan quoted in Le Blanc, *Lenin and the Revolutionary Party*, 167.
26. Melancon, *The Lena Goldfields Massacre*, 3, 103; Haimson, "The Russian Workers Movement on the Eve of the First World War" quoted in Le Blanc, *Lenin and the Revolutionary Party*, 179.
27. Haimson, "The Russian Workers Movement on the Eve of the First World War, "179.

5. ENGAGING WITH CATASTROPHE (1914–17)

1. Balabanoff, *My Life as a Rebel*, 113–14.
2. Taber, *Under the Socialist Banner*, 141, 105.
3. Shlyapnikov, *On the Eve of 1917*, 14, 17.

4. Krupskaya, *Reminiscences of Lenin*, 277, 285–6.
5. Ibid., 288.
6. Balabanoff, *Impressions of Lenin*, 36, 37.
7. Haupt, "War and Revolution in Lenin," in *Aspects of International Socialism 1871–1914*, 146; Luxemburg, "The Idea of May Day on the March," in Howard, ed., *Selected Political Writings*, 320–1.
8. Callinicos, "Lenin and Imperialism," in Rockmore and Levine, eds, *The Palgrave Handbook of Leninist Political Philosophy*, 459–60.
9. Lenin, "The Historical Destiny of the Doctrine of Karl Marx," *Collected Works*, Vol. 18, 584–5.
10. Lenin, "On the Question of Dialectics," *Collected Works*, Vol. 38, 360.
11. Lenin, "Karl Marx," *Collected Works*, Vol. 21, 54–5.
12. Serge, *From Lenin to Stalin*, 157.
13. Weeks, "Imperialism and the World Market," in Bottomore, ed. *A Dictionary of Marxist Thought*, 253.
14. Lenin, *Imperialism, the Highest Stage of Capitalism*, *Collected Works*, Vol. 22, 206–7, 226.
15. Ibid., 226, 237.
16. Ibid., 241.
17. Ibid., 243.
18. Ibid., 268–9, 253.
19. Ibid., 283.
20. Alexinsky, *Russia and the Great War*, 234.
21. Serge, *From Lenin to Stalin*, 157, 159.
22. Lenin, "Lecture on 'The Proletariat and the War,'" *Collected Works*, Vol. 36, 298–9.
23. Ibid., 299–300.
24. Lenin, "Socialism and the War," *Collected Works*, Vol. 21, 316, 317.
25. Lenin, *Two Tactics of Social-Democracy in the Democratic Revolution*, *Collected Works*, Vol. 9, 29; Krupskaya, *Reminiscences of Lenin*, 328.
26. Krupskaya, *Reminiscences of Lenin*, 328.
27. Lenin, "The Revolutionary Proletariat and the Right of Nations to Self-Determination," *Collected Works*, Vol. 21, 408–9; ibid., 328–9.
28. Marx and Engels, *Communist Manifesto*, in Marx, *The Political Writings*, ed. Fernbach, 63; Lenin, *Collected Works*, Vol. 25, 466.
29. Marx and Engels, *Communist Manifesto*, in Marx, *The Political Writings*, 60.
30. Lenin, *The State and Revolution*, *Collected Works*, Vol. 25, 468, 466, 464.
31. Ibid., 479.
32. Ibid., 479.
33. Ibid., 407.
34. Ibid., 497.

35. Kamenev in Richardson, ed., *In Defence of the Russian Revolution*, 103; also available on Marxist Internet Archive: www.marxists.org/archive/kamenev/1920/x01/x01.htm.

6. THE 1917 REVOLUTION

1. Lenin, "Lecture on the 1905 Revolution," *Collected Works*, Vol. 23, 253. There is an ambiguity here—what is meant by "the *decisive* battles of this coming revolution"? It would be possible to foresee an impending revolutionary victory in Russia but not to assume the decisive global victory will be immediately forthcoming. Thanks to John Molyneux for this thought.
2. Robert V. Daniels quoted in Le Blanc, *Lenin and the Revolutionary Party*, 215–16; Lieven, *The End of Tsarist Russia*, 303–7.
3. Krupskaya, *Reminiscences of Lenin*, 334–5; Haupt, "War and Revolution in Lenin," in *Aspects of International Socialism 1871–1914*, 149.
4. Wildman quoted in Le Blanc, *Lenin and the Revolutionary Party*, 217; Medvedev, *The October Revolution*, 42–4.
5. Chamberlin, *The Russian Revolution, 1917–1921*, Vol. 1, 73.
6. Trotsky, *History of the Russian Revolution*, Vol. I, 154, 153.
7. Anna Ulyanova and Maria Ulyanova quoted in McDermid and Hillyar, *Midwives of the Revolution*, viii.
8. Liberman, *Building Lenin's Russia*, 55.
9. Melancon, *Rethinking Russia's February Revolution*, 22.
10. Ibid., 35.
11. Levine, *The Russian Revolution*, 219–20, 223, 225.
12. Ibid., 227.
13. Ibid., 271, 278, 276; Suny, *Stalin*, 616.
14. Lenin, *Collected Works*, Vol. 24, 19–26.
15. Krupskaya, *Reminiscences of Lenin*, 348–9.
16. Blanc, "Did the Bolsheviks Advocate Socialist Revolution in 1917?"
17. Lars Lih, note to author, June 29, 2022, referring to the draft of a new essay, "The Bolshevik Adjustment in 1917."
18. Lenin quoted in Suny, *Stalin*, 609.
19. Krupskaya, *Reminiscences of Lenin*, 349.
20. Chernov, *The Great Russian Revolution*, 174.
21. Steinberg, *Spiridonova*, 174.
22. Kerensky, *Russia and History's Turning Point*, 368.
23. Ibid., 400.
24. Abramovitch, *The Soviet Revolution 1917–1939*, 63; Sukhanov, *The Russian Revolution 1917*, 505.

25. Abramovitch, *The Soviet Revolution 1917–1939*, 64; Trotsky, *The Struggle against Fascism in Germany*, 136.
26. Francis, *Russia from the American Embassy*, 193–4; Kerensky, *Russia and History's Turning Point*, 400.
27. Lenin, "Speech and Resolution on the Resignation of a Group of People's Commissars from the Council of People's Commissars," *Collected Works*, Vol. 26, 293.
28. Trotsky, *The Struggle against Fascism in Germany*, 185.
29. Reed, *Ten Days That Shook the World*, 292.
30. Lenin, "To the Population," *Collected Works*, Vol. 26, 297, 298–9.
31. Blanc, *Revolutionary Social Democracy*, 278.
32. Wade, *The Russian Revolution 1917*, 283.
33. Suny, *Stalin*, 665.
34. Baitalsky, *Notebooks for the Grandchildren*, 10.
35. Beatty, *The Red Heart of Russia*, 431.
36. Lenin quoted in ibid., 432.
37. Beatty, *The Red Heart of Russia*, 432–3.
38. Lenin quoted in ibid., 433.
39. Beatty, *The Red Heart of Russia*, 433–4.
40. Spiridonova quoted in Steinberg, *Spiridonova*, 191.

7. REVOLUTIONARY INTERNATIONALISM (1882–1922)

1. Halliday, "Three Concepts of Internationalism," 188–9.
2. Ibid., 194.
3. White, *Marx and Russia*, 1.
4. Leonhard, *Three Faces of Marxism*, 87–8.
5. Blanc, *Revolutionary Social Democracy*, 336.
6. Marx and Engels in Shanin, *Late Marx and the Russian Road*, 139.
7. Liberman, *Building Lenin's Russia*, 69, 8.
8. Ibid., 69; Lenin, *Collected Works*, Vol. 28, 75.
9. Mayer, *Wilson vs. Lenin*, 37, 38, 42, 51, 264. Mayer's quotation from Lenin's "On the Slogan of the United States Europe" (1915) can be found in Lenin, *Collected Works*, Vol. 21, 339–40.
10. Marx, *The Political Writings*, ed. David Fernbach, 766.
11. Ibid., 783, 1009.
12. Taber, *Under the Socialist Banner*, 126; Kautsky, "Revolutions, Past and Present" (online).
13. Luxemburg, "The Old Mole," in Robert Looker, ed., *Selected Political Writings*, 227.
14. Ibid., 228, 233, 234.
15. Lenin, "Letter to American Workers," *Collected Works*, Vol. 28, 74–5.

16. Haslam, *Russia's Cold War*, 2; Mayer, *Politics and Diplomacy of Peace-making*, 563.
17. Serge, *From Lenin to Stalin*, 155.
18. Ibid., 156.
19. Kautsky, *The Road to Power*, 82.
20. Traverso, *Fire and Blood*; Haslam, *The Spectre of War*; Mandel, *The Meaning of the Second World War*, 45; Westad, *The Cold War, a World History*, 5.
21. Riddell, ed., *Founding the Communist International*, 231–2.
22. Serge, *From Lenin to Stalin*, 45, 48.
23. Lenin, "Speech in Defence of the Tactics of the Communist International," *Collected Works*, Vol. 32, 470, 471, 474–5.
24. Lenin, *"Left-Wing" Communism—an Infantile Disorder*, *Collected Works*, Vol. 31, 24–5.
25. Ibid., 25. While Berkman refers to Lenin's blue eyes, others affirm they were brown.
26. Riddell, ed., *Toward the United Front*, 1158.
27. Lenin, *"Left-Wing" Communism—an Infantile Disorder*, *Collected Works*, Vol. 31, 95, 91.
28. Ibid., "Speech on the Italian Question," *Collected Works*, Vol. 32, 465, 467.
29. Rosmer, *Lenin's Moscow*, 46.
30. Gumperz and Volk quoted in Le Blanc, *October Song*, 208.
31. Lenin, "Draft Theses on National and Colonial Questions" and "To the Indian Revolutionary Association,' *Collected Works*, Vol. 31, 145–6, 138.
32. Lenin, "Report on the Tactics of the R.C.P.," *Collected Works*, Vol. 32, 479–80.
33. Lenin quoted in Lewin, *Lenin's Last Struggle*, 3–4.
34. Halliday, "Three Concepts of Internationalism," 197.

8. BESIEGED FORTRESS (1918–22)

1. Meyer, *Leninism*, 185–6.
2. Serge, *Notebooks 1936–1947*, 511; Luxemburg, *Socialism or Barbarism*, 237.
3. Kamenev, *The Dictatorship of the Proletariat*, in Richardson, *In Defence of the Russian Revolution*, 105.
4. Ibid., 106; Meyer, *Leninism*, 193.
5. Read, *Lenin*, 208.
6. Read, *From Tsar to Soviets*, 191.
7. Williams, *Through the Russian Revolution*, 276–7.

8. Serge, *Memoirs of a Revolutionary*, 155.
9. Lenin, "Report on the Work of the All-Russia Central Executive Committee and the Council of People's Commissars Delivered at the First Session of the All-Russia Central Executive Committee," *Collected Works*, Vol. 30, 327–8.
10. Serge, *Memoirs of a Revolutionary*, 140.
11. Spiridonova quoted in Osipova, "Peasant Rebellions," in Brovkin, ed., *The Bolsheviks in Russian Society*, 157.
12. Spiridonova quoted in Steinberg, *Spiridonova*, 235–6.
13. Burbank, *Intelligentsia and Revolution*, 19–20, 21; Getzler, *Martov*, 190.
14. Radek quoted in Le Blanc, *October Song*, 224.
15. Lenin, "Eleventh Congress of the R.C.P. (B.), Political Report of the C.C.," *Collected Works*, Vol. 33, 283.
16. Russell, *The Practice and Theory of Bolshevism*, 54.
17. Ibid., 60–1.
18. Ibid., 107.
19. Ibid., 21, 38, 10.
20. Kollontai, *Selected Writings*, 189, 192.
21. Ibid., 179, 170, 171.
22. Ibid., 199.
23. Carr, *The Bolshevik Revolution, 1917–1923*, Vol. 1, 198; Allen, *Alexander Shlyapnikov 1885–1937*, 160, 189, 183, 190.
24. Lenin, "Once Again on the Trade Unions, the Current Situation and the Mistakes of Trotsky and Bukharin," *Collected Works*, Vol. 32, 106.
25. Berkman, *The Bolshevik Myth*, 87, 90; Goldman, *Living My Life*, 764.
26. Berkman, *The Bolshevik Myth*, 319; Goldman, *My Two Years in Russia*, 198.
27. Luxemburg, *Socialism or Barbarism*, 233.
28. Ibid., 234.
29. *Rosa Luxemburg Speaks* (ed. Waters), 368; Luxemburg, *The Letters of Rosa Luxemburg*, 473.
30. Luxemburg, *Socialism or Barbarism*, 235; *Rosa Luxemburg Speaks* (ed. Waters), 393–4.
31. Lenin, "Eleventh Congress of the R.C.P. (B.), Political Report of the C.C.," *Collected Works*, Vol. 33, 290; Serge, *Memoirs*, 140.
32. Mayer, *The Furies*, 310–11; Read, *From Tsar to Soviets*, 191–2.
33. Suny, *Stalin*, 278, 486, 762 n30; Suny, *The Baku Commune, 1917–1918*, 352.
34. Suny, *Stalin*, 537; Carr, *The Bolshevik Revolution*, Vol. 1, 194, 195, 204, 212, 213; Medvedev, *Let History Judge*, 68–9.
35. Balabanoff quoted in Clark, *Lenin, a Biography* , 424.

36. Luxemburg, "Historical Responsibility" (January 1918), *Complete Works*, Vol. 5; *Rosa Luxemburg Speaks* (ed. Waters), 369, 395.
37. Serge and Sedova, *The Life and Death of Leon Trotsky*, 103.
38. Krausz, *Reconstructing Lenin*, 367; Arendt, *Origins of Totalitarianism*, 319.
39. Mayer, *The Furies*, 230–1.

9. UNEXPLORED MOUNTAIN (1921–23)

1. Lih, *Lenin*, 203, 205.
2. Lenin, "The Tasks of the Proletariat in the Present Revolution (April Theses)," *Collected Works*, Vol. 24, 24; Ross, *Russia in Upheaval*, 284.
3. Lenin, "They Have Forgotten the Main Thing," "The 'Crisis of Power,'" and "Speech against Bukharin's Amendment to the Resolution on the Party Programme," *Collected Works*, Vol. 27, 350, 334, 148.
4. Chamberlin, *The Russian Revolution, 1917–1921*, Vol. 1, 415.
5. Serge, *Year One of the Russian Revolution*, 353.
6. Ibid., 356.
7. Lih, *Bread and Authority in Russia, 1914–1921*, 134, 136, 137; Blanc, *Revolutionary Social Democracy*, 85.
8. Liberman, *Building Lenin's Russia*, 193.
9. Quoted in Le Blanc, *Leon Trotsky*, 50.
10. Paul Le Blanc, "Reflections on the Meaning of Stalinism," 87.
11. Lih, *Lenin*, 188.
12. Serge, *Notebooks 1936–1947*, 511–12.
13. Ryutin, *The Ryutin Platform*, ed. Datta Gupta, 123–4, 138, 134.
14. Lenin, "An Honest Voice in a Chorus of Slanderers," *Collected Works*, Vol. 27, 135.
15. Kennan, *Russia and the West under Lenin and Stalin* 243.
16. Liberman, *Building Lenin's Russia*, 7–11.
17. Chambers, *Ghosts on the Roof, Selected Essays*, ed. Teachout, 280; Lukács quoted in Le Blanc, *Revolutionary Collective*, 100.
18. The wording here is borrowed from Mike Taber, note to author, September 9, 2022.
19. Lenin, "Introduction to the Book by John Reed: *Ten Days That Shook the World*," *Collected Works*, Vol. 36, 519; Krupskaya's preface is available as "Introduction to the Russian Edition," which can be found in the 1987 Soviet edition of Reed's book, pp. 6–7.
20. Carmichael, "Preface," in Sukhanov, *The Russian Revolution 1917*, v.
21. Lenin, "Our Revolution," *Collected Works*, Vol. 33, 476.
22. Ibid., 477.
23. Ibid., 478.

24. Ibid., 478.
25. Ibid., 478.
26. Lenin, "Notes of a Publicist (1922)," *Collected Works*, Vol. 33, 204–5.
27. Ibid., 206, 207.
28. Liberman, *Building Lenin's Russia*, 94.
29. Strong, *The First Time in History*, 36–8.
30. Trotsky, "Preface," in ibid., 7.
31. Carr, *The Bolshevik Revolution, 1917–1923*, Vol. 2, 294, 295.
32. Leggett, *The Cheka*, 136–7, 163–4, 342; Lenin, *Collected Works*, Vol. 45, 389.
33. Lenin quoted in Shanin, "Chayanov's Message," in Chayanov, *The Theory of Peasant Economy*, 17 n26; Heinzen, *Inventing a Soviet Countryside*, 61, 66, 68.
34. Arendt, *Origins of Totalitarianism*, 318–19.
35. Lenin quoted in Zetkin, "Recollections of Lenin," in Lenin, *On Culture and Cultural Revolution*, 233, 234.
36. Fitzpatrick, *The Commissariat of Enlightenment*, xv–xvi.
37. Lenin, "The Tasks of the Youth Leagues," *Collected Works*, Vol. 31, p. 287; Lunacharsky quoted in ibid., 26, 97.
38. Lenin, "The Trade Unions, the Present Situation and Trotsky's Mistakes," *Collected Works*, Vol. 32, 24–5; Lenin, "Original Version of the Article 'The Immediate Tasks of the Soviet Government,'" *Collected Works*, Vol. 27, 209.

10. TESTAMENT AND AFTERMATH

1. Rosmer, *Lenin's Moscow*, 175–6.
2. Eastman, *Love and Revolution*, 335.
3. Fischer, *The Life of Lenin*, 603.
4. McNeal, *Bride of the Revolution*, 232.
5. Ibid., 243.
6. Ibid., 231.
7. Preobrazhensky quoted in Lih, *Lenin*, 190–1.
8. Kunstskaya, Mashtakova, and Subbotina, *Lenin—Great and Human*, 139–40; McNeal, *Bride of the Revolution*, 231–2.
9. Lenin, "On Cooperation," *Collected Works*, Vol. 33, 470, 474.
10. Ibid., 473.
11. Lenin, "Better Fewer, But Better," *Collected Works*, Vol. 33, 487.
12. Ibid., 487, 488–9.
13. Ibid., 489.
14. Ibid., 490.
15. Ibid., 498.

16. Rogovin, *Was There an Alternative?* 47, 112; Turton, *Forgotten Lives*, 120.
17. Lenin, "Letter to the Congress 1922 (Last Testament)," *Collected Works*, Vol. 36, 594–5.
18. Ibid., 596.
19. Quoted in McNeal, *Bride of the Revolution*, 242.
20. Duranty, *I Write as I Please*, 262.
21. Ibid., 274; Lewin, *The Soviet Century*, 308.
22. Lewin, *The Soviet Century*, 308.
23. Serge, *Notebooks 1936–1947*, 250.
24. Suny, *Stalin*, 612. See also Fitzpatrick, *On Stalin's Team*.
25. Le Blanc, *Leon Trotsky*, 113, 178; McIlroy and Campbell, "The Hippopotamus and the Giraffe," in Carlton, McCoy, and Smith, eds, *Dissenting Traditions*, 212, 241; Lewin, *The Soviet Century*, 379.
26. Rossi, *A Communist Party in Action*, 208–9.
27. Brandenberger and Zelenov, eds., *Stalin's Master Narrative*, 99, 101.
28. Ibid., 1, 39.
29. Heym, *Radek, a Novel*, 76.
30. Medvedev, *Let History Judge*, 869.
31. Serge, "The Socialist Imperative," 511–12.
32. Serge, "Thirty Years after the Russian Revolution," in *Year One of the Russian Revolution*, 484.
33. See Davies, *Soviet History in the Yeltsin Era*; Lipman, "Why Putin Won't Be Marking the Hundredth Anniversary of the Bolshevik Revolution"; Voice of America, "Putin Denounces Lenin, Says Stalin Got It Right."
34. Bill Nye on Cognitive Dissonance: www.youtube.com/watch?v=nXim4io4Pow (accessed January 27, 2023).
35. Lenin, *"Left-Wing" Communism—an Infantile Disorder*, *Collected Works*, Vol. 31, 62.
36. Budraitskis, *Dissidents among Dissidents*, 80.
37. Davis, *Old Gods, New Enigmas*, 215, 220.
38. Lenin, *What Is to Be Done? Collected Works*, Vol. 5, 509–10; Lenin draws from Dmitry Pisarev.
39. Rahv, *Essays on Literature and Politics, 1932–19723*, 53.

EPILOGUE: COMMIT YOURSELF AND THEN SEE …

1. See Kocka, *Capitalism: A Short History*, and Moody, *On New Terrain*.
2. Lenin, *What Is to Be Done? Collected Works*, Vol. 5, 412, 414.

3. Breitman, "The Current Radicalization Compared with Those of the Past," in Horowitz, ed., *Towards an American Socialist Revolution*, 101.
4. Dunne quoted in Le Blanc, *Left Americana*, 241.
5. Lenin quoted in Foner, "Lenin and the American Working-Class Movement," in Mason and Smith, eds. *Lenin's Impact on the United State* , 121–2; Lenin, *Lenin on the United States*, 95, 50.
6. Lenin, "Better Fewer, But Better," *Collected Works*, Vol. 33, 488–9.
7. Braverman in Evans, *James P. Cannon As We Knew Him*, 203–4. For rich, meticulously researched material on this mentor, see the two volumes by Palmer in the Bibliography.
8. *James P. Cannon, a Political Tribute*, 27, 18, 44.

Bibliography

*The works marked with an asterisk * may be helpful for beginners' next steps.*

Abramovitch, Raphael R. *The Soviet Revolution 1917–1939*. New York: International Universities Press, 1962.

Ahmed, Talat. *Mohandas Gandhi: Experiments in Civil Disobedience*. London: Pluto Press, 2019.

Alexinsky, Gregor. *Modern Russia*. New York: Charles Scribner's Sons, no date [1915].

——. *Russia and the Great War*. New York: Charles Scribner's Sons, 1915.

* Ali, Tariq. *The Dilemmas of Lenin: Terrorism, War, Empire, Love, Revolution*. London: Verso, 2017.

Allen, Barbara C. *Alexander Shlyapnikov 1885–1937: Life of an Old Bolshevik*. Chicago, IL: Haymarket Books, 2016.

Angus, Ian. *Facing the Anthropocene: Fossil Capitalism and the Crisis of the Earth System*. New York: Monthly Review Press, 2016.

Arendt, Hannah. *The Origins of Totalitarianism*, second edition. New York: Meridian Books, 1958.

Ascher, Abraham. *Pavel Axelrod and the Development of Menshevism*. Cambridge, MA: Harvard University Press, 1972.

——, ed. *The Mensheviks in the Russian Revolution*. Ithaca, NY: Cornell University Press, 1976.

——. *The Revolution of 1905*, 2 vols. Stanford, CA: Stanford University Press, 1988.

——. *Russia, A Short History*, revised edition. London: Oneworld Publications, 2017.

Avrich, Paul. *Kronstadt 1921*. New York: W.W. Norton, 1974.

——. *The Russian Anarchists*. New York: W.W. Norton, 1978.

Baitalsky, Mikhail. *Notebooks for the Grandchildren: Recollections of a Trotskyist Who Survived the Stalin Terror*. Atlantic Highlands, NJ: Humanies Press, 1996.

Balabanoff, Angelica. *Impressions of Lenin*. Ann Arbor, MI: University of Michigan Press, 1964.

——. *My Life as a Rebel*. Bloomington, IN: Indiana University Press, 1973.

Beatty, Bessie. *The Red Heart of Russia*. New York: Century Co., 1918.

Berkman, Alexander. *The Bolshevik Myth*. New York: Boni and Liveright, 1925.

Blanc, Eric. "Did the Bolsheviks Advocate Socialist Revolution in 1917?" *Marxist Essays and Commentary*, October 1, 2017, https://johnriddell.com/2017/10/13/did-the-bolsheviks-advocate-socialist-revolution-in-1917/.

——. *Revolutionary Social Democracy: Working-Class Politics across the Russian Empire (1882–1917)*. Chicago, IL: Haymarket Books, 2022.

Bogdanoff, A. [Alexander M. Bogdanov]. *A Short Course of Economic Science*, revised edition. London: Communist Party of Great Britain, 1925.

Bonch-Bruevich, V.D. "Meeting with Kropotkin," in Tamara Deutscher, ed., *Not By Politics Alone: The Other Lenin*. London: George Allen and Unwin, 1973.

Borkenau, Franz. *World Communism*. Ann Arbor, MI: University of Michigan Press, 1962.

Bottomore, Tom, ed. *A Dictionary of Marxist Thought*, second edition. Oxford: Blackwell, 1991.

Brandenberger, David and Mikhail V. Zelenov, eds. *Stalin's Master Narrative: A Critical Edition of the History of the Communist Party of the Soviet Union (Bolsheviks), Short Course*. New Haven, CT: Yale University Press, 2019.

Breitman, George. "The Current Radicalization Compared with Those of the Past," in Gus Horowitz, ed., *Towards an American Socialist Revolution*. New York: Pathfinder Press, 1971.

Brie, Michael. *Rediscovering Lenin: Dialectics of Revolution and Metaphysics of Domination*. Cham, Switzerland: Palgrave Macmillan, 2019.

Broué, Pierre. *Le Parti Bolchevique: Histoire du P.C. de L'U.R.S.S.* Paris: Minuit, 1963.

Brovkin, Vladimir, ed. *The Bolsheviks in Russian Society: The Revolution and Civil War*. New Haven, CT: Yale University Press, 1997.

Bruce, David. "The Seeds of Evil" (Review), *Revolutionary History*, Vol. 5, No. 4, [1995], online: www.marxists.org/history/etol/revhist/backiss/vol5/no4/bruce.html (accessed January 27, 2023).

Budgen, Sebastian, Stathis Kouvelakis, and Slavoj Žižek, eds. *Lenin Reloaded: Toward a Politics of Truth*. Durham, NC: Duke University Press, 2007.

Budraitskis, Ilya. *Dissidents among Dissidents: Ideology, Politics and the Left in Post-Soviet Russia*. London: Verso, 2022.

Bukharin, Nikolai. *Lenin as a Marxist*. London: Communist Party of Great Britain, 1925; reproduced in Al Richardson, ed. *In Defence of the Russian Revolution: A Selection of Bolshevik Writings, 1917–1923*. London: Porcupine Press, 1995, pp. 247–77.

Burbank, Jane. *Intelligentsia and Revolution: Russian Views of Bolshevism, 1917–1922*. New York: Oxford University Press, 1986.

Butler, Octavia. *Parable of the Sower*. New York: Grand Central Publishing, 2019.

——. *Parable of the Talents*. New York: Grand Central Publishing, 2019.

Callinicos, Alex. "Lenin and Imperialism," in Tom Rockmore and Norman Levine, eds., *The Palgrave Handbook of Leninist Political Philosophy*. London: Palgrave Macmillan, 2018.

Callinicos, Alex, Stathis Kouvelakis, and Lucia Pradella, eds. *Routledge Handbook of Marxism and Post-Marxism*. New York: Routledge, 2021.

Camfield, David. *Future on Fire: Capitalism and the Politics of Climate Change*. Oakland, CA: PM Press, 2023.

Cannon, James P. "The Revolutionary Party and Its Role in the Struggle for Socialism," in Ernest Mandel, ed., *Fifty Years of World Revolution, 1917–1967*. New York: Merit Publishers, 1968.

Carr, E.H. *The Bolshevik Revolution, 1917–1923*, 3 vols. London: Macmillan Press, 1950–53.

——. *The Interregnum, 1923–1924*. London: Macmillan Press, 1954.

——. *Michael Bakunin*. New York: Vintage Books, 1961.

* ——. *The Russian Revolution: From Lenin to Stalin 1917–1929*, second edition. London: Palgrave Macmillan, 2003.

Chamberlin, William H. *The Russian Revolution, 1917–1921*, 2 vols. Princeton, NJ: Princeton University Press, 1987.

Chambers, Whittaker. *Ghosts on the Roof, Selected Essays*, ed. Terry Teachout. New Brunswick, NJ: Transaction Publishers, 1996.

Chayanov, A.V. *The Theory of Peasant Economy*. Madison, WI: University of Wisconsin Press, 1986.

Chernov, Victor. *The Great Russian Revolution*. New Haven, CT: Yale University Press, 1936.

* Clark, Ronald W. *Lenin, a Biography*. New York: Harper and Row, 1988.

Clements, Barbara Evans. *Bolshevik Women*. Cambridge: Cambridge University Press, 1997.

Cliff, Tony. *Lenin*, 4 vols. London: Pluto Press, 1975–79.

Cohen, Stephen F. *Bukharin and the Bolshevik Revolution: A Political Biography, 1888–1938*. New York: Oxford University Press, 1980.

Cox, Judy. *The Women's Revolution, Russia 1905–1917*. Chicago, IL: Haymarket Books, 2017.

Dallin, David J. and Boris I. Nicolaevsky. *Forced Labor in Soviet Russia*. New Haven, CT: Yale University Press, 1947.

Dan, Theodore. *The Origins of Bolshevism*. New York: Schocken Books, 1970.

Daniels, Robert V. *Conscience of the Revolution: Communist Opposition in Soviet Russia*. New York: Simon and Schuster, 1969.

Davies, R.W. *Soviet History in the Yeltsin Era*. New York: St. Martin's Press, 1997.

Davis, Mike. *Old Gods, New Enigmas: Marx's Lost Theory*. London: Verso, 2018.

Deutscher, Isaac. *Stalin: A Political Biography*, second edition. New York: Oxford University Press, 1967.

——. *Lenin's Childhood*. London: Oxford University Press, 1970.

——. *The Prophet: The Life of Leon Trotsky*. London: Verso, 2007.

Deutscher, Tamara, ed. *Not by Politics Alone: The Other Lenin*. London: George Allen and Unwin, 1973.

Duranty, Walter. *I Write as I Please*. New York: Halcyon House, 1935.

Eastman, Max. *Marx, Lenin and the Science of Revolution*. London: George Allen and Unwin, 1926.

——. *Love and Revolution: My Journey through an Epoch*. New York: Random House, 1964.

Elbaum, Max. *Revolution in the Air: Sixties Radicals Turn to Lenin, Mao and Che*. London: Verso, 2006.

Elwood, R. Carter. *Inessa Armand, Revolutionary and Feminist*. Cambridge: Cambridge University Press, 1992.

——. *The Non-Geometric Lenin: Essays on the Development of the Bolshevik Party 1910–1914*. London: Anthem Press, 2011.

Engelstein, Laura. *Moscow 1905: Working-Class Organization and Political Conflict*. Stanford, CA: Stanford University Press, 1982.

Evans, Les, ed. *James P. Cannon as We Knew Him*. New York: Pathfinder Press, 1976.

Fischer, Louis. *The Soviets in World Affairs: A History of the Relations between the Soviet Union and the Rest of the World*, 2 vols. Princeton, NJ: Princeton University Press, 1951.

——. *The Life of Lenin*. New York: Harper and Row, 1964.

Fitzpatrick, Sheila. *The Commissariat of Enlightenment: Soviet Organization of Education and the Arts under Lunacharsky*. Cambridge: Cambridge University Press, 1970.

——. *Everyday Stalinism: Ordinary Life in Extraordinary Times, Soviet Russia in the 1930s*. New York: Oxford University Press, 2000.

——. *On Stalin's Team: The Years of Living Dangerously in Soviet Politics*. Princeton: Princeton University Press, 2015.

Foner, Philip S. "Lenin and the American Working-Class Movement," in Daniel Mason and Jessica Smith, eds., *Lenin's Impact on the United States*. New York: New World Review Publications, 1970.

Francis, David R. *Russia from the American Embassy, April 1916–November 1918*. New York: Charles Scribner's Sons, 1921.

Frankfurter, Marion D. and Gardner Jackson, eds. *The Letters of Sacco and Vanzetti*. New York: E.P. Dutton, 1960.

Freeman, Joseph, Joshua Kunitz, and Louis Lozowick, eds. *Voices of October: Art and Literature in Soviet Russia.* New York: Vanguard Press, 1930.

Frölich, Paul. *Rosa Luxemburg, Ideas in Action.* Chicago, IL: Haymarket Books, 2010.

Gerratana, Valentino. "Stalin, Lenin, and 'Leninism,'" *New Left Review* I #103, May–June 1977.

Getzler, Israel. *Nikolai Sukhanov: Chronicler of the Revolution.* London: Palgrave Macmillan, 2002.

——. *Martov: A Political Biography of a Russian Social Democrat.* Cambridge: Cambridge University Press, 2003.

Goldman, Emma. *Living My Life.* New York: Alfred A. Knopf, 1931.

——. *My Two Years in Russia.* St. Petersburg, FL: Black and Red Publishers, 2008. (This combines the two volumes: *My Disillusionment in Russia* and *My Further Disillusionment in Russia.*)

* Gorky [Gorki], Maxim. *Nikolai Lenin—The Man.* London: Daily Herald, 1924.

——. *Mother* (novel). New York: Collier Books, 1962.

——. *Untimely Thoughts: Essays on Revolution, Culture, and the Bolsheviks, 1917–1918.* New Haven, CT: Yale University Press, 1995.

Haimson, Leopold H. "The Problem of Social Stability in Urban Russia, 1905–1917," *Slavic Review* Vol. 23, No. 4 (1964): 619–42, and Vol. 24, No. 1 (1965): 1–22.

——. "The Russian Workers Movement on the Eve of the First World War." Unpublished paper, delivered at the annual meeting of the American Historical Association, December 1971.

——. *Russia's Revolutionary Experience, 1905–1917.* New York: Columbia University Press, 2005.

Halliday, Fred. "Three Concepts of Internationalism," *International Affairs*, Spring, 1988, Vol. 64, No. 2.

Halstead, Fred. *Out Now! A Participant's Account of the American Movement against the Vietnam War.* New York: Monad/Pathfinder, 1978.

Harcave, Sidney. *First Blood: The Russian Revolution of 1905.* New York: Macmillan, 1964.

Hardach, Gerd. *The First World War 1914–1918.* Berkeley, CA: University of California Press, 1981.

Harding, Neil, ed. *Marxism in Russia: Key Documents 1879–1906.* Cambridge: Cambridge University Press, 1983.

——. *Leninism.* Durham, NC: Duke University Press, 1996.

——. *Lenin's Political Thought: Theory and Practice in the Democratic and Socialist Revolutions.* Chicago, IL: Haymarket Books, 2009.

Haslam, Jonathan. *Russia's Cold War: From the October Revolution to the Fall of the Wall.* New Haven, CT: Yale University Press, 2011.

——. *The Spectre of War: International Communism and the Origins of World War II.* Princeton, NJ: Princeton University Press, 2022.

Haupt, Georges. "War and Revolution in Lenin," in *Aspects of International Socialism 1871–1914, Essays by Georges Haupt.* Cambridge: Cambridge University Press, 1986.

Haupt, Georges and Jean-Jacques Marie. *Makers of the Russian Revolution: Biographies of Bolshevik Leaders.* Ithaca, NY: Cornell University Press, 1974.

Heinzen, James W. *Inventing a Soviet Countryside: State Power and the Transformation of Rural Russia, 1917–1929.* Pittsburgh, PA: University of Pittsburgh Press, 2004.

Heller, Henry. *The Birth of Capitalism, A Twenty-First Century Perspective.* London: Pluto Press, 2011.

Heron, Kai and Jodi Dean. "Climate Leninism and Revolutionary Transition: Organization and Anti-Imperialism in Catastrophic Times," *Spectre*, online, June 26, 2022, https://spectrejournal.com/climate-leninism-and-revolutionary-transition/.

Heym, Stefan. *Radek, a Novel* (1995). New York: Monthly Review Press, 2022.

Ho Chi Minh. "Lenin and the Colonial Peoples," in Bernard B. Fall, ed., *Ho Chi Minh on Revolution.* New York: Signet Books, 1968.

Hughes, Langston. "Lenin," in Faith Berry, ed., *Good Morning Revolution: Uncollected Social Protest Writings by Langston Hughes.* New York: Lawrence Hill, 1973.

Hunt, Richard N. *The Political Ideas of Marx and Engels, Volume 1: Marxism and Totalitarian Democracy, 1818–1850.* Pittsburgh, PA: University of Pittsburgh Press, 1974.

____. *The Political Ideas of Marx and Engels, Volume 2: Classical Marxism, 1850–1895.* Pittsburgh, PA: University of Pittsburgh Press, 1984.

* James, C.L.R. "Lenin and the Vanguard Party," in Anna Grimshaw, ed., *The C.L.R. James Reader.* Oxford: Basil Blackwell, 1992.

——. *World Revolution, 1917–1936: The Rise and Fall of the Communist International.* Durham, NC: Duke University Press, 2017.

James P. Cannon, A Political Tribute (including five interviews from the last year of his life). New York: Pathfinder Press, 1974.

Kamenev, Lev. "The Literary Legacy and Collected Works of Illyitch," *Communist International*, No. 1, 1924; reproduced on Marxist Internet Archive: www.marxists.org/archive/kamenev/19xx/x01/x01.htm (accessed January 27, 2023).

——. *The Dictatorship of the Proletariat.* Detroit: Marxian Educational Society, 1920; reproduced in Al Richardson, ed. *In Defence of the*

Russian Revolution: A Selection of Bolshevik Writings, 1917–1923. London: Porcupine Press, 1995, pp. 102–10; also on Marxist Internet Archive: www.marxists.org/archive/kamenev/1920/x01/x01.htm (accessed January 27, 2023).

Kautsky, Karl. "Revolutions, Past and Present," *International Socialist Review*, January 1906; reproduced in Marxist Internet Archive: www.marxists.org/archive/kautsky/1906/xx/revolutions.htm (accessed January 27, 2023).

——. *The Class Struggle (Erfurt Program)*. New York: W.W. Norton, 1971.

——. *The Road to Power: Political Reflections on Growing into the Revolution*. Atlantic Highlands, NJ: Humanities Press, 1996.

Kellogg, Paul. *Truth Behind Bars: Reflections on the Fate of the Russian Revolution*. Edmonton, Alberta, Canada: AU Press, 2021.

Kennan, George F. *Russia and the West under Lenin and Stalin*. Boston: Little, Brown and Co., 1961.

Kerensky, Alexander. *Russia and History's Turning Point*. New York: Duell, Sloan and Pearce, 1965.

Khlevniuk, Oleg V. *The History of the Gulag: From Collectivization to the Great Terror*. New Haven, CT: Yale University Press, 2004.

Kocka, Jürgen. *Capitalism: A Short History*. Princeton, NJ: Princeton University Press, 2016.

Kollontai, Alexandra. *Selected Writings*. New York: W.W. Norton, 1980.

Krausz, Tamás. *Reconstructing Lenin, an Intellectual Biography*. New York: Monthly Review Press, 2015.

Kropotkin, Peter. *The Conquest of Bread*. New York: Vanguard Press, 1926.

* Krupskaya, N.K. *Reminiscences of Lenin*. New York: International Publishers, 1970.

____. "Introduction to the Russian Edition," in John Reed, *Ten Days That Shook the World*. Moscow: Progress Publishers, 1987.

Kunetskaya, L., K. Mashtakova, and Z. Subbotina. *Lenin—Great and Human*. Moscow: Progress Publishers, 1970.

Le Blanc, Paul. *Marx, Lenin, and the Revolutionary Experience: Studies of Communism and Radicalism in the Age of Globalization*. New York: Routledge, 2006.

——. *Unfinished Leninism, The Rise and Return of a Revolutionary Doctrine*. Chicago, IL: Haymarket Books, 2014.

* ——. *Lenin and the Revolutionary Party*. Chicago, IL: Haymarket Books, 2015.

——. *Leon Trotsky*. London: Reaktion Books, 2015.

* ——. *From Marx to Gramsci: A Reader in Revolutionary Marxist Politics*. Chicago, IL: Haymarket Books, 2016.

——. "Reflections on the Meaning of Stalinism," *Crisis and Critique*, Vol. 3, No. 1, March 2016.

——. "The Kornilov Coup," *Jacobin* (September 2017), www.jacobinmag.com/2017/09/russian-revolution-bolsheviks-kerensky-kornilov (accessed January 27, 2023).

——. *Left Americana: The Radical Heart of US History*. Chicago, IL: Haymarket Books, 2017.

——. *October Song: Bolshevik Triumph, Communist Tragedy, 1917–1924*. Chicago, IL: Haymarket Books, 2017.

——. "Was George Washington a French Agent?" *Socialist Worker*, online, June 27, 2017, https://socialistworker.org/2017/06/27/was-george-washington-a-french-agent.

——. *The Living Flame: The Revolutionary Passion of Rosa Luxemburg*. New York: Haymarket Books, 2020.

——. *Revolutionary Collective: Comrades, Critics, and Dynamics in the Struggle for Socialism*. Chicago, IL: Haymarket Books, 2022.

Leggett, George. *The Cheka: Lenin's Political Police*. Oxford: Clarendon Press, 1981.

Lenin, Vladimir Ilyich. *Collected Works*, 45 vols. Moscow: Progress Publishers, 1960–70.

——. *Lenin on the United States*, ed. C. Leitizen. New York: International Publishers, 1970.

* ——. *The Lenin Anthology*, ed. Robert C. Tucker. New York: W.W. Norton, 1975.

——. *Lenin's Final Fight, Speeches and Writings 1922–23*, ed. George Fyson. New York: Pathfinder Press, 1995.

——. *On Culture and Cultural Revolution*. Honolulu: University Press of the Pacific, 2001.

——. *Revolution at the Gates: Selected Writings of Lenin from 1917*, ed. Slavoj Žižek. London: Verso, 2002.

* ——. *Revolution, Democracy, Socialism: Selected Writings*, ed. Paul Le Blanc. London: Pluto Press, 2008.

——. *Lenin 2017: Remembering, Repeating, and Working Through*, ed. Slavoj Žižek. London: Verso, 2017.

Lenin, Vladimir Ilyich and Maxim Gorky. *Lenin and Gorky: Letters, Reminiscences, Articles*. Moscow: Progress Publishers, 1973.

Leonhard, Wolfgang. *Three Faces of Marxism*. New York: G.P. Putnam's Sons, 1974.

Leplat, Fred and Alex de Jong, eds. *October 1917: Workers in Power*. London: Merlin Press, 2016.

Levine, Isaac Don. *The Russian Revolution*. New York: Harper and Brothers, 1917.

____. *The Man Lenin*. New York: Thomas Seltzer, 1924.

* Lewin, Moshe. *Lenin's Last Struggle*. New York: Vintage Books, 1970.
——. *Russia/USSR/Russia: The Drive and Drift of a Superstate*. New York: The New Press, 1995.
——. *The Soviet Century*. London: Verso, 2016.
Liberman, Simon. *Building Lenin's Russia*. Chicago, IL: University of Chicago Press, 1945.
Liebman, Marcel. *Leninism under Lenin*. Chicago, IL: Haymarket Books, 2016.
Lieven, Dominic. *The End of Tsarist Russia: The March to World War I and Revolution*. New York: Penguin Books, 2015.
Lih, Lars T. *Bread and Authority in Russia, 1914–1921*. Berkeley, CA: University of California Press, 1990.
——. "Karl Kautsky as Architect of the October Revolution," *Jacobin*, online, https://jacobinmag.com/2019/06/karl-kautsky-vladimir-lenin-russian-revolution.
——. *Lenin Rediscovered. "What Is to Be Done?" in Context*. Chicago, IL: Haymarket Books, 2008.
* ——. *Lenin*. London: Reaktion Books, 2011.
Lipman, Masha. "Why Putin Won't Be Marking the Hundredth Anniversary of the Bolshevik Revolution," *The New Yorker*, November 3, 2017.
* Loginov, Vladlen. *Vladimir Lenin: How to Become a Leader*. London: Glagoslav Publications, 2019.
Löwy, Michael. *Fatherland or Mother Earth? Essays on the National Question*. London: Pluto Press, 1998.
——. *On Changing the World: Essays in Political Philosophy from Karl Marx to Walter Benjamin*. Chicago, IL: Haymarket Books, 2013.
Löwy, Michael and Paul Le Blanc. "Lenin and Trotsky," in Tom Rockmore and Norman Levine, eds., *The Palgrave Handbook of Leninist Political Philosophy*. London: Palgrave Macmillan, 2018.
* Lukács, Georg. *Lenin: A Study in the Unity of His Thought*. London: Verso, 2009.
Lunacharsky, Anatoly. *Revolutionary Silhouettes*. New York: Hill and Wang, 1968.
Luxemburg, Rosa. "The Russian Revolution," in Mary-Alice Waters, ed., *Rosa Luxemburg Speaks*. New York: Pathfinder Press, 1970.
——. "The Idea of May Day on the March," in Dick Howard, ed., *Selected Political Writings*. New York: Monthly Review Press, 1971.
——. "The Old Mole," in Robert Looker, ed., *Selected Political Writings*. New York: Grove Press, 1974.
——. *Socialism or Barbarism, Selected Writings*, ed. Paul Le Blanc and Helen C. Scott. London: Pluto Press, 2010.
——. *The Letters of Rosa Luxemburg*. London: Verso, 2011.

——. *Complete Works of Rosa Luxemburg*, Vol. 5, ed. Helen C. Scott and Paul Le Blanc. London: Verso, 2024 forthcoming.

Magdoff, Harry. *Imperialism: From the Colonial Age to the Present*. New York: Monthly Review Press, 1978.

Maguire, Robert A. *Red Virgin Soil: Soviet Literature in the 1920s*. New York: Columbia University, 1968.

Malm, Andreas. *Corona, Climate, Chronic Emergency: War Communism in the Twenty-First Century*. London: Verso, 2020.

Mandel, David. *The Petrograd Workers in the Russian Revolution: February 1917–June 1918*. Chicago, IL: Haymarket Books, 2018.

Mandel, Ernest. *The Meaning of the Second World War*. London: Verso, 1986.

*——. "The Leninist Theory of Organization: Its Relevance for Today," in *Introduction to Marxist Theory: Selected Writings*, Vol. 1. London: Merlin Press/Resistance Books/IIRE, 2021.

Marik, Soma. *Revolutionary Democracy: Emancipation in Classical Marxism*. Chicago, IL: Haymarket Books, 2018.

Marx, Karl. *The Political Writings*, ed. David Fernbach. London: Verso, 2019.

Mayer, Arno J. *Wilson vs. Lenin: Political Origins of the New Diplomacy 1917–1918*. Cleveland, OH: Meridian Books, World Publishing, 1964.

——. *Politics and Diplomacy of Peacemaking: Containment and Counterrevolution at Versailles, 1918–1919*. New York: Alfred A. Knopf, 1967.

____. *The Persistence of the Old Order: Europe to the Great War*. New York: Pantheon, 1982.

——. *The Furies: Violence and Terror in the French and Russian Revolutions*. Princeton, NJ: Princeton University Press, 2000.

McDermid, Jane and Anna Hillyar. *Midwives of the Revolution: Female Bolsheviks and Women Workers in 1917*. Athens, OH: Ohio University Press, 1999.

——. "In Lenin's Shadow: Nadezhda Krupskaya and the Bolshevik Revolution," in Ian Thatcher, ed., *Reinterpreting Revolutionary Russia*. London: Palgrave Macmillan, 2006.

McDermott, Kevin and Jeremy Agnew. *The Comintern: A History of International Communism from Lenin to Stalin*. London: Macmillan Press, 1996.

McIlroy, John and Alan Campbell, "The Hippopotamus and the Giraffe: Bolshevism, Stalinism, and American and British Communism in the 1920s," in Sean Carlton, Ted McCoy, and Julia Smith, eds., *Dissenting Traditions: Essays on Bryan D. Palmer, Marxism, and History*. Edmonton, Alberta, Canada: AU Press, 2021.

McNeal, Robert H. *Bride of the Revolution: Krupskaya and Lenin*. London: Victor Gollancz, 1973.

Medhurst, John. *No Less Than Mystic: A History of Lenin and the Russian Revolution for a 21st Century Left*. London: Repeater Books, 2017.

Medvedev, Roy. *The October Revolution*. New York: Columbia University Press, 1985.

——. *Let History Judge: The Origins and Consequences of Stalinism*, revised and expanded edition. New York: Columbia University Press, 1989.

Melancon, Michael. *Rethinking Russia's February Revolution: Anonymous Spontaneity or Socialist Agency?* Carl Beck Papers, Russian and East European Studies, Pittsburgh, PA: University of Pittsburgh, 2000.

——. *The Lena Goldfields Massacre and the Crisis of the Late Tsarist State*. College Station, TX: Texas A&M University Press, 2006.

Meyer, Alfred G. *Leninism*. New York: Frederick A. Praeger, 1967.

* Miéville, China. *October: The Story of the Russian Revolution*. London: Verso, 2017.

Mills, C. Wright. *The Marxists*. New York: Dell, 1962.

——. "Letter to the New Left," in Irving Louis Horowitz, ed., *Power, Politics and People: The Collected Writings of C. Wright Mills*. New York: Oxford University Press, 1963.

Molotov, V.M. (with Felix Chuev). *Molotov Remembers: Inside Kremlin Politics*. Chicago, IL: Ivan R. Dee, 1993.

Molyneux, John. *Marxism and the Party*. London: Pluto Press, 1978.

——. *Lenin for Today*. London: Bookmarks, 2017.

Moody, Kim. *On New Terrain: How Capital Is Reshaping the Battleground of Class War*. Chicago, IL: Haymarket Books, 2017.

Neale, Jonathan. *Fight the Fire: Green New Deals and Global Climate Jobs*. London: Resistance Books, 2021.

Nimtz, August H. *The Ballot, the Streets, or Both? From Marx and Engels to Lenin and the October Revolution*. Chicago, IL: Haymarket Books, 2019.

Osipova, Taisia. "Peasant Rebellions: Origins, Scope, Dynamics, and Consequences," in Vladimir Brovkin, ed., *The Bolsheviks in Russian Society: The Revolution and Civil War*. New Haven, CT: Yale University Press, 1997.

Palmer, Bryan. *James P. Cannon and the Origins of the American Revolutionary Left, 1890–1928*. Urbana and Chicago, IL: University of Illinois Press, 2010.

——. *James P. Cannon and the Emergence of Trotskyism in the United States, 1928–3 nm,8*. Chicago, IL: Haymarket Books, 2022.

Pearce, Brian, ed. *1903: Second Congress of the Russian Social Democratic Labor Party, Complete Text of the Minutes*. London: New Park, 1978.

Peters, J. *The Communist Party: A Manual on Organization*. New York: Workers' Library, 1935.

Piatnitsky, O. *Memoirs of a Bolshevik*. New York: International Publishers, 1930.

Pipes, Richard, ed. *Revolutionary Russia, a Symposium*. Garden City, NY: Anchor Books, 1969.

Pirani, Simon. *The Russian Revolution in Retreat, 1920–24: Soviet Workers and the New Communist Elite*. London: Routledge, 2008.

Pokrovskii, M.N. *Russia in World History, Selected Essays*. Ann Arbor, MI: University of Michigan Press, 1970.

Pomper, Philip. *Lenin's Brother: The Origins of the October Revolution*. New York: W.W. Norton, 2010.

Porter, Cathy. *Alexandra Kollontai, a Biography*, updated edition. Chicago, IL: Haymarket Books, 2014.

Pospelov, P.N. (chief editor). *Vladimir Ilyich Lenin, a Biography*. Moscow: Progress Publishers, 1965.

Possony, Stephen T. *Lenin, The Compulsive Revolutionary*. Chicago, IL: Regnery, 1964.

Rabinowitch, Alexander. *The Bolsheviks in Power: The First Year of Soviet Rule in Petrograd*. Bloomington, IN: Indiana University Press, 2008.

——. *The Bolsheviks Come to Power: The Revolution of 1917 in Petrograd*. Chicago, IL: Haymarket Books, 2017.

Rabinowitch, Alexander and Janet Rabinowitch, with Ladis K.D. Kristof, eds. *Revolution and Politics in Russia: Essays in Memory of B.I. Nicolaevsky*. Bloomington, IN: Indiana University Press, 1972.

Radek, Karl. "Lenin," reproduced in Al Richardson, ed. *In Defence of the Russian Revolution: A Selection of Bolshevik Writings, 1917–1923*. London: Porcupine Press, 1995, pp. 78–81; also on Marxist Internet Archive: www.marxists.org/archive/radek/1923/03/lenin.htm (accessed January 27, 2023).

Rahv, Philip. *Essays on Literature and Politics, 1932–1972*. Boston, MA: Houghton Mifflin Co., 1972.

Read, Christopher. *From Tsar to Soviets: The Russian People and Their Revolution, 1917–21*. New York: Oxford University Press, 1996.

——. *Lenin*. London: Routledge, 2005.

* Reed, John. *Ten Days That Shook the World*. New York: International Publishers, 1926.

Rees, Edward A. "Lenin and the New Economic Policy," in Tom Rockmore and Norman Levine, eds., *The Palgrave Handbook of Leninist Political Philosophy*. London: Palgrave Macmillan, 2018.

Rees, John. *The Algebra of Revolution: The Dialectic and the Classical Marxist Tradition*. London: Routledge, 1998.

Richardson, Al, ed. *In Defence of the Russian Revolution: A Selection of Bolshevik Writings, 1917–1923*. London: Porcupine Press, 1995.

Riddell, John, ed. *The Communist International in Lenin's Time. Lenin's Struggle for a Revolutionary International. Documents: 1907–1916, the Preparatory Years*. New York: Monad/Pathfinder Press, 1984.

——, ed. *The Communist International in Lenin's Time. The German Revolution and the Debate on Soviet Power. Documents: 1918–1919, Preparing the Founding Congress*. New York: Pathfinder Press, 1986.

——, ed. *The Communist International in Lenin's Time. Founding the Communist International. Proceedings and Documents of the First Congress: March 1919*. New York: Pathfinder Press, 1987.

——, ed. *The Communist International in Lenin's Time. Workers of the World and Oppressed Peoples, Unite! Proceedings and Documents of the Second Congress, 1920*, 2 vols. New York: Pathfinder Press, 1991.

——, ed. *Toward the United Front: Proceedings of the Fourth Congress of the Communist International*. Chicago, IL: Haymarket Books, 2013.

——, ed. *To the Masses: Proceedings of the Third Congress of the Communist International, 1921*. Chicago, IL: Haymarket Books, 2015.

Rockmore, Tom and Norman Levine, eds. *The Palgrave Handbook of Leninist Political Philosophy*. London: Palgrave Macmillan, 2018.

Rodney, Walter. *Decolonial Marxism: Essays from the Pan-African Revolution*, ed. Asha Rodney, Patricia Rodney, Ben Mabie, and Jesse Benjamin. London: Verso, 2022.

Rogovin, Vadim Z. *Was There an Alternative? 1923–1927*. Oak Park, MI: Mehring Books, 2021.

Rosdolsky, Roman. *Lenin and the First World War*. London: Prinkipo Press, 1999.

Rosmer, Alfred. *Lenin's Moscow*. Chicago, IL: Haymarket Books, 2016.

Ross, Edward Allsworth. *Russia in Upheaval*. New York: The Century, 1918.

Rossi, A. [Angelo Tasca]. *A Communist Party in Action*. New Haven, CT: Yale University Press, 1949.

Russell, Bertrand. *The Practice and Theory of Bolshevism*. London: George Allen & Unwin, 1920.

Ryutin, M.N. *The Ryutin Platform: Stalin and the Crisis of Proletarian Dictatorship, Platform of the "Union of Marxists-Leninists"* [1932], ed. Sobhanlala Datta Gupta. Kolkata, India: Seribaan, 2010.

Salvadori, Massimo. *Karl Kautsky and the Socialist Revolution, 1880–1938*. London: Verso, 1990.

Schwarz, Solomon. *The Russian Revolution of 1905: The Workers' Movement and the Formation of Bolshevism and Menshevism*. Chicago, IL: University of Chicago Press, 1967.

Scott, Helen C. and Paul Le Blanc, "Introduction," *The Complete Works of Rosa Luxemburg*, Vol. 5. London: Verso, 2024 forthcoming.

Scott, James C. *Seeing Like a State: How Certain Schemes to Improve the Human Condition Have Failed*. New Haven, CT: Yale University Press, 1998.

Serge, Victor. "The Socialist Imperative," *Partisan Review*, September–October 1947.

——. *Russia Twenty Years After*. Atlantic Highlands, NJ: Humanities Press, 1996.

* ——. *From Lenin to Stalin*. New York: Pathfinder Press, 1973.

——. "Lenin and Imperialism," *Inprecor*, September 13, 1923; reprinted in *From Lenin to Stalin* (New York: Pathfinder Press, 1973).

——. *Memoirs of a Revolutionary*. New York: New York Review of Books, 2012.

——. *Year One of the Russian Revolution*. Chicago, IL: Haymarket Books, 2015.

——. *Notebooks 1936–1947*. New York: New York Review of Books, 2019.

Serge, Victor and Natalia Sedova. *The Life and Death of Leon Trotsky*. Chicago, IL: Haymarket Books, 2016.

Service, Robert. *Lenin: A Political Life*, 3 vols. Bloomington, IN: Indiana University Press, 1985–95.

Seymour, Richard. "The Real Winston Churchill," *Jacobin*, November 11, 2018, www.jacobinmag.com/2018/01/winston-churchill-british-empire-colonialism (accessed January 27, 2023).

Shandro, Alan. *Lenin and the Logic of Hegemony: Political Practice and Theory in the Class Struggle*. Chicago, IL: Haymarket Books, 2015.

Shanin, Teodor, ed. *Late Marx and the Russian Road: Marx and the Peripheries of Capitalism*. New York: Monthly Review Press, 1983.

——. "Forward" to A.V. Chayanov, *The Theory of Peasant Economy*. Madison, WI: University of Wisconsin Press, 1986.

——. *Russia as a Developing Society*. New Haven, CT: Yale University Press, 1986.

——. *Russia 1905–07: Revolution as a Moment of Truth*. New Haven, CT: Yale University Press, 1986.

Shlyapknikov, Alexander. *On the Eve of 1917*. London: Allison and Busby, 1982.

Smith, Stephen A., ed. *The Oxford Handbook of the History of Communism*. Oxford: Oxford University Press, 2014.

——. *Revolution in Russia: An Empire in Crisis, 1890 to 1928*. Oxford: Oxford University Press, 2017.

Snyder, Louis L. *The World in the Twentieth Century*, revised edition. Princeton, NJ: D. Van Nostrand Co., 1964.

Souvarine, Boris. *Stalin, a Critical Survey of Bolshevism*. New York: Longman's Green and Co., 1939.

Stalin, Joseph. *The Essential Stalin: Major Theoretical Writings, 1905–1952*, ed. Bruce Franklin. Garden City, NY: Anchor Books, 1972.

Steinberg, Isaac. *Spiridonova: Revolutionary Terrorist*. London: Methuen and Co., 1935.

Strong, Anna Louise. *The First Time in History: Two Years of Russia's New Life (August 1921–December 1923)*. New York: Boni and Liveright, 1924.

Sukhanov, N.N. *The Russian Revolution 1917, a Personal Record*. Princeton, NJ: Princeton University Press, 1984.

Suny, Ronald Grigor. *The Baku Commune, 1917–1918: Class and Nationality in the Russian Revolution*. New York: Columbia University Press, 1972.

——. *The Soviet Experiment: Russia, the USSR, and the Successor States*. New York: Oxford University Press, 1998.

* ——. *Red Flag Unfurled: History, Historians, and the Russian Revolution*. London: Verso, 2017.

——. *Red Flag Wounded: Stalinism and the Fate of the Soviet Experiment*. London: Verso, 2020.

——. *Stalin: Passage to Revolution*. Princeton, NJ: Princeton University Press, 2020.

Swain, Geoffrey. *Russian Social Democracy and the Legal Labor Movement 1906–14*. London: Macmillan Press, 1983.

Taber, Mike, ed. *Under the Socialist Banner: Resolutions of the Second International, 1889–1912*. Chicago, IL: Haymarket Books, 2021.

Traverso, Enzo. *Fire and Blood: The European Civil War 1914–1945*. London: Verso, 2017.

Trotsky, Leon. *My Life, An Attempt at an Autobiography*. New York: Pathfinder Press, 1970.

——. *The Struggle against Fascism in Germany*, ed. George Breitman and Merry Maisel. New York: Pathfinder Press, 1970.

——. *On Lenin: Notes towards a Biography*, ed. Tamara Deutscher. London: George G. Harrap, 1971.

* ——. *The Young Lenin*. Garden City, NY: Doubleday, 1972.

——. *1905*. Chicago, IL: Haymarket Books, 2016.

——. *The History of the Russian Revolution*, 3 vols in one. Chicago, IL: Haymarket Books, 2017.

——. *Stalin*, ed. Alan Woods and Rob Sewell. Chicago, IL: Haymarket Books, 2019.

Tucker, Robert C. *Stalin as Revolutionary 1879–1929*. New York: W.W. Norton, 1973.

Turton, Katy. *Forgotten Lives: The Role of Lenin's Sisters in the Russian Revolution, 1864–1937*. London: Palgrave Macmillan, 2007.

Twiss, Thomas. *Trotsky and the Problem of Soviet Bureaucracy*. Chicago, IL: Haymarket Books, 2015.

Ulyanova-Yelizarova, A.I., D.I. Ulyanov, Maria Ulyanova, and N.K. Krupskaya. *Reminiscences of Lenin by His Relatives*. Moscow: Foreign Languages Publishing House, 1956.

United Nations. *Human Development Report 2021/2022: Uncertain Times, Unsettled Lives*. New York: United Nations Development Programme, 2022.

Valentinov, Nikolay. *Encounters with Lenin*. London: Oxford University Press, 1968.

——. *The Early Years of Lenin*. Ann Arbor, MI: University of Michigan Press, 1969.

——. "Nonparty Specialists and the Coming of the NEP," *Russian Review*, Vol. 30, No. 2, April 1971.

Voice of America. "Putin Denounces Lenin, Says Stalin Got It Right," *VOA News*, January 25, 2016, www.voanews.com/a/putin-denounces-lenin-says-stalin-got-it-right/3162079.html (accessed January 27, 2023).

Volkogonov, Dmitri. *Lenin, a New Biography*. New York: The Free Press, 1994.

Voronsky, Aleksandr Konstantinovich. *Art as the Cognition of Life: Selected Writings 1911–1936*. Oak Park, MI: Mehring Books, 1998.

Wade, Rex A. *The Russian Revolution 1917*. Cambridge: Cambridge University Press, 2000.

Weber, Gerda and Hermann. *Lenin: Life and Works*. London: Macmillan, 1980.

Weeks, John. "Imperialism and the World Market," in Tom Bottomore, ed., *A Dictionary of Marxist Thought*, second edition. Oxford: Blackwell, 1991.

Westad, Odd Arne. *The Cold War, a World History*. New York: Basic Books, 2017.

Weyl, Nathniel and Stefan T. Possony. *The Geography of Intellect*. Chicago, IL: Henry Regnery Co., 1963.

White, James D. *Lenin: The Practice and Theory of Revolution*. New York: Palgrave, 2001.

——. *Marx and Russia, The Fate of a Doctrine*. London: Bloomsbury Academic, 2019.

——. *Red Hamlet: The Life and Ideas of Alexander Bogdanov*. Chicago, IL: Haymarket Books, 2019.

Williams, Albert Rhys. *Lenin—the Man and His Work*. New York: Scott and Seltzer, 1919.

——. *Through the Russian Revolution*. New York: Boni and Liveright, 1921.

——. *Journey into Revolution: Petrograd 1917–1918*. Chicago, IL: Quadrangle Books, 1969.

Wolfe, Bertram D. *Three Who Made a Revolution, Biographical History*. New York: Dial Press, 1948.

——. *The Bridge and the Abyss: The Troubled Friendship of Maxim Gorky and V.I. Lenin*. Frederick A. Prager, 1967.

——. *Lenin and the Twentieth Century: A Bertram D. Wolfe Retrospective*. Stanford, CA: Hoover Institution Press, 1984.

Yarmolinsky, Avrahm. *The Road to Revolution, a Century of Russian Radicalism*. Princeton, NJ: Princeton University Press, 2014.

Zetkin, Clara. "My Recollections of Lenin," in *They Knew Lenin: Reminiscences of Foreign Contemporaries*. Honolulu: University Press of the Pacific, 2005.

——. *Rosa Luxemburg's Views on the Russian Revolution* (1922). New York: Red Star Publishers, 2017.

* Zinoviev, Gregory. *History of the Bolshevik Party, from the Beginnings to February 1917—a Popular Outline*. London: New Park Publications, 1973.

Index

The Pluto Press Newsletter

Hello friend of Pluto!

Want to stay on top of the best radical books we publish?

Then sign up to be the first to hear about our new books, as well as special events, podcasts and videos.

You'll also get 50% off your first order with us when you sign up.

Come and join us!

Go to bit.ly/PlutoNewsletter

Thanks to our Patreon subscriber:

Ciaran Kane

Who has shown generosity and comradeship in support of our publishing.